THE CONTEST FOR ABORIGINAL SOULS

EUROPEAN MISSIONARY
AGENDAS IN AUSTRALIA

Aboriginal History Incorporated
Aboriginal History Inc. is a part of the Australian Centre for Indigenous History, Research School of Social Sciences, The Australian National University, and gratefully acknowledges the support of the School of History and the National Centre for Indigenous Studies, The Australian National University. Aboriginal History Inc. is administered by an Editorial Board which is responsible for all unsigned material. Views and opinions expressed by the author are not necessarily shared by Board members.

Contacting Aboriginal History
All correspondence should be addressed to the Editors, Aboriginal History Inc., ACIH, School of History, RSSS, 9 Fellows Road (Coombs Building), Acton, ANU, 2601, or aboriginal.history@anu.edu.au.

WARNING: Readers are notified that this publication may contain names or images of deceased persons.

THE CONTEST FOR ABORIGINAL SOULS

EUROPEAN MISSIONARY AGENDAS IN AUSTRALIA

REGINA GANTER

PRESS

Published by ANU Press and Aboriginal History Inc.
The Australian National University
Acton ACT 2601, Australia
Email: anupress@anu.edu.au

Available to download for free at press.anu.edu.au

A catalogue record for this book is available from the National Library of Australia

ISBN (print): 9781760462048
ISBN (online): 9781760462055

WorldCat (print): 1037299501
WorldCat (online): 1037299354

DOI: 10.22459/CAS.05.2018

This title is published under a Creative Commons Attribution-NonCommercial-NoDerivatives 4.0 International (CC BY-NC-ND 4.0).

The full licence terms are available at creativecommons.org/licenses/by-nc-nd/4.0/legalcode

Cover design and layout by ANU Press. Cover photograph: Teacher H. A. Heinrich handing out sweets to the mission children with his son Denis watching, Finke River Mission, Hermannsburg, NT, P03757 07813, with kind permission of the Lutheran Archives Australia.

This edition © 2018 ANU Press and Aboriginal History Inc.

Contents

Abbreviations vii

Preface. ix

1. The quest for ecclesiastical territory – Catholics and Protestants . . . 1
2. Protestants divided 23
3. Empires of faith 49
4. The subtle ontology of power 81
5. Engaging with missionaries 107
6. The trials of missionary life. 147
7. The German difference 173
8. Conclusions 207

Bibliography. 223

Abbreviations

ABS	Australian Bureau of Statistics
ADB	*Australian Dictionary of Biography*
AIATSIS	Australian Institute of Aboriginal and Torres Strait Islanders
BFBS	British and Foreign Bible Society
CMS	Church Mission Society
CP	Congregatio Passionis Iesu Christi (Passionists)
DAA	Department of Aboriginal Affairs
ELSA	Evangelical-Lutheran Synod of Australia
ELSQ	Evangelical-Lutheran Synod of Queensland
FSC	Fratres Scholarum Christianarum (French Christian Brothers, De la Salle Brothers)
HMG	Hermannsburg Missionsgesellschaft (Hermannsburg Mission Society)
LAA	Lutheran Archives Australia
LMS	London Missionary Society
MSC	Missionaries of the Sacred Heart (Missionnaires du Sacré Coeur)
NATSIAC	National Aboriginal and Torres Strait Islander Anglican Council
OSB	Ordo Sancti Benedicti (Order of Saint Benedict)
PSM	Pious Society of Missions
RAAF	Royal Australian Air Force
RTS	Religious Tract Society (Religiöse Traktatgesellschaft)

SAC	Society of the Catholic Apostolate (Societas Apostolatus Catholici)
SJ	Society of Jesus
UELCA	United Evangelical Lutheran Church of Australia
UGSLSQ	United German and Scandinavian Lutheran Synod of Queensland
VELKA	Vereinigte Evangelische Lutherische Kirche in Australien
ZAPP	Zentralarchiv der Pallottinerprovinz

Preface

Accent-afflicted continental missionary patriarchs have left strong impressions in Aboriginal memories, and the collective Indigenous memory of mission evokes discipline, punishment, authority, confinement and loss. Indeed, missionaries from the Continent, but especially from Germany, have played an amazingly large role in the Australian mission effort. How strong their presence was, and why they were in Australia, is not widely understood.

Germany had a strong Pietist movement but no external empire until 1885, so German Protestant evangelists had to collaborate with Dutch and British organisations for mission placements. Because the former penal colonies were a relatively unattractive destination next to India, Africa or China, the British mission societies themselves strongly relied on German recruits for their first Australian missions, so that until the 1850s half of all mission efforts in Australia were staffed with German speakers. This strong participation continued up until World War I when it succumbed to strong anti-German agitations. But, remarkably in Western Australia, the German mission effort redoubled between the wars with the Catholic Pallottines maintaining a German-speaking presence in the Kimberley until 2000, and it is in regard to these that the Australian Research Council (ARC) Future Fellowship project (FT100100364) that underpins this book contributes the largest part of its original research.

What to expect of this book

This book is a short companion to the much more voluminous and detailed digital publication '**German Missionaries in Australia – A web-directory of intercultural encounters**'.[1] But, unlike the web-directory

---

1 Throughout this book you will find hyperlinks to that website styled **like this**.

ix

and practically all single-authored work on missions, this book reads laterally across the different missions. It is not about particular figures or places or language groups but about deciphering patterns and dynamics. This lateral reading generates a completely different type of knowledge about missions. We begin to see whether a practice was widespread or extraordinary, and we can begin to quantify, even if imperfectly. We see that missions were never the brainchild of individual innovators but part of a connected web of ideas and projects, with tides of baptisms, and veritable mission rushes in the attempt to build competing confessional empires on Australian territory.

This book is about the connections, confluences and patterns that cannot emerge from histories of particular places, people or institutions. For its quantitative approach, the book draws on data from all Australian missions of all denominations, but its detailed discussion is confined to the less well-researched Continental missionaries who left records in languages other than English. They were mostly either German speakers or closely collaborating with German speakers, so this book opens up its scope from the German speakers covered in the companion website to the broader rubric of Continental missionaries: besides German Lutherans, Moravians and Pallottines, it ranges across French, Dutch and Spanish Trappists, Italian Salesians, Austrian Jesuits, a French/German team of Missionnaires du Sacré Coeur (MSC) in the Northern Territory, an Italian/Swiss Passionist team at Stradbroke Island, the English/German teams of Wellington Valley, an Italian/German team at Guildford, and also the multinational Benedictines of New Norcia and Drysdale River.

Until now, only John Harris of the Evangelical History Society has attempted a comprehensive overview of Australian missions. His large and much-cited book *One Blood* covers an even wider spectrum of missions – not just the Continental ones – organised in a broad geographical and chronological framework. It already showed that new insights are generated by placing different mission histories alongside each other. The present book differs from *One Blood* in that it draws chiefly on primary sources, and it does not give condensed histories of particular missions – that is the task of the web-directory that accompanies this book.

Readers who seek to know more about particular missionaries, missions or mission societies are referred to the web-directory by means of live links, as well as links to some other authoritative websites like the *Australian Dictionary of Biography* or Trove. The web-directory contains entries on the persons, places and institutions involved with German-speaking missionaries in Australia. It drills down to detail on the 35 missions staffed by about 180 German-speaking missionaries, and includes illustrations and translated excerpts from letters and reports. It is built to a very large extent on primary material not previously accessed, mostly in German. This focus on German speakers seeks to capture a particular cultural and intellectual formation explicated in Chapter 7. The web-directory also hosts a time-dynamic **Map of Mission Locations**, which shows the entire Australian landscape of Christian missions as well as secular reserves from 1814 to 1967. The map shows the preponderance of German speakers among Australian missionaries, and how they gradually lost ground against non-German speakers, and against secular reserves. It also shows how quickly missions sprang up and disappeared across the Australian continent.

This book explores the agendas of mission societies, of missionaries on the ground and of the Indigenous people who most closely engaged with them, and enters into the subject position of all of them with both empathy and analytical rigour. Contradictory claims about missions are in current circulation – that they sought to civilise and assimilate, that they imprisoned Indigenous people, that they ensured the survival of Indigenous people, that they facilitated the survival of Indigenous languages. Under detailed historical investigation, all of these claims are true *to some extent*. In the process of this research, I have gained respect as well as empathy for the missionaries themselves, who were trained in theology to be thrown into force-fields of political manoeuvring; who came to look after souls and were left with the care of bodies.

An important and much neglected question is about the motivation of the Indigenous diplomats who facilitated the implantation of missions on Indigenous soils. Two unrelated namesake authors, Anna Kenny and Robert Kenny, addressed this intriguing question with regard to Hermannsburg and Ebenezer, both 'German-speaking missions' in my definition (see definitions below), and turned up interesting insights.[2] This book examines what we can reconstruct about Indigenous motivations from mission records. It also draws attention to the Pacific Islanders, Filipinos and other ethnic intermediaries who facilitated the emergence

---

2   Anna Kenny, *The Aranda's Pepa: An Introduction to Carl Strehlow's Masterpiece Die Aranda- und Loritja-Stämme in Zentral-Australien (1907–1920)*, ANU Press, Canberra, 2013; Robert Kenny, *The Lamb Enters the Dreaming: Nathanael Pepper and the Ruptured World*, Scribe Publications, Melbourne, 2007.

of missions, continuing the argument of my previous book, that ethnic relations in Australian history were triangulated, and cannot be properly understood across a black/white axis.[3]

At a glance

The detailed historical work in the companion website permits some quantitative judgements that have never before been available. When German missionaries in Australia are mentioned, South Australia generally springs to mind; but expressed as a proportion of the entire mission effort in each state, the German-speaking contribution to mission was greatest in the Northern Territory, followed by Victoria, South Australia and Queensland.

Until the turn of the nineteenth century, most new missions in the Australian colonies were located at the frontiers of settlement so that the missionaries entered sites of intense conflict. It was not unusual for them to arrive with police protection or soon request it, and several of the earliest missions were in or near government barracks and gaols, setting inauspicious signposts to Indigenous people.[4] When they were overtaken by colonial settlement, the missions were shifted away or closed down altogether, so that townships could be declared or the land otherwise divided. Throughout the mission period there were few years in which the Australian mission landscape remained unchanged, so that Aboriginal people as a whole needed to be highly adaptive and could not rely on any particular mission to reconstruct their lifestyle. The average lifespan of all Australian missions was 14 years – hardly enough to create a permanent shelter for an alternative future.

Regarding the number of people protected by missions from settler violence, we must be content with broad estimates. In most cases, the mission populations were layered into a small core of permanent residents,

---

3   Regina Ganter with Julia Martinez and Gary Lee, *Mixed Relations: Asian-Aboriginal Contact in North Australia*, University of Western Australia Publishing, Crawley, 2006; Regina Ganter, 'Turning the map upside down', *History Compass* 4.1 (2006): 26–35.
4   This was the case for **Ebenezer** mission, which was preceded by a spate of conflict in the Wimmera, on the **Daly River** after the Coppermine killings, for the Kimberley missions during the Kimberley land rush (see **Beagle Bay**), for **Hermannsburg** where, according to Pastor Schwarz, the government and settlers had 'attempted genocide', and the Coniston massacre renewed mission efforts in the Northern Territory (see **Gsell**).

surrounded by more or less seasonal camps, and a much larger population occasionally visiting. An outside estimate of 200 for such gatherings often occurs in the mission records. Assuming a generous average of 200 persons per mission, and mapping this estimate against the population estimates accepted as reasonably reliable by the Australian Bureau of Statistics (ABS), it appears that in 1888 about 5.5 per cent of the Aboriginal population was in reach of a mission, rising to 5.8 per cent in 1901. According to the ABS, the nadir in the Aboriginal population probably occurred in the first two decades of the twentieth century, reflected in the 1921 census as a dip to 72,000 persons. In that year, 28 missions encompassed perhaps 7.7 per cent of the Aboriginal population. The greatest number of missions operated from 1947 to 1954, when 53 missions might have reached around 14 per cent of the Aboriginal population. This means that in Australia the 'century of missions' was not the nineteenth, but the twentieth century – that is, after the frontier wars were over, and missions had shifted their character from places of refuge to places of confinement because they had become part of government policy and mostly catered for children of mixed descent removed from their families. It also means that the claim that missions prevented the annihilation of Indigenous populations is tenuous.

To flesh in the 'amazingly large role' of German-speaking missionaries in Australia with some data, they were almost equally divided between Catholics and Protestants,[5] and the average lifespan of the 35 missions staffed by German speakers is 14 years, which is also the average lifespan of all Australian missions to 1915.

By *mission*, I mean denominational missions supervised by religious, not the secular government reserves generally called 'mission' in New South Wales. I have excluded town orphanages and any mission attempts that lasted for less than one year (these are, however, included in the Australian

---

5 Of the 95 Protestants captured by this study, 44 were ordained priests, 14 were lay helpers from Germany, and 37 lay helpers were first-generation migrants from the southern Australian communities. The Catholics sent altogether 34 German-speaking Fathers, about 49 Brothers and two medical professionals (one female). This count excludes the accompanying spouses and the Catholic Sisters, and it also excludes the Australian-born children of German migrant parents, such as John Haussman, Paul Albrecht, Ted Strehlow and the Stolz/Reuther sons. But it includes the travelling missionaries Waldeck, Kramer and Doblies, and the Moravian Rev. Adolf **Hartmann**, about whose place of birth and education I am unsure. It also includes persons associated with other German religious, who came from what had been German-speaking territories (Jesnowski, Ratjaski, Tanzky, Contemprée, Sboril, Hulka, Longa, Girschnik, Claussen, Norup, Kierkegaard, Larson), including F.W. Albrecht from Poland and Fr F.X. Gsell from Alsace.

Government's website on the history of child welfare institutions, **Find & Connect**). By *missionaries*, I mean Brothers, Fathers, Pastors and lay helpers, which in many cases were the wives of Protestant pastors. The Catholic Sisters dropped out of my quantitative approaches because German-speaking Sisters only entered the Kimberley in the 1950s, at the outer end of the timeframe of my investigation, and were administered by separate organisations. '*German-speaking*' means that their first language was a form of German, not that they necessarily interacted in German. In trying to ascertain the number of *German-speaking missionaries*, I exclude the Australian-born staff (although some of them may also have been speaking German) and the non-employed wives and children of missionaries. *German-speaking missions* is a shorthand reference to the missions on which German-speakers were present. It does not necessarily mean that German was spoken on these missions, or that the missions were conducted by German organisations. It is meant to capture the encounter between Indigenous people and German speakers.

The strength of the German-speaking presence might be expressed by the number of missions on which they were present, or by the proportion of such missions in a given state or territory. However, the Australian mission landscape changed from year to year, and a short-lived mission had much less impact than a longlasting one. To arrive at a more meaningful quantification, I devised the concept of '*mission-years*', where a calendar year during which four missions were active counts as four mission-years.

In the Northern Territory until 1915, such German-speaking missionaries staffed six of the eight missions and made up 87 per cent of a total of 75 mission-years. In Victoria, German-speakers made up 67 per cent of its 212 mission-years, on four of nine missions to 1915. In South Australia, German-speakers made up 46 per cent of its 270 mission-years to 1915, on nine out of 13 missions. In Queensland, German-speakers staffed 45 per cent of mission-years on 10 out of 26 missions to 1915. In Western Australia, German-speakers made up 17 per cent of mission-years to 1915, but here they became more dominant after World War I. Reckoning up to 1950, German-speakers made up 26 per cent of mission years in Western Australia in seven out of a total of 25 mission locations. New South Wales as the oldest state underwent many changes in territorial boundaries. The mission period in NSW ended in 1849, with many stops and starts and a low average mission lifespan of 11 years. In the current geographical territory of NSW, German-speakers only contributed 10 per cent of mission years in only one of 10 locations to 1915. But, in the territories actually administered by the colony of NSW,⁶ German-staffed missions made up 16 per cent of mission years in three of 16 locations until 1915 with an average lifespan of just eight years. Tasmania never had Christian missions in the sense understood here.

Christianising versus civilising

It has generally been taken for granted that Christianising and civilising were two sides of the same coin. However, recent work by Christine Lockwood engages in particular with the men from the Dresden Mission Society to distinguish between the aims of secular governments, whose support was essential, and of the churches who sought to save souls and seed Indigenous churches. These goals were not naturally aligned. The Christianising/civilising complex arose from strategic alliances between church and state, and these alliances were always brittle.

Secular forces targeted a civilising function: pacifying the frontiers of white settlement to abate violence, gathering Indigenous people on reserves to free land for settlement, instilling the habits of industry and the sanitary behaviour required for a sedentary lifestyle, providing basic education and training to provide a labour force. On this register, the indicators of success were neatly dressed children, orderly song performances, the ability to read, write and speak English, engagement in housewifery, and the productive activities and income-earning capacities that promised independence from welfare.

The missionaries themselves were generally more focused on Christianising. Their register of success revolved around baptism and any expression of interest in the gospel and its associated objects, rituals and stories. Questions about the cross (strikingly similar to an Indigenous pictogram), about afterlife and heaven, about Jesus or Mary were joyfully reported and recorded as signs of interest, steps towards conversion and therefore salvation in the afterlife. The distinction between Christianising and civilising is blurred because not all missionaries adopted the same standards. A German Moravian pastor at **Yorke Peninsula**, for example, insisted that '[a]ll must properly comb and brush themselves, or they get

---

6   Historically, NSW included Zion Hill, Stradbroke Island, Port Essington, the Yarra mission, Buntingdale and some of the period of Lake Boga mission.

no breakfast'.⁷ The Dresden missionaries in Adelaide, on the other hand, did not care whether the children attending their school were dressed. Needless to say, the latter had much less public support than the former.

The sacred and secular objectives left much room for strategic alliance between church and state. The missionaries mostly agreed that, in order to be taught, Aboriginal people had to adopt sedentary lifestyles and rescind much of their tradition. This created its own set of pressing problems as seasonal adaptations could no longer be observed and growing sedentary communities were quickly eating themselves out of their ecological niches.⁸ For sedentary communities, food and accommodation had to be supplied, so that much of the missionary effort became quickly directed towards material conditions.

This holistic attitude to change magnified the funding problem. Colonial and Westminster governments might have been disposed towards facilitating a humanitarian reform agenda, but they were not prepared to carry its cost. They might provide some seed-funding, pay for a government schoolteacher to implement a government-approved curriculum, make some land available on revocable leases, deliver blankets and rations, or even pay a per capita allowance. In a number of instances where the available records allow a calculation, the government subsidy averaged to three pennies a day for each mission resident, a penny a meal. But even these piteous government subsidies were not reliable and could be withdrawn at short notice if expectations were not met: if English was not used as the language of instruction, if an ordained priest was not resident, if the missionary in charge was not married.

Because the missions had to engage in income-earning activities, many of them transformed into farms and cattle stations. Only the Aborigines Inland Mission departed from the model of missions as providers, by placing unsupported missionaries in Aboriginal communities who were themselves dependent on Aboriginal support. Elsewhere, income earning and productive engagement meant that the Fathers and pastors had to rely on Brothers and lay helpers who had practical skills but little theological training. It also meant that mission residents learned a host of skills in the farms, gardens, orchards, stations, woolsheds, smithies, workshops,

---

7   T.S. Archibald, *Yorke's Peninsula Aboriginal Mission: A Brief Record of its History and Operations*, Hussey and Gillingham, Adelaide, 1915.
8   Deborah Bird Rose, 'Signs of life on a barbarous frontier: Intercultural encounters in north Australia', *Humanities Research* 2 (1998): 17–36.

kilns, bakeries, butcheries, kitchens and sewing rooms – skills that might be useful for the different futures awaiting them, and that could equip them for self-reliance. Despite all this exertion, the missions were never actually self-supporting and therefore relied to a great degree on public subscriptions, and finally ended in welfare dependence.

The churches and the states agreed on the need for a sedentary lifestyle, but the question of land became the greatest impediment to a secure future for Indigenous communities. While missionaries often expressed the sentiment that they were, after all, on Indigenous land, which involved certain responsibilities, the state considered the whole territory as crown land.[9] Missionaries wanted to have secure access to land in order to engage in productive, self-supporting activities, and many of them had the idea of parcelling out small allotments to Indigenous Christian couples, starting with outstations, but aiming for secure tenure (see **Mapoon**, **Daly River**, **Rapid Creek**, **Cape Bedford**, **Weipa**, **Point Pearce**). However, the Constitution Acts of the Australian colonies made no provision for a secure land tenure except by purchase, which was far too expensive for the mission societies (see **Wellington Valley**, **Flierl**). Had secure tenure been granted to the Christian couples on the missions, the future of many Indigenous people in Australia would have looked very different.[10]

Insecure tenure meant that many missions were shifted from one location to another. This involved the loss of some people from the mission population and the dislocation of those who moved (for example, from Broome to **Cygnet Bay** and Drysdale River, from **Lake Condah** to Lake Tyers, from **Mari Yamba** to Hopevale, from **Bloomfield** to Yarrabah, and the various shifts of Little Flower mission). Such forced removals expedited the fragmentation of organic communities capable of exercising their own methods of governance. In the twentieth century, Chief Protectors signed off on massive numbers of forced removals, and often missions became the receptacles of such removed persons. This rendered it compulsory to remain on a mission – anyone brought in

---

9 'The Aborigines considered us as intruders in their country and considered our sheep their property. I had to learn a great deal and it was difficult for me to understand and work with Aborigines … The land was their property and they wanted us to give them food and supplies in return for using it.' Fr Alphonse Bleischwitz, founding Balgo mission in 1939, cited in Brigida Nailon, *Nothing is Wasted in the Household of God: Vincent Pallotti's Vision in Australia 1901–2001*, Spectrum, Richmond, 2001, p. 127.
10 Helen MacFarlane and John Foley, Kimberley Mission Review – Analysis and Evaluation of Church and Government involvement in the Catholic Missions of the Kimberley (n.d., ca 1981), State Records of Western Australia.

by police could not leave without permission. It also made it difficult to adhere to a local language for teaching and preaching. Only very few punitive removals of adults were initiated by missionaries (e.g. Weipa), but, ironically, an unsympathetic Chief Protector could object and intervene when missionaries asked some of their trusted Aboriginal staff to accompany them for tasks off the mission, such as helping to establish new sites (see, for example, Chief Protector Neville's objections to workers from Beagle Bay at **Rockhole**).

Tensions between protectors and missionaries became frequent as governments increasingly developed their own policies for the management of Indigenous populations, which were often in conflict with those of the missions. In general, German-speaking missionaries preferred to prevent outside employment and the mixing of different language groups, whereas governments aimed for the opposite, long before they formulated the policy of Assimilation. An apt expression of the anti-denominational intent of government bureaucracies is the way in which officials insisted on calling the missions by their geographical name instead of the name used by the mission societies: Moreton Bay instead of **Zion Hill**, Lake Hindmarsh instead of Ebenezer, Cape Bedford instead of Hope Valley, Daly River instead of St Joseph's, Cooper's Creek instead of Bethesda (later **Killalpaninna** named after the lake), Finke River instead of **Hermannsburg**.

Missionaries were quite aware of the loss of independence associated with government handouts and favours. The German-speaking bishops in charge of northern missions (**Gsell** and **Raible**) were very wary of accepting government appointments as local protectors and of accepting government grants tied to certain expectations. Pastor **Schwarz** at Hopevale also refused a subsidy as long as possible, and Rev. **Hey** preferred to raise money through the Presbyterian Women's Mission Union of Victoria for a teacher at Mapoon: 'I don't think we should beg everything we can get from the government because it might make us too dependent which could have dire consequences'.[11]

Most missionaries realised that their project would not be achieved within a generation. They felt that the hope of Christianising lay at best in the second generation, and therefore focused their efforts on children.

---

11 Hey to La Trobe, 28 March 1898, The Moravian Mission in Australia Papers, MF 186, Australian Institute of Aboriginal and Torres Strait Islanders (AIATSIS).

This might mean removing children entirely from their parents and country (**Stradbroke Island**, Wellington Valley, Mari Yamba and, after World War II, **Beagle Bay** and the Kimberley missions), or it might involve dormitories at the core of the mission, still within reach of the parents on the perimeters. A few missions actually commenced with children whom the missionaries themselves removed (**Drysdale River** see Nicholas **Emo**) or who were removed by police (**Bathurst Island**, **Wandering Brook**, **Garden Point**). In the long run, the missionaries were not in a position to fend off the demands of governments and had to accept removed adults and children together with pro rata funding. At Mapoon, the number of children in the dormitories tripled within a year once removals of children began. Two years after the first removed children arrived, their entire access area including gardens, play areas and dormitories were wire-fenced, and the doors were controlled through wires from the mission house. Rev. Hey wrote with regret: 'We are now a penitentiary'.[12]

The missions were in a pincer of expectations, and missionaries could come under fire from criticism from all sides – interfering government officers, jealous settler neighbours, inquisitive journalists, resentful Indigenous people and, most difficult to cope with, their own ranks.

Chapter preview

This book is organised thematically, and therefore does not attempt to provide a comprehensive account of any of the missions, missionary figures or mission societies, all of which is provided in the accompanying web-directory. The first three chapters address the geopolitics of mission and the circumstances that led to competitive mission 'rushes' in Australia, looking through the lens of the organisations that oversaw and managed the mission effort. The first chapter focuses on the tension between Protestants and Catholics and the emerging jealousies within the early Catholic Church in Australia. Chapter 2 explores the remarkable factionalism of Australian Lutherans and explains the different intellectual formation provided in various mission colleges. Chapter 3 traces the competitive northward extension of mission where the shape of colonial empires provided the framework for confessional empire building, so that the rise and decline of missions is mapped onto geopolitical circumstances.

---

12 Walter Roth, Annual Report of the Chief Protector of Aborigines, *Queensland Votes and Proceedings*, 1903, Vol. 2, p. 470.

The second half of the book explores the intentions, or agendas, of two other stakeholders: the missionaries on the ground and Indigenous people who engaged with them, again proceeding inductively from the mission records. Chapter 4 examines the ontological dynamics from which meaning was created in early mission contact settings where the Christian focus on the supernatural became interesting and decipherable to Indigenous Australians. Chapter 5 explores the local diplomats and imported workers from the Pacific Rim who inserted themselves as intermediaries into the culture clash between foreign missionaries and local populations. This resists the portrayal often encountered in mission narratives of a lonely missionary encountering 'wild natives' and gives due credit to the mission pioneers from a range of ethnic backgrounds who were not formally members of staff. Chapter 6 looks at mission life from the point of view of staff, including the motivations they claimed for mission work. The Lutheran Church tends to claim a characteristic engagement with Indigenous languages, and therefore vernacular language maintenance. The Indigenous language revival in South Australia is entirely underpinned by German missionary sources, but can we make these claims across the board of German-speaking missionaries? These hard questions about the 'German difference' are addressed in Chapter 7.

What the chapters all have in common is that they delve into the major sources of tension: between Catholics and Protestants, between German and British missionaries, between the Church and the State, and between Indigenous and White expectations, all located in complex force fields of diverse opinions, factions and alliances, so that the monolithic force-field of 'missionaries' or 'colonisers' crumbles in the face of diverse concrete realities. When one takes into consideration the rifts between English and German approaches, between religious and scientific approaches, between the pragmatic and egalitarian Moravians and the mysticism and hierarchy-devoted Catholics, there is not much left of a monolithic Western knowledge system encountering the Indigene. This in itself should be empowering for the postcolonial project.

The uses of mission historiography

Indigenous historiography has not been particularly interested in differentiating between colonisers. For Eve Fesl, the 'Dresden missionaries incarcerated Nungga in what could be described as concentration camps'.¹³ According to Christine Lockwood, the Dresden missionaries were the least likely of all missionaries to concern themselves with material conditions, discipline and surveillance. Fesl, at this early stage of Indigenous-authored historiography in 1993, was more interested in theorising broad antagonisms than in detailed examination. Broad sketches of contradictory interests (like workers/capitalists, men/women, Orient/Occident, Black/White, Muslim/Christian) can mobilise populations into political action and bring about change. But they can also be disempowering and misleading.

Because missions became so drawn into government policies, histories of Aboriginal policy have not clearly distinguished between Christian missions and secular government reserves. In the 1970s, Charles Rowley applied Irving Goffman's then fashionable concept of the total institution to reserves and missions. Later Foucauldian ideas, such as governmentality, were used to probe to the underlying power relations.¹⁴ According to Michel Foucault's history of prisons, the total institutions that became so expert at reshaping and re-forming individual selves were driven by the impulse of humanitarian reform. These reforms introduced new regimes of disciplining the body so that torture was replaced by the chain gang, and the chain gang gave way to the panoptical prison affording constant surveillance.¹⁵ In analogy, we might say that the Australian colonial regimes shifted from open warfare to retributive policing to incarceration on reserves for constant surveillance. These were not strictly speaking regimes of punishment for doing something, they were regimes for being something, for being a member of a group 'most likely' to cause objection or obstruction. Foucault's deconstructions are persuasive, but they are not empowering. Even the humanising discourse of psychiatry (and, by analogy, the humanist discourse of mission and conversion) appears as a ploy of oppression. Such a defeatist analysis fixates the underlying power relations as remaining essentially the same, without ever acceding that a prisoner may indeed prefer surveillance to torture – if liberty is not an option on the table. Foucault doesn't just switch on light bulbs, he stuns the reader with floodlight: power relations do not

---

13 Eve Fesl, *Conned! Eve Mumewa D. Fesl Speaks Out on Language and the Conspiracy of Silence: A Koorie Perspective*, University of Queensland Press, St Lucia, 1993, p. 210.
14 Charles Rowley, *Aboriginal Policy and Practice: The Destruction of Aboriginal Society*. Vol. 1, Australian National University Press, Canberra, 1970; Rosalind Kidd, *The Way We Civilise: Aboriginal Affairs, the Untold Story*, University of Queensland Press, St Lucia, 1997.
15 Michel Foucault, *Discipline and Punish: The Birth of the Prison*, Vintage, New York, 1977.

shift, oppression becomes inexorable, any 'exit' signs are obscured and we remain caught in a straight-jacket of self-perpetuating power relations. For the disempowered, this means a loss of hope, and must give rise to anger. A historically differentiated account of individuals and groups of people with often conflicting agendas and interests is better suited to Reconciliation – if revolution is not an option on the table. This book attempts to look at the Continental missionaries from the 'other side of the altar' – in approbation of Henry Reynolds who demonstrated how much Australian historiography can gain by examining the different sides of a contest. Here, the 'other side of the altar' means the space occupied by the few at the front, the missionaries themselves.

Missionary writings are among the earliest records of contact, and missionaries also made a significant contribution to anthropology and ethnography in Australia. They collected legends and myths, and acquired, and taught in, local Indigenous languages. They could not foresee how – in today's native title environment where historical connection to land needs to be demonstrated – such mission practices may assume far-reaching significance when it is through such stories that Indigenous claims to land might be substantiated.[16]

Chris Anderson observed 20 years ago that with the development of anthropological training in Australian universities, and increasing opportunities for fieldwork, missionary sources fell out of favour and were for a long time 'all but left out' of a scholarship in which 'the battle lines have been too sharply drawn'.[17] On one side of the 'battle lines' were the missionary voices captured in their own records and those historians – mainly of the cloth – who argued that they sheltered Aboriginal people from extinction, extermination and abuse. On the other side were secular historians and anthropologists focusing on the dysfunctions on missions – excessive punishments, sexual transgressions and the erosion of traditional social structures – and Indigenous people who primarily referred to the confinement and paternalism on mission reserves and the prohibitions on traditional practices.

---

16   R.M.W. Dixon, *The Languages of Australia*, Cambridge University Press, Cambridge, 1980; Luise Hercus and Kim McCaul, 'Otto Siebert: The missionary-ethnographer', in Walter Veit (ed.), *The Struggle for Souls and Science: Constructing the Fifth Continent: German Missionaries and Scientists in Australia*, Occasional Paper No. 3, Strehlow Research Centre, Alice Springs, 2004, pp. 36–50.
17   Christopher Anderson (ed.), *Politics of the Secret*, Oceania Monograph 45, University of Sydney, Sydney, 1995, p. 1.

Tony Swain and Deborah Rose tried to shift that perspective around the time of the Australian Bicentennial when interest in missions was at a low ebb.[18] Since then, under the impact of native title research, mission records have been mined for information on claims to land, family connections and cultural maintenance, for language reclamation and the study of linguistic shifts. Indeed, more than one PhD per year on average has been produced since the 1950s on Aborigines and missions in Australia generally. Much of this work was not primarily interested in the missions themselves, but rather in what their records reveal about Indigenous people, culture and history.

Mission history proper has come into academic focus in the framework of transnational history that looks for connections and cross-influences in empires and colonies. The Catholic Church is the transnational institution *par excellence*, and Rebekka Habermas notes that missionaries with their international networks were among the best-connected professions.[19] New questions have been asked of the material, such as about the role of women on missions, the importance of Indigenous evangelists and the role of missions in pacifying the frontiers of expanding empires. In Western Australia, Jacqueline van Gent investigated gender issues of mission history for her postdoctoral work, and Peggy Brock, Gareth Griffiths and Norman Etherington contributed to collections of more comparative work.[20] In Melbourne, Pat Grimshaw, Andrew Brown-May, Amanda Barry and others began to collaborate on an ARC discovery grant in 2006 to produce two edited collections on missions in the British Empire.[21] The history of English-speaking missions in Australia, and their positioning in the British Empire, is now well researched.

---

18 Tony Swain and Deborah Bird Rose (eds), *Aboriginal Australians and Christian Missions: Ethnographic and Historical Studies*, Australian Association for the Study of Religions, Bedford Park, SA, 1988.
19 Rebekka Habermas, 'Mission im 19. Jahrhundert – Globale Netze des Religiösen', *Historische Zeitschrift* 287 (2008): 641; Wayne Hudson, 'Religious citizenship', *Australian Journal of Politics & History* 49.3 (2003): 425–29.
20 Peggy Brock (ed.), *Indigenous Peoples, Christianity and Religious Change*, Brill, Leiden, 2005; Norman Etherington (ed.), *Missions and Empire*, Oxford University Press, New York, 2005.
21 Pat Grimshaw and Andrew May (eds), *Missionaries, Indigenous Peoples and Cultural Exchange*, Sussex Academic Press, Eastbourne, 2010; Amanda Barry, Joanna Cruickshank and Andrew Brown-May (eds), *Evangelists of Empire? Missionaries in Colonial History*, Melbourne University Conference series Vol. 18, eScholarship Research Centre in collaboration with the School of Historical Studies and with the assistance of Melbourne University Bookshop, Melbourne, 2008.

A substantial literature also engages with the German-speaking missions in central and southern Australia, although few were able to access the German materials.[22] Interest in Lutheran histories has been primarily directed towards their South Australian involvements rather than their missions in Queensland and Victoria. Linguists associated with the University of South Australia such as Rob Amery, Mary-Anne Gale and Peter Mühlhäusler, as well as Luise Hercus in Canberra, have done much to appraise the language records of Lutheran missionaries, and continue to inspire detailed postgraduate work on Indigenous languages such as by Clara Stockigt and Heidi Kneebone. Also, the South Australian Museum holds extensive collections of material culture and manuscripts from Lutheran missionaries. Its anthropologists, particularly Peter Sutton and Philip Jones, have created interest in some of the Lutheran missionaries.[23] Interest in this material was also spawned by Christine Steven's popular history of the Lutheran missions in South Australia, *White Man's Dreaming* (1994), which relied on translated materials and secondary sources, and more recently by the higher degree research of

---

22   W.H. (Bill) Edwards, *Moravian Aboriginal Missions in Australia 1850–1919*, Uniting Church Historical Society (SA), Adelaide, 1999; Kay Saunders (Kay Evans), 'Missionary Effort Towards the Cape York Aborigines, 1886–1910, a Study of Culture Contact', Honours thesis, University of Queensland, 1969; Joc Schmiechen, 'The Hermannsburg Missionary Society in Australia 1866–1894, a Study in Aboriginal and European Interaction During First Contacts', Honours thesis, University of Adelaide, 1971; Noel Pearson, 'Ngamu-ngaadyarr, Muuri-bunggaga and Midha Mini in Guugu Yimidhirr history: Dingoes, Sheep and Mr Muni in Guugu Yimidhirr History: Hope Vale Lutheran Mission 1900–1950', Honours thesis, University of Sydney, 1986; Christine Choo, *Mission Girls: Aboriginal Women on Catholic Missions in the Kimberley, Western Australia, 1900–1950*, University of Western Australia Press, Perth, 2001; Robert Kenny, *The Lamb Enters the Dreaming*. German materials were accessed by Anna Kenny, *The Aranda's Pepa*; and Felicity Jensz, *Moravian Missionaries in the British Colony of Victoria, Australia, 1848–1908: Influential Strangers*, Brill, Leiden, 2010.
23   Rob Amery, *Warrabarna Kaurna! Reclaiming an Australian Language*, Swets & Zeitlinger, Lisse, Netherlands, 2000, pp. 105–06; Rob Amery, 'Beyond their expectations: Teichelmann and Schürmann's efforts to preserve the Kaurna language continue to bear fruit', in Walter Veit (ed.), *The Struggle for Souls and Science: Constructing the Fifth Continent: German Missionaries and Scientists in Australia*, Occasional Paper No. 3, Strehlow Research Centre, Alice Springs, 2004, pp. 9–28; Mary-Anne Gale, *Dhanum Djorra'wuy Dhäwu: A History of Writing in Aboriginal Languages*, Aboriginal Research Institute, University of South Australia, Underdale, 1997; Peter Mühlhäusler, 'Exploring the missionary position', *Journal of Pidgin and Creole Languages* 14.2 (1999): 339–46; Peter Mühlhäusler, *Linguistic Ecology: Language Change and Linguistic Imperialism in the Pacific Region*, Routledge, London, 2002; Stephen A. Wurm, Peter Mühlhäusler and Darrell T. Tryon (eds), *Atlas of Languages of Intercultural Communication in the Pacific, Asia, and the Americas*. Vol. 3, Mouton de Gruyter, Berlin, 1996; Clara Stockigt, 'Early descriptions of Pama-Nyungan ergativity', *Historiographia Linguistica* 42.2–3 (2015): 335–77; Clara Stockigt, 'Pama-Nyungan Morphosyntax: Lineages of Early Description', PhD thesis, University of Adelaide, 2016; Philip Jones, Peter Sutton and Kaye Clark, *Art and Land: Aboriginal Sculptures of the Lake Eyre Region*, South Australian Museum, Adelaide, 1986; Philip G. Jones, '"A Box of Native Things": Ethnographic Collectors and the South Australian Museum, 1830s–1930s', PhD thesis, Department of History, University of Adelaide, 1997.

Heidi Kneebone on Lutheran missionaries from Hermannsburg, and of Christine Lockwood on Lutheran missionaries from Dresden, both strongly grounded in primary research at the Lutheran Archives Australia (LAA). The most recent works on particular Lutheran missionaries are by Anna Kenny, who tackles the intellectual formation of Carl Strehlow, and by Susanne Froehlich, who released the unabridged diary of her ancestor Johann Flierl in the original German with extensive annotations. Johann Flierl's life spans the South Australian Lutheran missions, the Lutheran foray into north Queensland and the missionary colonisation of Papua New Guinea. The latter became a much more important field for German missionaries than Australia, so that in Germany the mission historians tend to focus their attention on mission history in Papua New Guinea, Africa or India, rather than Australia, with very few exceptions.[24]

The northern histories of German engagement on missions are comparatively neglected. Research on the north Queensland Lutheran missions was propelled mainly by anthropological inquiry and without much access to German materials.[25] The German speakers in the Northern Territory and Western Australia are even less well researched by academics. Deborah Rose accessed the English translation of the Daly River Diary for the Malak Malak land claim.[26] Christine Choo was more concerned to tell the Indigenous side of the Kimberley mission experience and used oral history as her primary research tool. Attention has sometimes turned to notable figures in mission history, particularly scholars who have produced ethnographic or linguistic work. The linguist William McGregor has

---

24 Theo Ahrens, 'Concepts of power in a Melanesian and biblical perspective', *Missiology: An International Review* 5.2 (1977): 141–73; Theo Ahrens, 'On grace and reciprocity: A fresh approach to contextualization with reference to Christianity in Melanesia', *International Review of Mission* 89.355 (2000): 515–28; Wilfried Wagner (ed.), *Kolonien und Missionen: Referate des 3. internationalen kolonialgeschichtlichen Symposiums 1993 in Bremen*. Vol. 12, Lit, Münster, 1994; Heinz Schütte, 'Lokale Reaktionen auf evangelische Missionsbemühungen im kolonialen Neuguinea 1887-1914', in Wilfried Wagner (ed.), *Rassendiskriminierung, Kolonialpolitik und ethnisch-nationale Identität*, Bremer Asien-Pazifik Studien Vol. 2, Lit, Münster/Hamburg, 1992, pp. 497–509; Christine Winter, *Looking After One's Own: The Rise of Nationalism and the Politics of the Neuendettelsauer Mission in Australia, New Guinea and Germany (1921–1933)*, Peter Lang Verlag, Frankfurt am Main, 2012. Britta Duelke, *'Same but Different' Vom Umgang mit Vergangenheit: Tradition und Geschichte im Alltag einer nordaustralischen Aborigines-Kommune*, Studien zur Kulturkunde 108, Rüdiger Köppe Verlag, Köln, 1998 is a notable exception.
25 Anthropologist Chris Anderson described the Kuku Yalanji in his 1985 PhD thesis, Bruce Rigsby engaged with the languages of Cape York Peninsula, and Peter Sutton collaborated with Rigsby on several publications. Sutton requested translations for the Wik Native Title case. Peter Sutton and Bruce Rigsby. 'People with "politicks": Management of land and personnel on Australia's Cape York Peninsula', *Resource managers: North American and Australian hunter-gatherers* (1982): 155–71.
26 Rose, 'Signs of life on a barbarous frontier'.

engaged with the work of Fr Ernst Worms and Fr Hermann Nekes in the Kimberley. McGregor edited their massive manuscript on *Australian Languages* and published several commentaries on their work.

The history of the Kimberley, Daly River and MSC missions has been largely left in the hands of the churches. Margaret Zucker produced a history of the Kimberley missions commissioned by the late Bishop John Jobst and was therefore able to access the diocesan archives in Broome closed to other researchers. Other publications focused on individuals or were geared towards the commemoration of beginnings, and carry a strong flavour of progress narrative.[27] However, in 2005, Sister Brigida Nailon published the correspondence of the redoubtable Fr Nicholas Emo, which allows access in English for the first time to the turbulent Trappist history of Beagle Bay to 1899. Because Nailon's book is of much interest for the people of the Kimberley, but is difficult to locate, I have drawn on it extensively for the web-entries on **Beagle Bay** and **Emo**.

With regards to the Kimberley missions, these were strongly dominated by the Pallottine Society based in Limburg. Their history in Australia does not conform to the worldwide pattern of implosion during World War I, on the contrary, the loss of the German external empire only reinvigorated their Australian presence. The major focus of my research on the Pallottines was on the first 15 years to World War I, but I have also attempted to cover their subsequent activities in Australia as far as possible, mindful that several of the Pallottine staff were still alive during my research.

Spelling and naming conventions

Wherever known, the religious affiliation of authors and the linguistic affiliation of Aboriginal people is specified. However, it is fallacious to assume that an Aboriginal person is, say, Bardi merely because they are at Beagle Bay. The Indigenous diplomats who helped to establish missions were not necessarily locals, and the people who settled on missions were not necessarily traditional owners. Many mission sites were strategically located at the meeting sites of several different groups. It is therefore

---

27   Francis Byrne, *A Hard Road: Brother Frank Nissl 1888–1980: A Life of Service to the Aborigines of the Kimberleys*, Tara House, Nedlands, 1989; Margaret Zucker, *From Patrons to Partners: A History of the Catholic Church in the Kimberley 1884–1984*, University of Notre Dame Press, Broome, 1994.

not advisable to be more specific than the sources themselves. I use non-specific collective terms like 'locals', 'Aboriginal people' or 'mission residents', unless their linguistic affiliation has been determined in reliable sources.

Where language groups are specified, it is nigh impossible to be orthographically correct, since each orthography is an approximation based on the writer's linguistic background and that of the intended readership, such as Strehlow's Aranda and Spencer's Arrernte. The AIATSIS language database does not settle such differences, and some of the ethnic descriptors used by missionary sources cannot be matched to that database. Working from very diverse sources and across vast regional differences, I have not attempted to impose a consistent orthographic standard (preferred by English or German speakers) across the spelling of language names. I indicate alternative spelling in brackets at least once to facilitate keyword searches.

Mission archives

There is little awareness in the communities of the type of material held in mission archives, including rich mines of photographs, and few academic historians have used mission records extensively because they are so difficult to access. Most of the German handwritten manuscripts are in Sütterlin and related forms of old German lettering that is very difficult to decipher for modern German speakers, so that some mission archives now offer training in Sütterlin to help their users access the materials. A sample of this handwriting style appears on the **Introduction** to the web-directory.

Mission archives differ greatly from each other. The archival holdings for the Pallottine missions in the Kimberley are dispersed between the Archives of the Pallottine Community in Rossmoyne (Perth), the Zentralarchiv der Pallottinerprovinz (ZAPP) in Limburg (Germany), unarchived diocesan records in Broome not accessible to research, records of the Irish St John of God Sisters held in Broome, the Trappist archives in Sept Fons (France) and in the mother houses of the Trappists and Pallottines in Rome. Of these, I only accessed the Rossmoyne and Limburg archives, and could have spent several more fruitful years of research there. A meticulously researched institutional history of the German Province of the Society of the Catholic Apostolate by Antonia Leugers, written as the history of an enterprise that sidestepped questions of faith, proved to be an excellent orientation aid.[28] The Pallottine archives in Limburg hold records of the ordained Fathers as well as the Brothers, and these often give insightful counter-narratives of events on the missions. The material is mostly in German, mostly handwritten and includes stenographic annotations, many abbreviations and easily four languages in a single sentence, like this entry in the diary of Beagle Bay mission:

> Cape l'Ev. mail per Salv. geschickt. Sr. Fl. malade – 28 Sept.[29]

Mission diaries are full of such humdrum and yield very little to a superficial reading, but they offer a marvellous amount of detail to sustained investigation. In the case of Daly River, it was possible to reconstruct insightful biographies of several mission residents. Much of the Daly River records are held by Society of Jesus archive in Melbourne. Other Catholic archives with material relevant to Australian missions are the MSC archives in Sydney and Issoudun, and the Benedictine archives of New Norcia. Except for the latter, these archives are not equipped for public access. They have no schedule of fees and charges for archive use, are not publicly funded and have no onus to release institutional records to the public. Responding to the requests of visitors merely adds to the workloads of part-time and, in some cases, honorary archivists.

The Protestant archives are in general more habituated to public access. The LAA in Adelaide have a circle of 'friends of the archives', including a band of volunteers who have for many years been transcribing and translating the German records. This renders them easily accessible and the LAA records have been used extensively by linguists, anthropologists and regional and family historians. The staff and friends of the LAA are very used to the presence of researchers who are 'not our people'.[30] An extremely valuable scaffold for research is the LAA's 'Weiss index' of all German Lutheran (and Moravian) pastors in Australia. Digitised transcripts of a growing number of records as well as images can be ordered electronically.

---

28   Antonia Leugers, *Eine geistliche Unternehmensgeschichte: Die Limburger Pallottiner-Provinz 1892–1932*, EOS Verlag, St Ottilien, 2004.
29   It means: 'Forwarded mail on to Cape Leveque on the San Salvador, Sister Flight sick until 28 September'. Diary of Wilhelm Droste, (Pater), P1 Nr 17, Zentralarchiv der Pallottinerprovinz (ZAPP).
30   Comment by Dr Lois Zweck, then president of the Friends of the Lutheran Archives, Adelaide, 2007.

The Neuendettelsau archives (now Mission EineWelt) have long been difficult to access and were recently moved to the state church archives in Nürnberg (Landeskirchliches Archiv). Similarly, the few surviving records of the Gossner Mission and Berliner Missionsgesellschaft (Berlin Mission Society) are administered by the Kirchliches Archivzentrum in Berlin. The records of the Hermannsburg Mission Society and of the Basel Mission Society (now Mission 21) are still held by the respective societies and are accessible to researchers, and Mission 21 has a comprehensive website for ordering images.

As far as Moravian missions in Australia are concerned, much of their material is in English. It has been used by Bill Edwards, Hilary Carey, Robert Kenny, Jane Lydon and Felicity Jensz.[31] Little use has been made of the microfilms held by AIATSIS of material from the Moravian archives in Herrnhut (Archiv der Brüderunität). I translated some of these for the Wik Native Title case in 1995 and since found that it is far easier to navigate through this correspondence in the original in Herrnhut than on the microfilms at AIATSIS.[32]

Acknowledgements

In several archives not designed for public admittance, I was humbled by the generous access I was granted, including the use of photocopiers, scanners and desk space, informative conversations and often invitations to partake in the meals.

In the archives of the Limburg monastery, I was the first Australian 'not of the cloth'. The personal files I requested had never been inspected, and Br Georg Adams SAC, who patiently piled them up for me, acquisitioned them as I was requesting them, which is why they are numbered from P1 for Personal File 1. They contained anything from an Iron Cross, to a Vatican Passport, to files on court cases and correspondence with descendants, and were clearly only meant as an internal repository.

---

31 Edwards, *Moravian Aboriginal Missions*, 1999; Kenny, *The Lamb Enters the Dreaming*; Jensz, *Moravian Missionaries*; Jane Lydon, *Fantastic Dreaming: The Archaeology of an Aboriginal Mission*, Rowman Altamira Press, Lanham, MD, 2009; Hilary M. Carey, 'Companions in the wilderness? Missionary wives in colonial Australia, 1788–1900', *Journal of Religious History* 19.2 (1995): 227–48.
32 Regina Ganter, 'Letters from Mapoon: Colonising aboriginal gender', *Australian Historical Studies* 29.113 (1999): 267–85.

I thank Br Adams and the Provinzial for the trust vested in me, and for the hospitality during several periods in the monastery – a remarkable experience.

At the Pallottine Archives in Rossmoyne (Perth), also not equipped for public access, Australian Pallottine Regional Fr Eugene San kindly granted admission. Its part-time archivist, Dr Roberta Cowan, became a staunch source of valuable information, pointing me to published and unpublished materials, and patiently proofread and corrected my web-entries on the Pallottines with a great investment of time. Fr John Winson SAC and the retired Brothers in Kew (Melbourne) also received me with kindness and hospitality, and granted undisturbed access to the library of Fr Ernst Worms, who spent his last years there.

At the MSC archives in Issoudun, reserved for members of the cloth, Fr Pierre Bailly MSC prepared for me all published sources regarding F.X. Gsell and gifted me Gsell's autobiography in French. At the Chevalier Centre in Kensington (Sydney), Br Anthony Caruana MSC guided me to valuable resources, including the enormous photo collection from the MSC missions in the Northern Territory in the process of getting digitised, Fr Gsell's card index of mission residents and Caruana's own almost complete book manuscript of a history of the Australian MSC missions.

In the archives of the Society of Jesus in Hawthorn (Melbourne), I was able to access the Catalog of the Austrian Mission and the Daly River mission diaries and correspondence translated from Latin by Paddy Dalton SJ and F.J. Dennett SJ. The archivist, Br Michael Head SJ, gifted me a copy of the very useful *Australian Dictionary of Jesuit Biography 1848–1998*.

The staff and 'friends of the archives' at the LAA in Adelaide, Lyall Kupke, Rachel Kuchel and Dr Louis Zweck made it a welcoming and generous research site that I visited and contacted often. In the archives of Mission 21 (Basel), director Dr Guy Thomas and archivist Claudia Wirthlin offered assistance and provided access; in the Hermannsburg Missionsgesellschaft, Dr Hartwig Harms welcomed me; and in Herrnhut, archivist Rüdiger Kröger provided access and guidance. The directorate of Mission EineWelt in Neuendettelsau provided access to files while the archives were closed in the absence of the archivist Frau Hagelauer. Director of the Kirchliches Archivzentrum in Berlin Dr Wolfgang Krogel made every effort to guide me to the patchy holdings of the former mission societies in Berlin that were in the process of getting digitised.

A special thank you to Pastor Ivan Roennfeldt and his wife Olga (née Reuther) in Brisbane for historical advice on the Lutheran missions in Queensland, for the use of their extensive historical library, for access to materials on missionary Georg Reuther and his family, and for many good introductions. They became esteemed friends and mentors. The hospitality and generosity of Maria Schwarz in Hoechst (Frankfurt) resulted in a study-abroad semester at Griffith University of her grandson Sebastian Gangel, during which he repatriated many of the photographs from his family's albums to Hopevale and deposited the albums of Fr Georg Schwarz in the Queensland State Library for digitising.

Apart from making new contacts, I also leaned on older networks. Help with translations was kindly provided by Br Brian Cunningham FSC and two unbeatable Latin scholars, Emeritus Prof. Bob Milns and Don Murray. My childhood pen pal Catherine Clautour assisted my excursion into France by researching and facilitating contacts, interpreting during my visit and translating texts. She organised contact with Benoît Gsell in Benfeld and his nephew in Strasbourg, historian Fabien Baumann-Gsell, both of whom liberally contributed material and stories from F.X. Gsell. Christa Loos and the octogenarians Elizabeth Hahn and the late Franz Müll (my primary schoolteacher) spent many hours with me poring over letters in Sütterlin. Thanks are due to Marie Gehde, one of my former students, for her stalwart web-entry support. Research and writing contributions came from my history students, Karen Laughton, Jillian Beard and Zoe Dyason. I was also able to draw on the contributions to the website by Laurie Allen, Dr Rob Amery, Dr Amanda Barry, Dr Susanne Froehlich, Dr Felicity Jensz, Dr Anna Kenny and Dr Christine Lockwood. An interactive map of missions and reserves in Australia was designed by Griffith IT students Kevin Bauer, Tim Grillmeier, Marissa Grayson and Zach Hilhorst, supervised by Dr Andrew Lewis. I thank Geoff Hunt for his diligence in imposing the ANU Press house style on this manuscript and Dr Rani Kerin at Aboriginal History Inc. for her energetic support.

For enlightening discussions with people other than those already mentioned, particularly in the early stages of this work, I thank Professor Theo Ahrens in Hamburg, Professor Heinz Schütte in Paris, Professor Wilhelm Wagner in Bremen, the linguists Professor Nicholas Evans, Dr Luise Hercus, Professor Bill McGregor, Professor Peter Mühlhäusler and Clara Stockigt, the anthropologists Dr Philip Jones and Dr Anna Kenny, the mission historians Rev. Dr Bill Edwards, Professor Pat

Grimshaw, Dr Heidi Kneebone, Professor Jane Lydon, Professor Kay Saunders, Joc Schmiechen, John Strehlow and Dr Christine Winter, and the Humanities scholars Professor Wayne Hudson, Professor Janet McCalman, Professor Peter Monteath, Professor Tim Rowse, Professor Paul Turnbull and Professor Walter Veit. Most of all, I am indebted to the generous funding of a Future Fellowship from the Australian Research Council.

1

The quest for ecclesiastical territory – Catholics and Protestants

For its first 50 years, the martial law of the British colony of New South Wales acknowledged only the Church of England and a few Protestant churches as legitimate religious denominations. After the liberalising Church Act of 1836,[1] other denominations flooded into the new British territory, reflecting the diversity of its settler population. The multiplicity of denominations lent a distinction to the settler townships where Catholic and a plethora of Protestant churches coexisted in close proximity. With the perceptive eyes of a newcomer, Bishop Otto **Raible** observed on his arrival in Australia in 1928, 'a curious competition of church towers in the towns' not found in Europe, where the religious differences had a more regional character.

Whereas the settler towns were crowded with competing denominations, in their remote mission enterprise the churches maintained this regional character, and accommodated themselves into informal territories. The conquest of these territories drew the Australian colonies into the mission era, lagging somewhat behind the 'century of missions' when European mission societies formed and missionary training colleges were established at an astounding rate. Between the founding of the London Mission

---

1 *An Act to promote the building of Churches and Chapels and to provide for the maintenance of Ministers of Religion in New South Wales 1836* (NSW).

Society in 1795 and the Steyler Mission Society in 1875, new mission societies were formed at the rate of one in every five years in England and the German-speaking regions of the Continent.

In the colony of New South Wales – and therefore on the whole Australian continent – the emergence of missions was haphazard. After 15 years of British settlement, a school for Aboriginal children at Parramatta was the lone beacon of effort (1814–26) until an attempt was made at a government station in Wellington Valley behind the Blue Mountains (1821, 1824–26). The next mission attempt was by Rev. Lancelot Threlkeld for the London Missionary Society (LMS) at Lake Macquarie near Newcastle (1826–28). By 1830, all these efforts were dormant, though several new starts were made during the following decade.

The Catholic outreach to Australia (1830s)

The Catholic Church in the nineteenth century was in active renewal, reaching out to the world. In the period of the Napoleonic wars, the Italian Risorgimento and the 1848 revolutions, prosperous and influential monasteries were secularised, their treasures looted, the buildings burnt or made available as quarries of ready-made building material for townsfolk. Moreover, the rising bourgeoisie and disappearing aristocracy meant that the Church lost its traditional support and source of patronage. To survive this social upheaval, the Church needed to reinvent itself to appeal to the rising classes, and to women, as its new power base. The adoration of the sacred heart became a popular signal for the greater inclusion of laity in church functions, and the veneration of the blessed virgin, especially through recitation of the rosary, became a central tenet of western Catholicism, as it had long been in the Orthodox Church. The Vatican adopted the principle of the Immaculate Conception in 1854.

This renewal brought forth a proliferation of new monastic societies. Between 1850 and 1870, the Vatican approved 116 new religious congregations, and several of them took root outside of Italy, including in nations that were not predominantly Catholic.[2] Some of these directly addressed themselves to the inclusion of laity and evangelising mission, and, of these, the **Society of the Catholic Apostolate** (SAC) (1835) and

---

2   Anne Cunningham, *The Rome Connection: Australia, Ireland and the Empire, 1865–1885*, Crossing Press, Darlinghurst, 2002, p. 53.

1. THE QUEST FOR ECCLESIASTICAL TERRITORY – CATHOLICS AND PROTESTANTS

the **Missionaries of the Sacred Heart** (MSC) (1854) became particularly active in Australia – the SAC (or Pallottines) in the Kimberley and the MSC in the Northern Territory.

Across the English-speaking Protestant world, this became a time of strong foment between Catholics and Protestants. Malta, with a predominantly Catholic population, had become part of the British Empire in 1800, resulting in political stand-offs between the churches in the 1840s.[3] In the United States, the anti-Catholic movement was becoming institutionalised with the formation of an American Republican Party (1854), which emerged out of nativist anti-foreign sentiments and the emergence of a militant Protestantism. At the same time, Catholic Ireland was getting rapidly impoverished from oppressive land laws and crop failures (1845–57), which were also giving rise to religious tension.[4]

In countertendency, the Oxford movement of the 1830s and 1840s achieved an approximation of liturgies between the High Anglican Church and Catholics and created some elbow room for the Catholic Church in the British colonies. In New South Wales, civic society was beginning to gain numerical strength and began to lobby for the cessation of convict transportation and the replacement of martial law with civic government. During the period of office of the liberal Sir Richard **Bourke** as governor of New South Wales (1831–37), public grants for churches, schools, teachers and chaplains became available, and the active suppression of Catholics eased.

This created an opportunity for a more decisive presence of the Catholic Church in New South Wales, and Benedictines at Downside (Bath) were the first to respond to these political shifts. This Benedictine community had established itself at Downside in 1814, after a long period of exile in France, so they were keenly aware of political opportunities in a changing world, and, unlike other monastic orders, the Benedictine congregation consisted of autonomous communities who were able to make their own decisions. The headmaster at St Gregory's College was Dr John Bede **Polding**, special protégé of the president of the English Benedictines. He had been orphaned early in life (his father originally named Polten, from Germany) and raised in the Benedictine fold by his maternal uncle, Rev. Dr Bede Brewer. Polding had declined a bishopric

---

3   H.I. Lee, 'British policy towards the religion, ancient laws and customs in Malta 1824–1851', *Melita Historica: Journal of the Malta Historical Society* 3.4 (1963): 1.
4   Cunningham, *The Rome Connection*, p. 53.

in Madras, preferring what he referred to as semi-retirement as one of the professors at Downside.⁵ On the advice of Polding, one of the former students at St Gregory's, William **Ullathorne** OSB, was established in New South Wales in 1832 as vicar general of Bishop Morris to erect a formal Benedictine presence. Ullathorne took charge of the Catholic priests already labouring in Sydney (John Joseph **Therry** and Philip **Conolly**) and oversaw the completion of three churches and St Mary's cathedral in Sydney. Encouraged by Governor Bourke's reforms, he suggested it was time to appoint a bishop. Polding now offered himself, so Ullathorne was given the opportunity to decline his appointment as vicar apostolic of New Holland and Van Diemen's Land in favour of his esteemed mentor Polding.

Polding was consecrated in May 1834 and arrived as the first Catholic bishop in Australia in September 1835, to become embroiled in a lively battle of wits in the press that pitted him against his Protestant counterpart, the Anglican Bishop William Grant **Broughton**. For the Anglicans, the one redeeming feature of the new Catholic bishop was that he was not Irish. Polding formed schools and began to recruit priests for his new vicariate when the convict period was coming to an end and the 1836 Church Act made room for a more solid Catholic institutional presence. In 1838, the Marist Bishop Jean Baptiste Pompallier arrived in New Zealand and a large group of Irish clergy (including Rev. John **Brady**) arrived in Sydney.

Arrival of German Protestant missionaries (1838)

That same year two groups of German Protestant missionaries also arrived. One group was hastily put together as pioneer missionaries for the Moreton Bay region near the secondary convict station. They were sponsored by the Presbyterian migration advocate J.D. **Lang** and formed **Zion Hill** mission to pacify this new frontier. The Aboriginal people of Moreton Bay had received bad press resulting from the shipwreck of the *Stirling Castle*, particularly after the rescue of the captain's wife Eliza **Fraser** in August 1836. This missionary group included two ordained pastors, one trained in Basel (Christopher **Eipper**) and one in Halle

---

5   **Advertising**, *The Sydney Morning Herald*, 24 April 1848, p. 2, National Library of Australia, Trove (henceforth Trove).

(K.W.E. **Schmidt**), eight missionary wives and initially nine artisans who were the first contingent of men trained by the recently formed **Gossner** Mission Institute in Berlin. They were farewelled from Berlin in July 1837 and arrived in Sydney in January 1838.

The other group consisted of two ordained missionaries from the **Dresden Mission Society**, sponsored by George Fife **Angas** as chair of the South Australian Company, along with a large group of German immigrants. The company sought to attract agricultural settlers to form model communities, and made it a condition of funding that the German settlers must be accompanied by missionaries to address the problems that would be created by the dispossession of Aboriginal land. In both cases, the missionaries were expected to form 'Moravian-style' missions, which meant that lay colonists were to form a small agricultural settlement to support two ordained pastors who were to acquire the local language and conduct school and religious instruction among local Aboriginal people, with minimal support from the state. At Zion Hill, the 'Moravian model' worked reasonably well because the colonists and Pastor Schmidt were all trained by Gossner, and the whole group arrived together having shared the strains of the journey, including the death of one of the men. But in South Australia, the two missionaries arrived from the Dresden Mission Society in Saxony in October 1838, a month before the Prussian community led by Lutheran Pastor August **Kavel**. Pastors Clamor **Schürmann** and Christian Gottlob **Teichelmann** commenced a school in Adelaide, whereas the Lutheran migrants moved 6 km out of town to form the settlement of Klemzig. Kavel's people understood themselves as religious refugees with a quite different theological formation, so the missionaries – reinforced in 1840 by pastors Samuel **Klose** and Eduard **Meyer** – worked in isolation from the German migrants, who provided minimal assistance.[6]

In the end, it mattered little what the missionaries were actually doing or how well they worked with their colonists. The Zion Hill group created fertile fields and orchards, primarily to support themselves; offered casual work to Aboriginal people; and conducted a school, also primarily populated with the children of the colonists. They praised the learning capabilities of their Indigenous pupils and attempted to acquire the language, while the various local Aboriginal groups of the Moreton Bay region invited them to important functions and diplomatic missions

---

6 Christine Lockwood, 'The Two Kingdoms: Lutheran Missionaries and the British Civilizing Mission in Early South Australia', PhD thesis, University of Adelaide, 2014.

and tried to work out just how these newcomers could contribute to society. After five years, Governor **Gipps** asked the missionaries to move 'further afield', because he planned to disband the convict station and release the Moreton Bay region for settlement. Government funding had been tied to public subscriptions and decreased every year due to waning public interest, and ceased altogether in October 1843. By this time, the 'Moravian-style' experiment, with its massive investment of human capital, had been declared a failure by all but the missionaries themselves, and their agricultural success became one of the arguments used against them. The Moreton Bay region, with advancing settlement, seemed open for a Catholic initiative.

Benedictine conquest of the Australian colonies (1840s)

Bishop Polding really wanted the whole Australian Catholic diocese to be a Benedictine one. What was needed was a Benedictine monastery to train religious in the colonies. In November 1840, Polding embarked with the Vicar General of New South Wales William Ullathorne and Rev. Henry Gregory on a lengthy European tour, departing on the *Orion* via Valparaiso, on the direct shipping route from Sydney. Rev. Osmund Thorpe CP describes the public spectacle of their departure:

> In order to give the Catholics an opportunity of expressing in a striking manner their respect for their Bishop, the steamer *Clonmel* was chartered to accompany the *Orion* down the Harbour ... the *Clonmel* was rushed and more than four hundred and fifty pushed their way on board. In spite of threats none would disembark. Eventually the steamer moved away from the wharf ... and from the decks of the *Clonmel* men, women and children kept up a ceaseless cheering.
>
> But these four hundred and fifty people were but a small section of the crowd that had assembled in Sydney to show honour to Bishop Polding. Seven thousand people walked with him from St Mary's Cathedral to the wharf. Non-Catholics were nearly as interested as the Catholics. All business was suspended that day, and the entire population seemed to be down by the foreshore. All the ships were flying their colours, and when the *Clonmel* and the *Orion* began to move down the Harbour, the guns boomed out and from the crowd came a great burst of cheering.[7]

---

7   Osmund Thorpe, *First Catholic Mission to the Australian Aborigines*, Pellegrini & Co., Sydney, 1950, p. 21.

1. THE QUEST FOR ECCLESIASTICAL TERRITORY – CATHOLICS AND PROTESTANTS

In *The Australian* newspaper, directed at a largely Anglican audience, the event sounded much less spectacular. After commenting that 'Our metropolis affords a very beggarly account of public amusements, and therefore we fain gladly accept whatever is presented to us', the paper merely noted about the ceremonious departure of the Catholic clergy:

> A large concourse of the Roman Catholic community accompanied them to the place of embarkation, and cheered them as they left the shore. Another large party of ladies and gentlemen on board the *Clonmel* steamship, followed the *Orion* outside the heads to bid them a last farewell.[8]

The papers reported that Polding and Gregory reached the Benedictine convent of St Callixtus in Rome on Christmas Eve, and that Polding was delivering a series of sermons in February and was arranging 'with his Holiness for a subdivision of his extensive vicariate'.[9] Bishop Polding must have created the idea of a very large Catholic population in New South Wales and adjacent colonies. Ullathorne later said, with some exasperation, that Polding 'never detailed a case very well':

> Seldom was a case put to me, or a circle of facts communicated, but something or other, that was important to decision, and had to be kept in view in action, was received and never came out … One got fragments, never being certain of having got the most essential ones. It is this which has embarrassed so many of his affairs with the Holy See, and caused him to be so often misapprehended. He never detailed a case well …[10]

Polding's return to Sydney on 10 March 1843, with a 19-strong retainer, was a triumph. He arrived with only two Benedictine Fathers (Garoni and Gregory), but brought five aspirants to the sanctuary and some Irish Christian Brothers to conduct urban schools, as well as four Passionist priests destined to form the first Catholic Aboriginal mission in Australia.[11] One of these described their arrival at Sydney:

---

8 '**Port Macquarie**', *The Australian*, 17 November 1840, p. 3, Trove.
9 '**Middle District**', *Geelong Advertiser*, 25 July 1842, p. 3.
10 Ullathorne, *From Cabin-Boy to Archbishop*, Chapter 26, cited in Thorpe, *First Catholic Mission*, p. 24.
11 Cardinal Moran's history mentions the Benedictines F.F. Garoni and Gregory, four Passionist Fathers, three Irish Christian Brothers, two secular priests, and five aspirants to the sanctuary for a monastery. Patrick Francis Moran, *History of the Catholic Church in Australasia: From Authentic Sources*, Frank, Coffee & Co., Sydney, n.d., Vol. 1, p. 227. **Shipping Intelligence** on 11 March 1843 announced the following arrivals: The Most Reverend Dr Polding, Archbishop of Sydney; Rev. Dr Gregory, Rev. Messrs. Canoni, Snell, Viccari, Sanchioli, Pacheali, Young, McCarthy, Hallaman; Messrs. Healy, Dume, Smith, McClennon, Roach, Murray, Carroll, Larkin, Scannel. The Italian names are all wrong. *Australasian Chronicle*, 11 March 1843, p. 3, Trove.

Our disembarkation and our entrance into the City was indeed a glorious affair surrounded with all solemnity, for the Archbishop and we with him, were welcomed by the Catholics who number over 18,000, in a way that the people are accustomed to welcome only the Sovereign Pontiff in Italy. A special procession consisting of many school-girls, fifty or more boys of the college of the two Confraternities, all the clergy with a band and many distinguished laymen, was organised to escort us. The clergy, the band, many laymen and the heads of the Confraternities boarded a large steamer and came out to our ship *Templar*. In the meantime a huge crowd was gathered on the shore. Then the Archbishop and ourselves were conducted to the landing-stage to the sound of band music and shouts of welcome from the people, shouts that grew louder as we approached the land. A procession was formed and we passed through the City to the accompaniment of welcoming cries from the crowds of people. In that way we reached the Cathedral where the bells were ringing in a festive tone and the organ was being played. Then the *Gloria in Excelsis Deo* was sung to a sweet and touching air. Afterwards the Solicitor-General read a short but forcible address of welcome to the Archbishop in the name of all the Catholics of the City. The Archbishop replied in words so full of feeling that most of those present had tears in their eyes. Then the *Te Deum* was sung. And finally the Archbishop gave his blessing to the large number of people present. When all this was over we left the cathedral in the same order in which we entered it and proceeded to the Archbishop's House, accompanied all the time by the band and by cries of welcome from the people. This solemn entry is such a tender and glorious mark of respect towards our holy Catholic religion that one cannot help feeling joyful to the point of tears.[12]

The local press, predictably, gave a more sober account, and pointedly alleged that to welcome Archbishop Polding the St Patrick's Total Abstinence Society Band played 'See the Conquering Hero comes'. The press reported with its usual superficial diligence that to staff the Moreton Bay Catholic mission 'five Italian' priests accompanied the archbishop and Rev. Gregory: **Snell** (actually Swiss), Viccari (actually Raimondo Vaccari), Canoni (actually Garoni OSB), Sanchioli (actually Maurizio Lencioni) and Pacheali (actually Luigi Pesciaroli).[13] After his return to Sydney as archbishop, Polding rescripted St Mary's as a Benedictine cathedral and his residence as a Benedictine monastery with obligatory choral recitation of the Divine Office, although most of his religious were not Benedictines.[14]

---

12   Vaccari in Sydney to Mgr Lione Colmo, 15 March 1843, in Thorpe, *First Catholic Mission*, p. 208.
13   *Sydney Morning Herald*, 11 March 1843; and '**Shipping Intelligence**', *Australasian Chronicle*, 11 March 1843, p. 3, Trove.
14   Thorpe, *First Catholic Mission*, p. 80.

1. THE QUEST FOR ECCLESIASTICAL TERRITORY – CATHOLICS AND PROTESTANTS

During his European tour, Polding had successfully conducted a sensitive diplomatic mission for the Holy See to Malta, gaining such favourable disposition from the Pope that he was appointed Count of the Holy Roman Empire and Bishop Assistant at the Papal Throne. He was also raised to the Archiepiscopal See of Sydney, meaning a promotion both of the bishop and of the vicariate, which now received its own Australian hierarchy of jurisdictions. Adelaide and Hobart became separate episcopal Sees, and Western Australia became an apostolic prefecture.[15] All this meant that Polding returned to Sydney with an armful of titles suggesting that he was more learned, noble and elevated than the Anglican bishop: a doctor of theology, a count and an archbishop. It was like throwing down the gauntlet, and the press had a feast.

The Anglican Bishop of Sydney Broughton lodged a very formal and public objection, claiming that the 'Bishop of Rome' (meaning the Pope) had no authority whatsoever to institute any episcopal See within an already existing diocese, and that this act was 'in breach and contravention of the canonical laws, usages, and common order of the household of faith' and infringed on the Anglican's 'undoubted ecclesiastical rights and independence, according to the principles of that Catholic Church to which we have never ceased to belong'. Bishop Broughton felt that this 'attempted invasion of the See of Rome' was 'an act of direct and purposed hostility towards us' and instructed all his ministers to read his protest out in public. The Protestant press referred to it as an 'attempt on the part of a foreign prince to confer a title and territorial jurisdiction within the realm of England'.[16] Lord Stanley in the Colonial Office, who had sanctioned Polding's elevation with a 'grand dinner', ignored the Australian protests.[17]

There arose some confusion about how to properly address and refer to an archbishop, who was also a count and a doctor, and whose status relative to the Anglican bishop was under dispute. After a personal interview between Polding and Earl **Grey** in April 1847, a circular was sent to Governor Fitzroy and other governors of the colonies, clarifying that an act of parliament now formally recognised the rank of the Irish Roman Catholic prelates 'by giving them precedence immediately after the prelates of the Established Church of the same degree'. Subsequently,

---

15   Thorpe, *First Catholic Mission*.
16   '**The Church in Australia**', *The Courier* (Hobart), 14 April 1843, p. 4, Trove.
17   **Advertising**, *The Sydney Morning Herald*, 24 April 1848, p. 2, Trove. Bede Nairn, '**Polding**, John Bede (1794–1877)', *Australian Dictionary of Biography*, National Centre of Biography, The Australian National University (henceforth *ADB*).

'the Roman Catholic prelate in New South Wales will be addressed as the Most Reverend Archbishop Polding, and in Van Diemen's Land as the Right Reverend Bishop Wilson'. Archbishop Polding would in future be officially addressed as 'Your Grace'.[18]

The Scottish promoter of Presbyterian immigration, J.D. Lang, relished this public battle, never failing to substitute 'popish' for 'papal', 'Romish' for 'Catholic', and 'Popery' for 'Vatican'. He was keen to show up rifts within the Catholic Church. Such a rift was just occurring in Germany, where in 1844 the Bishop of Trier had put on public display, for the first time in over 30 years, the cathedral's most sacred relic – the seamless robe of Jesus – to encourage pilgrimages and donations. This so outraged a young priest, Johannes Ronge, that he wrote an incensed public letter to the bishop, was excommunicated and, with Johannes Czerski, formed a breakaway sect of German Catholics (Deutschkatholiken) who renounced indulgences, confession, celibacy and submission to Rome. The holy coat in Trier was not displayed again until 1898, and only three times since then. Lang penned what he called a Litany of the Holy Coat.[19]

> Dr. Lang is going to England, Holy Coat ! pray for us !
> To bring out both Swiss and Germans, Holy Coat ! pray for us !
> To cultivate the vine at Port Phillip !!! Holy Coat ! pray for us !
> He 's worse than Ronge and Czerski, Holy Coat ! pray for us !
> Those heretical Silesian priests, Holy Coat ! pray for us !
> Who, madly daring to think for themselves, Holy Coat ! pray for us !
> And to examine the word of God, Holy Coat ! pray for us !
> Have renounced the Pope and all his work !!! Holy Coat ! pray for us !
> Including thee, Most Holy Coat !!! Holy Coat ! pray for us !
> He will defeat our grand conspiracy, Holy Coat ! pray for us !
> In which Bishop Polding and Bishop Murphy, Holy Coat ! pray for us !
> With all the French priests in Tahiti, Holy Coat ! pray for us !
> Are now engaged with might and main, Holy Coat ! pray for us !
> To ROMANIZE THIS SOUTHERN HEMISPHERE !!!
> Holy Coat ! pray for us !

To 'romanize the southern hemisphere', Polding had appointed two vicars general. The Rev. Dr John Brady, who had been among the group of clergy arriving in New South Wales in 1838, became vicar general in Perth

---

18 **'Sydney news'**, *The Maitland Mercury & Hunter River General Advertiser*, 22 April 1848, p. 4, Trove. Presumably, the reference is to the Church Act of 1836, which placed all religions on an equal footing, removing the privileged position of the Anglican Church in New South Wales.
19 **'Original correspondence'**, *The Sydney Morning Herald*, 14 March 1846, p. 3, Trove.

1. THE QUEST FOR ECCLESIASTICAL TERRITORY – CATHOLICS AND PROTESTANTS

in 1843, where he was elevated to Bishop of Western Australia in May 1845, and Rev. John Joseph Therry, one of the first two Catholic priests in New South Wales, became vicar general in Van Diemen's Land.[20] In the same year that Polding extended the Catholic mantle to the west and south, he also dispatched the four Passionists to the north to form the first Catholic mission in Australia at Moreton Bay. It did not escape J.D. Lang's notice that the Catholics were setting up ecclesiastical jurisdictions in areas where the Catholic populations were sparse:

> the real character of all this, as a regularly organised plan for the establishment of Romish domination in these regions, is evident from the case of Swan River, where the entire population does not exceed four or five thousand souls, of whom a large majority are Protestants. What the real object is of appointing a bishop, with a whole array of priests and sisters of charity, for such a mere handful of people as the Roman Catholics of that Lilliputian colony must necessarily be, it is not difficult to divine.[21]

Lang was prominently involved in the colonisation of Moreton Bay in the 1840s and 1850s and intended this as a Protestant region, preferably Presbyterian. The Catholic mission on Stradbroke Island was a direct competition to the Lutheran one set up with the help of Lang at Zion Hill. While scoping a site, Archbishop Polding noted, not without satisfaction, that the Lutheran mission counted as a 'house of hunger' among local Aborigines, and had thoroughly failed:

> a native settlement had been undertaken by German Lutherans, and had completely failed, all the ministers connected with it being farmers. I did not deem it prudent to begin our mission on the same site.[22]

> It has done little good and it is not likely to do more. The children are taught in English; and it was lamentably ludicrous to see so much good pains, as Mr Smith [Rev. Schmidt] evinced, to make these little creatures answer precisely as parrots might. The blacks have taken a prejudice against them. They call their house a house of hunger, because they get nothing. … They complain bitterly that the Germans invited them to work and then kept the crops for their own families.[23]

---

20 The Catholic Archdiocese of Perth, '**History**'; J. Eddy, '**Therry**, John Joseph (1790–1864)', *ADB*, published first in hardcopy 1967.
21 'Original correspondence', *The Sydney Morning Herald*, 14 March 1846, p. 3, Trove.
22 Polding to Cardinal Franzoni, Sydney, 10 April 1845, in Thorpe, *First Catholic Mission*, p. 194.
23 Polding to Murphy, Moreton Bay, 2 July 1843, in Thorpe, *First Catholic Mission*, p. 191.

The first Australian Catholic mission (Stradbroke Island, 1843–47)

The Indigenous people visited Zion Hill mission (now Nundah in Brisbane) as it suited them, and the Quandamooka of Stradbroke Island drew their lesson from the experiences of Zion Hill. The island men agreed to work for the Passionist missionaries in the garden, but only on the condition that they would be entitled to the harvest.[24] At any rate, Polding decided that the site was not suitable for agriculture (he claimed there was no fresh water!) and that it was only temporary. The mission soon faltered.

Money had become a major issue straight away. The Passionists arrived in the year of Australia's first wave of bank failures in which six banks collapsed, the largest being the Bank of Australia in 1843. Depression and confusion caused a run on the Savings Bank of NSW in May 1843, and resulted in a Select Committee on Monetary Confusion in August 1843.[25] The missionaries remained at the archbishop's residence in Sydney for nearly three months, so the latter complained that he was forced to provide for about 20 persons sitting down to dinner every day.[26] The Passionist relations with the archbishop quickly soured to the point that Vaccari and Polding communicated by correspondence in Latin. Polding was not only in charge of financing the mission, he also micromanaged its planning. Tensions soon arose between Vaccari, who had been appointed as prefect apostolic in charge of a separate 'apostolic mission', and Polding, who treated him as a subordinate.

When Polding had asked for missionaries before he left on his recruitment drive in Europe in 1840, the Protestant mission effort was expanding. The South Australian Lutherans were about to start two new mission locations besides Piltawodli, at Encounter Bay and Port Lincoln, and the Wesleyans had opened a mission at Buntingdale near Geelong in Victoria. A government protectorate station also operated in Victoria and another one at Flinders Island (Tasmania). German speakers were so predominant

---

24   Polding to Franzoni, Sydney, 10 April 1845, in Thorpe, *First Catholic Mission*, p. 194.
25   Bryan Fitz-Gibbon and Marianne Gizycki, 'A History of Last-Resort Lending and Other Support for Troubled Financial Institutions in Australia', System Stability Department, Reserve Bank of Australia, Research Discussion Paper 2001-07, October 2001.
26   Polding to Therry, May 1843, in Thorpe, *First Catholic Mission*, p. 190.

1. THE QUEST FOR ECCLESIASTICAL TERRITORY – CATHOLICS AND PROTESTANTS

in this mission effort that of the seven missions in Australia by the end of 1840, five had German speakers (**Wellington Valley**, **Zion Hill**, **Piltawodli**, **Encounter Bay** and **Port Lincoln**).

Polding wanted to see a more institutional Catholic participation in the expanding mission activity. He had wanted to recruit Benedictines, was met with a refusal and then chanced upon Father Raimondo Vaccari through his ecclesiastical friends at the Retreat of Saints John and Paul on the Coelian Hill.[27] Vaccari had several influential friends, among them Cardinal Oriolo, a highly esteemed Franciscan, and Vincent Pallotti (canonised in 1963) who had just formed a new order in 1835 (the **Pallottines**). 'To have been a friend of such a man is an honour no degree of subsequent failure can obliterate', wrote Fr Thorpe.[28]

Subsequent failure indeed eventuated at the Stradbroke Island mission, which had no reliable supply line, so the missionaries suffered famine and had nothing to offer to Aboriginal people after the 60 government blankets and the calico dresses made by Sydney Catholic women had been distributed. The three Italians had no facility for language acquisition so they did not even attempt a school, neither did they have funds to take in and feed children. They were merely trying to survive their difficult situation on the island at a disused and leaky government station on a two-year lease. Aboriginal people who lived around Dunwich were acquainted with Europeans from their contact with convicts and military and spoke English, but only the Swiss Fr Joseph Snell was multilingual (German, French, Turkish and Italian) and had some English. The missionaries struggled to understand the frontier stories of deceit, betrayal and abuse that the Indigenous people were trying to relate to them. For the first seven months, Aboriginal people only stayed at the mission for about 10 weeks altogether, though sometimes the missionaries were taken on travels around the island, just like the Zion Hill missionaries.

The mission was doomed to fail because from the beginning Polding had no faith in the Passionists. He referred to them as 'bunglers', 'ignorant of the world' and 'contracted in their notions', and sought to prevent a direct line of communication between them and the Propaganda Fide. 'I am determined to procure if I can our own people.'[29] The Passionists did not

---

27 Thorpe, *First Catholic Mission*, p. 23.
28 Thorpe, *First Catholic Mission*, p. 36.
29 Polding at Moreton Bay to Heptonstall, 9 June 1843, in Thorpe, *First Catholic Mission*, p. 191. Rev. Thomas Heptonstall OSB was Polding's cousin and the procurator of the Benedictine Brothers in London.

report to Polding, and Polding did not report to the Propaganda Fide about the mission. By the end of the second year, Rome criticised Polding for the failing mission compared with Bishop Pompallier's thriving Māori missions. Polding's 'own people' were invited to make another attempt at mission in Western Australia. The three Passionist priests left their superior, Vaccari, on Stradbroke Island and made their way to Sydney in June 1846 in the hope of joining the proposed Benedictine mission in Western Australia. When they reached Sydney, Archbishop Polding was on his second European tour, and the Western Australian mission party had itself also encountered many tribulations. They were reassigned to Bishop Dr Francis **Murphy** in Adelaide, where they were separated and quietly unhappy.[30]

The Catholic extension to Western Australia (1846)

The first vicar general of Western Australia, Rev. Dr John Brady, 'lived in a miserable hovel without comforts of any kind, on the simplest food', according to Catholic historian Dr R.R. Madden, who was the colonial secretary of Western Australia at the time, and a devout Irish Catholic. Madden found that 'the colony was administered by Irish Orangemen in the interests of Orangemen ... unprincipled astute bigots in authority'.[31] Actually, Brady only spent two months in the tiny residence in Victoria Avenue with Fr John Joostens and catechist Patrick O'Reilly, before setting off to Rome in early 1844 to recruit more staff and seek an elevation.[32]

During his two-year European tour, Brady submitted a manuscript for publication, in Italian and English editions, *A Descriptive Vocabulary of the Native Language of W. Australia*.[33] It does not specify which language it deals with, other than indicating the Swan River colony area, and Brady must have gathered the information it contains within a few weeks before his departure to Rome – or borrowed it from an unspecified source. The Vatican was led to believe that there was a substantial population in the new Swan River colony, with at least two million Indigenous and 3,000 Catholics.[34] Madden commented on this gross exaggeration:

---

30   **Departures**, *The Sydney Morning Herald,* 9 December 1847, p. 2, Trove.
31   Madden to Rev. Dr Meagher, Vicar-General of Dublin, 27 September 1853, in Thorpe, *First Catholic Mission*.
32   The Catholic Archdiocese of Perth, 'History'.
33   John Brady, *A Descriptive Vocabulary of the Native Language of W. Australia*, Rome, 1845.
34   The Catholic Archdiocese of Perth, 'History'.

1. THE QUEST FOR ECCLESIASTICAL TERRITORY – CATHOLICS AND PROTESTANTS

> A map has been printed in Rome … wherein the whole continent of Australia is divided into Roman Catholic Bishoprics, and therein the Catholic population the town of Perth is set down at 3,000. Now when I left the colony in 1848, long after this map was made out, the Roman Catholic population having increased in the meantime, the total number of Catholic did not amount to ninety, resident in Perth and in a circuit of ten miles round it … The total number of Catholics throughout the entire colony of Western Australia was about three hundred.[35]

Brady was anointed as Bishop of Western Australia in May 1845, and in early 1846 he returned with 27 new staff from France, Ireland, Italy and Spain, an event covered extensively in the press. The Sydney *Morning Chronicle* reported the arrival of 12 priests, six Sisters of Mercy, eight Irish students, in a party of 27 altogether.[36] Other sources give different figures for the composition of this group. Fr Georg Walter SAC is surely wrong in referring to 20 priests.[37] Dom Salvado OSB, one of the group, mentioned six priests in the party consisting of three French and one Irish priest, himself and Dom Serra; six Sisters of Mercy; and 14 novices, students and lay people.[38] His count of 26 omitted the Italian priest Angelo Confalonieri. Stefano Girola specifies that there were seven priests in this group, and that only one of these could speak English.[39]

Bishop Brady divided the team to cover the southern, middle and northern parts of his bishopric. The Sisters of Mercy were to stay in Perth. The French priests were sent south to Albany to commence an Aboriginal mission. They walked to Mt Barker where they had trouble interacting with the Indigenous people and were treated with suspicion by the English settlers, who gave them no support. They nearly starved to death and left for Mauritius within a couple of years.[40]

---

35 Madden to Meagher, 27 September 1853, in Thorpe, *First Catholic Mission*, p. 244.
36 **British Extracts**, *Morning Chronicle* (Sydney), 24 January 1846, p. 3, Trove.
37 Georg Walter, *Australien: Land, Leute, Mission*, Limburg, 1928, p. 118.
38 Rosendo Salvado, *Memorie Storiche dell' Australia*, S. Congreg. de Propaganda Fide, Rome, 1851, translated E.J. Stormon, *The Salvado Memoirs: Historical Memoirs of Australia and Particularly of the Benedictine Mission of New Norcia and of the Habits and Customs of the Australian Natives*, University of Western Australia Press, Nedlands, 1977, p. 22.
39 Stefano Girola, 'Fr. Confalonieri's legacy in the Australian church', *L'Osservatore Romano*, Weekly Edition in English, 28 October 2009, p. 23.
40 Walter, *Australien*, 1928, p. 118; Girola, 'Confalonieri's legacy', p. 23; Neville Green, 'Aborigines and white settlers in the nineteenth century', in C.T. Stannage (ed.), *A New History of Western Australia*, University of Western Australia Press, Nedlands, 1981, p. 91.

Northern outreach at Port Essington (1846–48)

Father Angelo Bartolomeo **Confalonieri** and two young Irish catechists, James Fagan and Nicholas Hogan, were sent north to the latest British outpost at Port Essington, established in 1838. They travelled on the *Heroine*, which had just brought back the German explorer Ludwig Leichhardt from his triumphant overland voyage to the new outpost (1844–45). The *Heroine* struck a reef in Torres Strait and the only two survivors of the wreck were the ship's captain and Fr Confalonieri, who were picked up by a passing vessel and landed at the struggling port of Essington.

Father Confalonieri had been trained in a Capuchin monastery and hardened in the Italian Alps. He arrived at his destination with his bare life, stripped of all material possessions except a cross and a scapular. He separated himself from the military settlement and adopted instead an Indigenous lifestyle at Black Point from 1846 to 1848. The Iwaidja had a long history of contact with Macassan trepang fishermen, who were actually the reason for establishing an outpost at Port Essington, and they had the custom of addressing strangers in a form of trade Malay. The Iwaidja suffered from malaria, bronchitis and an influenza epidemic that claimed many lives. Confalonieri attempted to use his traditional medical skills to alleviate the suffering of the afflicted, until he himself succumbed to malaria.

Confalioneri brought the future potential of this trading area to the attention of the Vatican, which quickly erected the diocese of Victoria – a vast ecclesiastic territory stretching all across the north and into Queensland, so called before the separate colony of Victoria was formed, and named after the Port Essington outpost. Archbishop Polding gained Papal approval for three new dioceses in May 1847: Melbourne with Bishop J.A. **Goold**, Maitland with Bishop Burchall and Victoria (in the north-west) with Bishop J. **Serra**. Polding was responding to the news that the Anglicans were about to form four bishoprics in Australia and were 'making every attempt to take possession of those very vast states, and consequently it will be necessary to oppose their plans energetically'.[41]

---

41   Polding to Fransoni, 22 and 25 February 1847, cited in Ralph M. Wiltgen, *The Founding of the Roman Catholic Church in Oceania, 1825 to 1850*, Princeton Theological Monograph Series, No. 143, Wipf and Stock Publishers, Eugene, OR, 2010, p. 389.

Polding proposed a Spanish bishop for the north because 'it seems to me that a Spanish bishop deprived of subsidies could successfully call upon the charity of his fellow countrymen in the Philippine Islands. The churches there are very rich and Christianity has done so much good among the indigenes that they now number four million Catholics'.[42] Thus, the practice of leaning on the help of Filipino Catholics was established from the beginning of the Catholic extension to northern Australia (see Chapter 5). The British outpost of Port Essington, however, was abandoned in 1849.[43]

The Benedictines of New Norcia (1846)

Two of the most colourful characters in the group of Catholic clergy arriving in January 1846 were Dom José (Joseph) Serra OSB and Dom Rosendo **Salvado** OSB, who established the Benedictine monastery and Aboriginal mission at New Norcia, about 140 km north of Perth. These two were from the splendid Benedictine monastery San Martin Pinario in the centre of Santiago de Compostela. The monastery, built in 1494 and now one of the most important baroque buildings in Spain, had become a refuge for the multitudinous pilgrims who annually flocked to the Santiago cathedral that forms the destination point of the now popular Camino de Santiago (St James Way, Jakobsweg), one of the three most important Catholic pilgrim routes next to Rome and Jerusalem. Dom Salvado (1814–1900) was from a wealthy and musical family, a gifted pianist and composer who became the organist at St Martin's in Compostela in 1832. However, in 1835 the Spanish Benedictines had to flee Santiago de Compostela and they took refuge in southern Italy, at the Benedictine monastery of La Cava, which had already been restored after its closure under Napoleon. (The abbey church that the Benedictines built at New Norcia, incongruous in its Western Australian landscape, shows striking similarities to the façade of the La Cava monastery in Salerno.) When Bishop Brady was recruiting for Western Australia in 1845, the Spanish Benedictines had given up hope of being allowed to return to Santiago de Compostela, so the two friends, Serra and Salvado,

---

42   Polding to Fransoni, 22 and 25 February 1847, cited in Wiltgen, *Founding of the RC Church in Oceania*, p. 389.
43   Regina Ganter with Julia Martinez and Gary Lee, *Mixed Relations: Asian–Aboriginal Contact in North Australia*, University of Western Australian Publishing, Crawley, 2006; Girola, 'Confalonieri's legacy'.

volunteered for the Australian mission. The Benedictine colonisation of Western Australia, in effect, arose from the suppression of monasteries in the Spanish revolution.

Setting up a mission site took more than a year. A Catholic squatter, John Scully, invited the Benedictines to form a mission near his property about 130 km north of Perth and gave liberal assistance to settle the party of five missionaries at Badji Badji. During the absence in Perth first of Salvado and then of Serra and Denis Tootle OSB from Downside early in 1846, the Irish catechist John Gorman died and the only remaining missionary, Dom Leander Fontaine, became extremely distraught. Serra and Salvado returned from Perth with two volunteers to shift the site to Moore River, then all of them drifted back to Perth to finally negotiate a lease for the site. On their return in December 1846, they found the mission site destroyed, and they received a notice to vacate because they had inadvertently settled on a sheep run. They then selected 20 acres on the northern banks of the Moore River and, supported by 17 French and Irish volunteers, cleared the land so that on 1 March 1847, the feast of Saint Rosendo and nameday of Rosendo Salvado, the founding of the mission was repeated on the same day as the previous year, but now on a third and final site in Victoria Plains, among Murara-Murara people.[44]

Liberal funding was made available in Rome for the mission and, while Serra and Salvado lobbied for home rule of their mission efforts, Bishop Brady in Perth sought to retain control of the mission and its funding. While in Europe to raise funds for the mission in 1848, Dom Serra was elevated to the first Bishop of 'Victoria', but after an intervention from Bishop Brady, Serra was demoted to coadjucator of Bishop Brady. Serra left for Western Australia in September 1849 with 38 Spanish and Italian Benedictines and an Irish monk to set up a monastery. A dispute arose between Serra, who now sought to focus his efforts on the Perth region, and Salvado, who wanted to advance the northern mission.[45] Serra started a monastery on the outskirts of Perth called New Subiaco after the monastery founded by St Benedict in the sixth century.

---

44   Dom William, '**Salvado**, Rosendo (1814–1900)', *ADB*, published first in hardcopy 1967.
45   E. Perez, '**Griver**, Martin (1814–1886)', *ADB*, published first in hardcopy 1972.

1. THE QUEST FOR ECCLESIASTICAL TERRITORY – CATHOLICS AND PROTESTANTS

By this time, Salvado was in Europe accompanied by two Aboriginal converts[46] to show the results of their mission activities and publicise the promise and achievements of emerging mission.[47] Salvado was consecrated as Bishop of 'Victoria' in August 1849, but by this time the Port Essington outpost was getting disestablished, so there was barely a Catholic flock in this vast northern bishopric.

While Salvado was in Europe to raise interest in an effort in the north, Brady and Serra ended up in terrible clashes over funding. The Perth diocese fractured along ethnic lines – between Brady with the Irish and Serra with the Continental Catholics. Brady became embroiled in legal action with Serra, was admonished during his visit to the Vatican in 1850 and, after a disciplinary visit from Archbishop Polding in 1852, Brady withdrew to Kilmore, Ireland.[48]

Salvado returned to Western Australia in 1853 with 36 more Benedictines, but remained at Subiaco during Serra's absence (1853–55) before returning to New Norcia in 1857. The mission was finally declared independent of the Perth diocese in April 1859 (after Serra's final departure), with Salvado as its administrator, whereupon 47 monks from Perth chose to move to New Norcia. Serra returned to Europe to try to reverse this decision, and being unsuccessful severed his links with Western Australia and did not return.

Fr Martin Griver from Barcelona, who had arrived together with Serra in 1849, became Bishop of Perth after Serra, though he was not a Benedictine monk. Griver hoped to continue the work of Confalonieri in the far north but was caught up in the rivalry between Salvado and Serra.[49] He was 'a man of wonderful asceticism; after his death a wooden cross 12 inches long was found attached to his shoulders, fastened permanently into his flesh by five iron spikes'.[50] It was during Griver's tenure that Salvado achieved home rule for New Norcia with Salvado's appointment as Lord

---

46 One of the Aboriginal converts was Francis Xavier Conaci, a gifted student who died in 1853 of a chest complaint, the other was John Baptist Dirimura, who also died soon after their return. They were robed in Benedictine habits by Pope Pius IX, and were met by the king of Sicily and Naples, who promised financial support.
47 Rosendo Salvado's *Memorie Storiche* was published in Italian (1851), in Spanish (1853) and in French (1854).
48 Ernest MacGregor Christie, 'Angelo Confalonieri: First missionary to Port Essington, North Australia', ca 1950, PMS 3686, Australian Institute of Aboriginal and Torres Strait Islanders (AIATSIS).
49 Perez, 'Griver, Martin (1814–1886)', *ADB*.
50 New Advent, The Catholic Encyclopedia, '**Perth**'.

Abbot of New Norcia in March 1867. New Norcia by now controlled up to 1 million acres, bred horses for the British army in India and had access to the convict labour that flooded into Western Australia from 1849 to 1868.

The Benedictine colonisation of Western Australia, with its massive importation of new staff and ecclesiastical authority over a vast territory, was only reined in with the arrival of Austrian Jesuits in Darwin in 1882, to which Salvado reluctantly consented (see **Jesuits in the Northern Territory**), and with the appointment of the Irish Matthew **Gibney** as Bishop of Perth in January 1887, who facilitated the arrival of French Trappists in the Kimberley in 1890 (see **Beagle Bay**). Salvado's northern diocese was too vast and too underpopulated to extend a Catholic, let alone a Benedictine, colonisation. But it served as an effective block to the extension of Protestant activity into the west and north for decades.

Early Protestant mission effort in Western Australia

By the time the first 27 Catholic missionaries arrived with Bishop Brady in 1846, Protestant missionaries had already made a start in Western Australia. Wesleyan minister Francis Armstrong conducted a government-funded mission at Mt Eliza from 1834 to 1838. A German/Italian group made an attempt at Guildford (Giustiniani 1836–38), and this was followed by Smithies, which was relocated twice before it failed (1840–54).

Two years before German Lutheran missionaries attempted 'Moravian-style' missions in Moreton Bay and South Australia, another Moravian-style experiment was initiated by the 'Western Australian Missionary Society',[51] which also included German speakers. The party consisted of the Italian scholar and physicist Rev. Dr Louis Giustiniani and his German wife Maria, and the catechists Abraham Jones, Friedrich Waldeck and Frederike Wilhelmine Ludovika Kniest. They arrived at the Swan River colony on 26 June 1836 on the *Addingham*, and established a mission at Guildford outside Perth where Friedrich and Frederike were married on 14 August 1836.[52] Giustiniani was a former Roman Catholic who

---

51 The Australian Church Missionary Society in Dublin was integrated into the Western Australian Missionary Society in London in September 1835.
52 Dave Nutting, '**German Australia**'.

1. THE QUEST FOR ECCLESIASTICAL TERRITORY – CATHOLICS AND PROTESTANTS

preached in English, German, French and Italian, and had some knowledge of Hebrew, Syriac, Greek and Latin. He became an outspoken critic of the government and named settlers who were engaged in abuses to the Colonial Office, so he was soon surrounded by enemies and allegations. The only other clergyman in Western Australia was the Anglican Rev. John Wittenoom who had no interest in mission activities. Wittenoom was also a Justice of the Peace and magistrate, and the two priests often occupied opposite sides of the courtroom when Giustiniani defended and Wittenoom sentenced Aboriginal prisoners. Giustiniani was refused naturalisation and the allocation of mission land, and complained to Lord Glenelg about the xenophobic British culture of the Swan River colony. Borowitzka agrees that this was a 'period of intense British nationalism and patriotism' and describes Giustiniani's efforts to civilise the settlers and protect Aborigines from lawful abuse as a complete reversal of settler expectations.[53] Moreover, Giustiniani engaged himself in social justice activities for labourers and was seen as a class traitor and a threat. One catechist left within three months, another was charged with indecent conduct with Aboriginal women, in a colony where settlers were chopping the ears off mutilated Aboriginal corpses and engaged in what they called 'mercy killings' of wounded Aborigines. Giustiniani was forced to leave and finally departed in February 1836.[54] He was the first, but not the last, missionary to be driven out of Western Australia. His replacement, Rev. William Mitchell, with experience in India, gave up almost immediately, due to the 'low level of civilisation'. The Guildford citizens were no more welcoming of the Catholic Fr Griver and 17 brethren in 1849.[55]

A Wesleyan initiative tried to pick up from Giustiniani's efforts at Guildford. The Methodist Rev. John Smithies arrived with his family in June 1840 and set up a mission school in Perth where the children worked as domestic servants, sleeping in dormitories. After a spate of deaths, the school was relocated in 1845 to a farm, called Wanneroo. Visiting from Adelaide, Anglican Matthew **Hale** was inspired to open Poonindie mission near Port Lincoln, which took over Schürmann's already existing mission in 1853.[56] Poor soil at Wanneroo caused Smithies to relocate to

---

53 Lesley J. Borowitzka, 'The Reverend Dr Louis Giustiniani and Anglican conflict in the Swan River Colony, Western Australia 1836–1838', *Journal of Religious History* 35.3 (2011), p. 357.
54 Borowitzka, 'Reverend Dr Louis Giustiniani'.
55 Perez, 'Griver, Martin (1814–1886)', *ADB*; and entry in Catholic Encyclopaedia, also available at **Wikisource**.
56 A. De Q. Robin, '**Hale**, Mathew Blagden (1811–1895)', *ADB*, published first in hardcopy 1972.

York in 1852, but by 1854 only three children were left in his care and Smithies moved to Tasmania in 1855. Wybalenna had closed down in 1847, but Smithies did not attempt to commence a mission in Tasmania.

Conclusion

The intense competition between Catholics and Protestants that coloured public life in the Australian colonies also manifested in the mission effort. In 1846, when the Catholics arrived in Western Australia to commence a mission, the whole continent had only 10 missions, of which five were staffed with German speakers, although two of them were already declining (Zion Hill was on notice to vacate and on **Stradbroke Island** Vaccari was left alone). Wellington Valley in New South Wales had already been wound down. The emerging colony of Victoria had four government protectorate stations and Buntingdale mission, and in South Australia four Lutheran missionaries were struggling along with three mission stations.

There was no cooperation between these various mission efforts. On the contrary, they were flagships of territorial competition, between Benedictines and other Catholics; between Catholics and Protestants, and among Protestants between Anglicans and Dissenters; between English-speaking and German-speaking missions; and, as we shall see, even between different Lutheran denominations. Despite observable xenophobia, the Scottish Presbyterians collaborated with German speakers first at Moreton Bay (Zion Hill), in the 1860s in Victoria (**Ebenezer**) and in the 1890s at Cape York (**Mapoon**, **Aurukun**, **Weipa**, Mornington Island).

2
Protestants divided

Lutheran factionalism

At Light Pass in South Australia's Barossa Valley, a pair of church towers could be taken from a distance for the two spires of a cathedral (see **Rechner**). But they belong to two Lutheran churches, each with their own cemetery at the back, defiantly facing each other on either side of the narrow Light Pass Road. The 'Strait Gate' church prominently displays its name with the inscription 'ENTER YE AT THE STRAIT GATE – MATTHEW 7:13' as if to remind the members of the opposing synod that they will likely have trouble passing through the narrow gate of heaven, because according to the gospel of Matthew 'strait is the gate, and narrow is the way which leads to life, and few be there be that find it'.[1] One of these churches is the Immanuel Lutheran church, originally built by Kavel's people,[2] the other was built by a breakaway synod led by Julius Rechner which formed in 1860.[3]

---

1 **Matthew 7:14**.
2 Schubert, David A. and John Potter, *Kavel's People: From Prussia to South Australia*, sound recording, Royal Society for the Blind of South Australia, Gilles Plains, 1990; Lois Zweck, 'Kavel and the missionaries', *Lutheran Theological Journal* 47.2 (2013): 91.
3 The breakaway synod dedicated its church 'Zur Engen Pforte' in 1861. A new Immanuel Church (which now stands) was dedicated without a church tower in 1886, and in 1887 the breakaway synod added a church tower to house a bell from the Moravian village of Kleinwelka. The Immanuel Synod added an almost identical tower in 1930. In 1960, the breakaway synod replaced its church with a modern structure but retained the bell tower. '**Strait Gate Lutheran Church**', Organ Historical Trust of Australia.

Breakaway synods characterised German Protestantism. Martin **Luther** gave Germans the Bible in their own language in 1534 so that they could interpret it for themselves, and this they did. Alongside the Lutheran church emerged the reformed churches inspired by Calvin and Zwingli in Switzerland. John **Calvin** (Jehan Cauvin, 1509–64) is known for his insistence on predestination and Huldrych **Zwingli** (1484–1531) disputed Luther's insistence on the real presence of Christ in the Eucharist at a **Marburg colloquy** in 1529. Exactly these issues of interpretation were to bedevil Protestantism.

In the course of Prussian nation-building under Friedrich Wilhelm III, several attempts were made between 1798 and 1840 to meld Protestants together into a 'union church'. In Bavaria, there was relatively little resistance to the church union, but further north resisters considered themselves 'true Lutherans' (Alt-Lutheraner) and formed 'free churches' (Freikirchen) that became subject to various kinds of persecution after 1817. An 1830 decree on church rites caused particular resistance, and led to Lutheran migrations to the expanding empire of Russia and to the United States, promoted for its freedom of religion. It also led to the first organised migration of Germans to Australia in 1838 under Pastor August **Kavel**. Kavel had been removed from his ministry because of his opposition to the prescribed new worship order, therefore the members of the first German community in South Australia considered themselves religious refugees with a licence for stubborn dogmatism. Kavel's people disassociated themselves from the missionaries sent from Dresden in 1838 and 1840 and rejected the second group of immigrants arriving in 1841 under Pastor G.D. **Fritzsche**. Their irreconcilable difference was based on **Revelations 20**, out of which some constructed the expectation of a thousand-year Reich, while others were suspicious of such millenarian leanings.

More Germans arrived in South Australia, as well as in Queensland and Victoria, as a result of the failed German Revolution of 1848 and the discovery of gold in Victoria, and the synodal split in South Australia was carried into the other colonies, even though these subsequent migrations were driven by economic rather than religious motives. The pastors required for these new migrant communities were supplied by the German missionary training colleges that supplied pastors to 'heathen mission' (here referred to as mission) and to 'inner mission' (here referred to as migrant communities). Some had been sent to the Australian colonies for the purpose of heathen mission but eventually became migrant community pastors (**Teichelmann**, **Schürmann**, **Meyer**, **Klose** in South Australia, and **Schmidt** and **Eipper** in Queensland). Training colleges mushroomed in Germany with different confessional orientations within Lutheranism and also from a pre-Lutheran protestant movement, the Unity of Brethren (Unitas Fratrum or Brüderunität), colloquially called **Moravians** (Märenbrüder).

The German missionary training colleges

The Moravians, based at **Herrnhut** in Saxony on the **Zinzendorf** estate since 1722, became a model for Lutheran evangelism. They were a strongly pious community of dissenters whose lives were organised around devotion, arranged in choirs – men's choir, young women's choir, married couples' choir, and so on.[4] They began heathen mission in 1732 by sending out colonists to the slavery economy of the West Indies to settle as Christian communities, along the Catholic model of monastic colonisation. The Moravian mission effort was itself preceded by bible societies[5] and by the Halle mission established by August **Francke** in 1705. The Halle pietist movement inspired a number of societies in Germany and Switzerland in a spirit of Counter-Enlightenment 'Awakening', which fostered transnational links across Europe and a strong evangelist outreach. In terms of Hegelian dialectics, the Catholic thesis, which produced the Enlightenment anti-thesis, resulted in the evangelist mission outreach as its synthesis.

William **Carey**, inspired by the Zinzendorf initiative, formed the Particular Baptist Society for Propagating the Gospel (1792) and sent Baptist missionaries to India in 1793. Then three Protestant mission societies were formed in quick succession in the United Kingdom – the initially Calvinistic and later interdenominational London Missionary Society (LMS) in 1795 attending to China, South-East Asia and the South Seas; the Presbyterian Scottish Missionary Society in 1796; and the Anglican Church Mission Society (CMS) in 1799, whose first missionaries were German Lutherans. The influential Dr Karl **Steinkopf**

---

4   Felicity Jensz, *German Moravian Missionaries in the British Colony of Victoria, Australia, 1848–1908: Influential Strangers*, Brill, Leiden, 2010; W.H. (Bill) Edwards, *Moravian Aboriginal Missions in Australia 1850–1919*, Uniting Church Historical Society (SA), Adelaide, 1999.
5   Early Bible societies included the Society for Promoting Christian Knowledge (1698), Society for the Propagation of the Gospel (1701), Deutsche Christentumsgesellschaft (1780), Religiöse Traktatgesellschaft (1799).

in London facilitated their placements.⁶ Steinkopf had been Secretary of the Deutsche Christentumsgesellschaft in Basel for five years before he was sent to London as minister for the German Lutheran Savoy Church in 1801 (during which time the French/Italian/Swiss alpine region of Savoy was occupied by French revolutionary forces). From Basel, he had connection with the Religious Tract Society (Religiöse Traktatgesellschaft [RTS], formed in London in 1799) and with the LMS. He also became a member of the CMS and helped to form the interdenominational British and Foreign Bible Society (BFBS) in London in 1804. As foreign secretary of the RTS and BFBS, he travelled extensively and helped to seed bible societies on the Continent. This German–English network flourished in a period of intellectual 'Anglomania' when the royal Hanoverian connection promoted such links.⁷

A number of missionary training institutes emerged in Germany, initially in collaboration with the British mission societies. Here we examine only those from where Lutheran missionaries were recruited to Australia – initially from Dresden/Leipzig (Saxony), Berlin (Prussia) and Basel (Switzerland), and eventually from Hermannsburg (Hanover) and Neuendettelsau (Bavaria). These training centres had different confessional orientations that manifested as tensions in the mission work. Moreover, 'inner mission' and 'heathen mission' invoked quite different demands for requisite training. The missionary training seminaries were constantly fine-tuning their curricula in an attempt to provide comprehensive alternative pathways to ordination, bridging the gap between barely adequate schooling and higher learning, and providing an affordable shortcut for pious candidates who lacked the wherewithal to attend the theological faculties.⁸

Jänicke's Mission Institute (1800)

The first German mission school, the Jänickesche Missionsinstitut in Berlin, emerged in 1800 in association with the LMS and dedicated to 'heathen mission' (*Mission unter den Heiden*). Its director, Johannes

---

6   Timothy Stunt, *From Awakening to Secession: Radical Evangelicals in Switzerland and Britain, 1815–35*, Bloomsbury Publishing, London, 2000; Timothy Larsen, *A People of One Book: The Bible and the Victorians*, Oxford University Press, Oxford, 2011.
7   Michael Hoare, *The Tactless Philosopher: Johann Reinhold Forster (1729–98)*, Hawthorne Press, Melbourne, 1976, p. 68.
8   The scribbled sub-headings will help the reader through the following notes on the characteristics distinguishing the mission institutions from each other.

Jänicke (1748–1827), was a religious refugee from Bohemia who had fled from Saxony to Prussia during the Counter-Reformation. He studied in Leipzig and ministered in the Bohemian Bethlehem Church in Berlin, which accommodated both old-Lutheran and Reformed Church Bohemians, so there was a tendency towards supra-confessional tolerance. Jänicke took in mostly artisans and began the four-year training program with arithmetic and writing, but also offered German, Latin and English, and a little Greek and Hebrew. He produced many notable candidates working for the LMS in China, Korea, South India and Namibia.[9]

After Jänicke's death, two organisations claimed to continue his work. One was the Berliner Missionsgesellschaft, formed in 1824 and aligned with the Prussian State Church. It opened its own training seminary in 1829 and was able to attract the public funding formerly allocated to Jänicke, and to continue Jänicke's collaboration with the LMS (see below, Gossner).[10] The other successor was Jänicke's son-in-law J.W. Rückert, who remained doggedly 'old Lutheran' and was drained of funding and support. His collaboration with the LMS, which organised and funded the placements of missionaries, became beset by tensions. This competition eroded the strong reputation of the Berlin colleges.

By this time, other Lutheran seminaries had emerged. Basel partnered with the CMS and Barmen was oriented towards Dutch territories. This brotherly division of labour disintegrated as more institutions began to compete for the same funding and placements in the Protestant empires.

Basler Missionsgesellschaft

German pietists, mostly from Baden and Württemberg, formed the interdenominational **Basel Mission Society** (1815), which collaborated with the CMS in London to train candidates for 'heathen mission'. The Basel training seminary opened in 1816. The Basel Mission Society was a daughter organisation of the Deutsche Christentumsgesellschaft, in which C.G. **Blumhardt**, the first director at Basel, had succeeded Steinkopf. The Basel Mission Society had a well-organised grassroots support network of 'Hilfsvereine'. With these support societies and its

---

9   Deutsches Historisches Museum, '**Afrika in Berlin** – ein Stadtspaziergang des DHM – Mauerstraße/Bethlemenskirchplatz: Das Jänickesche Missionsinstitut'.
10 The Berlin Mission Society only adopted this name in 1908. It originally adopted the name of Rückert's school, the Gesellschaft zur Beförderung der evangelischen Missionen unter den Heiden.

mission newsletter, the *Evangelischer Heidenbote* (Protestant Heathen Messenger), it conducted public awareness campaigns to solicit donations and gifts. The network extended across Switzerland and Germany as far away as Saxony, drawing support from the Berlin institutions.

The Basel seminary offered a three-year course to an intake of up to 15 candidates per year, who had to be at least 20 years old. The LMS sponsored between four and nine places each year, and other places at the seminary were funded by the Hilfsvereine, so that candidates who could not afford a university education could be trained as missionaries ready for ordination. The first curriculum at Basel, occupying 36 hours per week (plus three hours of singing), offered a balance of theological studies and practical skills (each making about 40 per cent of all courses offered) with only minimal language studies (about 20 per cent of courses were devoted to English, Dutch, German grammar and philology). The candidate moved from the more practical studies in the first two semesters – arithmetic, calligraphy, orthography, rhetoric, map-making, non-European geography, bible studies and bible passages – to the more theoretical in the final semesters – homiletics and catechesis, mission history and method, logic, and history of Christianity. The two permanent teaching staff also offered courses in anatomy, botany, surgery and basic medicine, and supplementary instruction in drawing, music, singing, reading, technical work, parish record keeping and 'interacting with Catholic missions'. It was a pragmatic education that aimed to qualify candidates for ordination in the Lutheran or Anglican Church without extending the full theological training provided by universities.

This shortcut route to ordination caused consternation among German and British theologians. Moreover, some of the staunchly Lutheran candidates (including Christopher **Eipper** from Basel and **Teichelmann** and **Schürmann** from Dresden) refused to swear allegiance to a bishop requisite for ordination into the Anglican Church. The British mission societies for their part also had reservations about the English-language competence of the German candidates. The mission directors of Sierra Leone (where Johann **Handt** was sent in 1827) decided to only accept native English speakers. For placement in India, the British required at least a grounding in the Bible languages, which were completely absent from the pragmatic Basel curriculum of the first few years. The first college director at Basel, Inspektor Blumhardt, became disillusioned with the demands made from London. He pointedly observed that the fine CMS college in London's fashionable Islington was equipped to receive

50 students, but had only been able to recruit 12. Blumhardt felt that the high standards set in London, which arose from the 'high church' ambitions driven by the Oxford movement, could be implemented neither in London nor Basel. He began to develop mission fields for Basel candidates independent of the British and Dutch mission societies by sending candidates to the Caucasus, from 1827 to Liberia and from 1834 to India.[11] After 1839, Blumhardt's successor Hoffman yielded to the academic pressures. He added Latin, Greek and Hebrew, as well as English and the option of an oriental language, to an increasingly academic curriculum, which swelled into a demanding workload over four years of study, still starting from basic school knowledge (reading, writing, arithmetic). The Anglo-German Protestant missionary alliance disintegrated further.

Heterodox grassroots

Placing candidates in colonial missions without the conduit of the British mission societies further eroded the Anglo-German Protestant missionary alliance. A scriptural dispute with political implications no doubt exacerbated these Anglo–German rifts. In 1824, Pope Leo XII condemned the free circulation of bibles that included the Aprocrypha, and the Anglican Church, with its aspirations for high church status, distanced itself from such texts that were not authorised by the Roman Catholic Church. In 1825, the English Bible Society severed its links with the Continental ones, who continued to include the Apocrypha in their translations, so the English–German network of bible societies built up to a large degree by Steinkopf disintegrated.

The network of mission societies (Hilfsvereine), on the other hand, blossomed in the German-speaking areas. In the 1830s, the Leipzig Mission Society corresponded with mission societies in Bremen (formed in 1819), Lübeck (since 1820), Hamburg (1822), Dresden, Leipzig, Halle, Barmen, Klemzig, Tübingen, Zürich, Homburg, Weissenfels, Lüneburg, Calw, Elberfeld, Naumburg and Rostock. Other Hilfsvereine

---

11   Kehinda Olabimtan, '**Basel Mission**', *The Encyclopedia of Christian Civilization*, 25 November 2011.

included Grossmunzel (1829), Hildesheim (1833), Hameln (1834), Strasbourg (1836), Hannover, Stade, Lehe, Celle, Breklum (North Fresia) and East Fresia.[12]

These networks had little structural hierarchy and were orientated towards international contacts, leaning on the model of the Moravians of the Brüderunität (Unitas Fratrum). Strong pressures were exerted to join the Union Church of Prussia in the 1830s, but since Germany still had no external empire, the state churches showed little interest in heathen mission.[13] The supra-confessional aspirations of the mission networks resulted in tensions between old-Lutheran dogma and Reformed Church aspirations, so that there were frequent shifts in allegiance in this heterodox movement. For example, one of Basel's Hilfsvereine, the Barmer Verein, conducted a preparatory school to send candidates to Basel until 1825, when it opened its own training seminary from which candidates were posted particularly in the Dutch territories of Sumatra, Borneo, Nias and the Cape Colony. In 1828, this became the Rheinische Missionsgesellschaft (Rhenish Mission Society), which eventually became the largest Lutheran mission society in the German empire (but without direct involvement in Australia and not covered here). The mission societies in Hamburg, Bremen and four other northern townships merged in 1836 into the Norddeutsche Missionsverein and included reformed and old-Lutheran members. In its attempt to enter the New Zealand mission field, it was pre-empted by British missionaries.[14] Like all direct action grassroots movements, this mission movement driven by the personal commitment of pietist awakening and charismatic leadership was fluid and unpredictable.

Gossner Mission (1836)

Also in 1836, Johannes Evangelista **Gossner** (1773–1858) broke away from the Berlin Mission Society to form the **Gossner Mission** in Berlin. Gossner was a former Catholic who had recently converted to Lutheranism and had taken on Jänicke's ministry in the Bohemian Bethlehem Church in Berlin. He had a supra-confessional orientation and little patience

---

12   Detlef Döring, *Katalog der Handschriften der Universitätsbibliothek Leipzig*, Otto Harrassowitz Verlag, Wiesbaden, 2005.
13   Volker Stolle, 'Wozu war ein konfessionelles Hilfswerk nötig?', **Lernprozesse für unsere Mission** Nr 74, Evangelisches Missionswerk Deutschland (n.d.).
14   Ilse Theil, *Reise in das Land des Totenschattens: Lebensläufe von Frauen der Missionare der Norddeutschen Mission in Togo/Westafrika (von 1849 bis 1899)*, LIT Verlag, Münster, 2008, p. 32.

for the doctrinal enmities that were corroding Lutheranism, particularly in Berlin where Rückert's old-Lutheran stance emphasised confessional divisions. Gossner did not aim to provide theological training that could lead to ordination. What was required were not theologians but many practical workers – 'Godly mechanics' he liked to call them – and his mission newsletter was called *Die Biene auf dem Missionsfelde* (The bee on the mission field). The Gossner Mission was born with six young artisans who had been turned away by other missionary training institutions. Gossner recruited six more, including Wilhelm Schmidt who was already a pastor in the Bethlehem Bohemian church in Berlin, and personally instructed his first apostolic twelve in Bible readings and hymn singing. Gossner entered into correspondence with Steinkopf in London and with the CMS to arrange placements for his missionaries. Gossner's very first cohort was recruited after less than a year of training by the Australian immigration activist John Dunmore **Lang**, to form a mission at Moreton Bay (see **Zion Hill**). Other candidates in the 20-year history of the Gossner mission were destined for the New Hebrides (1844), the Chatham Islands (1845) and north India (1845) where Gossner churches still exist. The Gossner men were practical, unorthodox and undogmatic. This did not recommend them to old-Lutheran purists who would give up their homeland for the correct liturgy.

Rückert conducted a campaign against Gossner, whom he called an unorthodox competitor, a 'propagandist' and a 'Catholic'. Gossner had no institutional organisation and no staff, so that in Rückert's opinion it was 'envy and malice and slander' to speak of two mission institutes in Berlin. Rückert wrote to the LMS that 'Our pupils are instructed by six teachers in Latin, Greek, Hebrew, English, History, Logic, Mathematics, Music and the several branches of theological knowledge. They live in my own house and are provided a monthly allowance with all necessaries'. He claimed to have graduated 10 missionaries in 10 years, including Schürmann and Teichelmann.[15] Rückert urged the LMS to support his seminary, similar to the funding provided by the CMS for places at the Basel seminary. Rückert died in 1854 and Gossner in 1858, and the Berlin Mission Society became caught up in disputes over the direction of missionary training, some arguing for more theological training and some for the pragmatic model adopted by Gossner in Berlin and

---

15   Rückert to LMS, 10 December 1838, Correspondence, Berliner Missionsgesellschaft, Signatur 572, Archiv der Berliner Missionsgesellschaft.

Harms in Hermannsburg (see below).[16] In 1855, the curriculum of the Berlin Mission Society consisted of six hours of instruction per day with six theology courses (Dogma, Epistles, Catechesis, Bible Studies, Libri symbolici, Church History), two German language courses (Synopsis, Grammar), three bible languages (Greek, Hebrew, Latin) as well as recitals, church service and a course in 'South African Mission'. Unlike Rückert's earlier school, it did not offer English, Logic and Mathematics.

Neuendettelsau Mission Society (1841)

The proliferation of Lutheran training institutes and mission societies with different aims and orientations continued. Near Basel, the St Chrischona Pilgermission (Lutheran travelling missionary society) formed in 1840, and in 1841 Wilhelm **Löhe** set up the Lutheran **Neuendettelsauer Missionsgesellschaft** near Nürnberg. This was formally called 'Gesellschaft für innere Mission im Sinne der Lutherischen Kirche' (Society for Inner Mission in the spirit of the Lutheran Church), flagging a focus on migrant mission and a more narrow confessional orientation than Basel, Hamburg and Berlin. Neuendettelsau accepted candidates at age 17 and preferred aspirants in their 20s who had to be 'decidedly confessionally oriented' (not supra-confessional). Its newsletter, *Kirchliche Mitteilungen* ('Church News'), commenced in 1843. The Neuendettelsau institute started as a preparatory school to send candidates to Lutheran theological seminaries in the United States. A seminary for deaconesses opened in 1854, and the new seminary building in Neuendettelsau opened in 1867. Neuendettelsau did not send candidates into heathen mission until 1878 with a first placement to Australia (see **Johann Flierl**), which opened the way to missions in Papua New Guinea. The curriculum initially comprised English, Latin and Greek, with Hebrew offered as an elective, theological training, writing and oratory, and – in accordance with Luther's emphasis on music – singing, piano and violin. Since many candidates commenced from a low standard of education (unlike at the Leipzig institute), there was much catching up to do in literacy, geography and numeracy, and the curriculum was often tailored to the requirements of the candidates. In 1878, the textbooks on ethics and dogma by German linguist Bauer had not yet been printed, so each student copied them from the handwritten manuscript. The final exams were marked by sympathetic pastors, and for languages there was no minimum threshold. Candidates who could

---

16   *Berliner Missionsberichte*, no. 11, 1858, p. 167.

not afford the 600–700 Mark annual fee were taken in on credit, and could even be supplied with clothing and books by the institute, and at graduation signed for their accumulated debt, which in Flierl's case was 2,000 Mark.[17] The day began at 5am and ended at 10pm with evening prayer and liturgy, so the days were already full. As the curriculum became increasingly demanding, the program grew to four years in 1892 and to six years by 1913, approximating the training received in theological faculties.

Hermannsburg Mission Society (1849)

Whereas the curriculum in Basel and Neuendettelsau mushroomed under the pressure to prepare candidates for ordination, a back-to-basics missionary training institution emerged in a small township about halfway between Hannover and Hamburg. The Norddeutsche Mission in Hamburg splintered off into a Reformed Church faction in Bremen, while the old-Lutheran Ludwig **Harms** set up his own training centre in 1849 at **Hermannsburg**. Like Gossner in Berlin, Harms leaned on the 'Moravian model' of missionising, although the Herrnhut Moravians themselves did not yet provide formal missionary training (until 1869). Both Gossner in Berlin and Harms in Hermannsburg provided minimal training in order to send pious artisans (and their wives) as colonists to support a core of one or two ordained pastors.

Harms, too, started with an apostolic twelve, mostly farm boys from the surrounding heathlands of Lüneburg. The earliest group photos show brotherly affection with linked arms and hands. In one image, the heads of candidates are superimposed over figures in dark suits and polished shoes, which these boys most likely did not own. After the first year of study, Hermannsburg was willing to support its students in the Missionshaus.[18] Some brought substantial fortunes with them, including a whole local farm in 1854. Teachers were not paid until this policy of 'communism' was abolished in 1870.[19]

---

17   Susanne Froehlich (ed.), *Als Pioniermissionar in das ferne Neu Guinea: Johann Flierls Lebenserinnerungen*, 2 vols, Harrassowitz Verlag, Wiesbaden, 2015, Vol. 1, p. 115.
18   Barbara Henson, *A Straight-out Man: FW Albrecht and Central Australian Aborigines*, Melbourne University Press, Carlton, Vic., 1992, p. 6.
19   Ernst-August Lüdemann (ed.), *Vision: Gemeinde weltweit – 150 Jahre Hermannsburger Mission und Ev. Luth. Missionswerk in Niedersachsen*, Verlag der Missionshandlung, Hermannsburg, 2000, p. 57.

The Hanoverian church authority (Konsistorium) refused to ordain the first Hermannsburg cohort because of an insurmountable 'defectus scientiae' in their training, which lacked the Bible languages, science and theology.[20] The Lutheran Church refused to recognise the Hermannsburg school as a Lutheran church institution and referred to it instead as a private initiative (until 1977).

However, Pastor Harms enjoyed enormous local support in his congregation. He spoke and instructed in Platt, the local dialect, and was a highly charismatic figure dominating the Hermannsburg township. His deft storytelling sermons and lectures often invoked the devil. Contrary to the church law of 1864, he insisted that baptism must expressly include an avowal of Satan. When he took up his post as Hermannsburg parish pastor in 1849, he conducted a public ceremony in which the parishioners were asked to 'rise up and speak after me' a vow of personal allegiance to himself 'never to divorce from me until God doeth us part'.[21]

This pipe-smoking 'man of the people' addressed his candidates as his children. Their strictly celibate monastic life was highly regimented in daily rhythm from 6am to 10pm with 28 hours per week of instruction, and the remainder spent in physical labour, so that they would become 'as dexterous with axe and dung fork as with book and pen'. Two young men died under the rigours of these demands in the first few years, and those who left the institute were subjected to public chastisement. In 1853, one student died, two left and at least one was expelled. In 1857, three were expelled because they demanded the right to get engaged to marry. They had all had to swear an oath of personal allegiance to Harms and were therefore opprobriated as 'oath-breaking scoundrels' (*bundbrüchige Schurken*). Another 10, who were expelled for demanding changes in the teaching style, emigrated and attached themselves to the Wisconsin Synod. Students subject to punishment had to show repentance, admit their guilt and had to thank Harms for the punishment they received. The patriarchal personal cult surrounding Ludwig Harms had something 'dark, sharp, and ruthless' even in the eyes of other Lutherans.[22]

---

20 Lüdemann, *Vision*.
21 Lüdemann, *Vision*, p. 42.
22 Lüdemann, *Vision*, pp. 53, 41.

Harms attracted students from Scandinavia and the Baltic, but had difficulty in forging links with the Protestant mission societies overseas. After four years of training, with no placements in sight, Harms therefore commissioned his own boat, the *Candace* (after the Ethiopian Queen in Apostles 8:27) and the first cohort was sent to Ethiopia in 1853, reputedly on the strength of sailors' reports that the Galla (Oromo) people would profit from a mission. The Sultan of Muskat (Oman) repelled the missionaries. Harms then turned towards the Zulu in South Africa. American and LMS missionaries had been active in Zulu mission since the 1830s, and they had recently been colonised by Wesleyans (1841), Lutherans from Stavenger in Norway (1845), Lutherans from Berlin (1847) and Anglicans (1850). Harms sent 40 candidates between 1856 and 1860 and called his first Zulu mission 'Hermannsburg'. From Hermannsburg in Hanover, Harms held the micromanagement of the Zulu missions where it was a requirement that if Zulu parents left the mission, their children would still be detained. The missionaries themselves were equally subject to discipline, and observers were astounded that 'a dozen families live in one large dwelling and eat at a common table, having all their affairs, with the concerns of the entire mission, managed by a single person'. The experiment was 'watched with the deepest interest by Christians throughout the world'.[23]

Harms forged his own theology with little difference between his own opinion and God's word, and other pastors considered his sermons divisive, polarising and factionalist.[24] Harms enjoined his students not to engage in supra-confessional laxities:

> We Lutherans have the purest and most unadulterated confession. This is why I do not want you to have a confessional union with Catholics and Reformed Protestants. You are not to enter into a union with the others, but we shall remain unshakably true to our confession.[25]

This dogmatism of Hermannsburg candidates continued to fester in the Australian mission effort.

---

23 William Ireland, *Historical Sketch of the Zulu Mission, in South Africa, as also of the Gaboon Mission in Western Africa*, American Board of Commissioners for Foreign Mission, Boston, 1865, p. 24.
24 Lüdemann, *Vision*, p. 53, 41.
25 Ludwig Harms, 1849 speech at the opening of the Hermannsburg Mission Institute, cited in ***Biographisch-Bibliographisches Kirchenlexikon***, Vol. 2.

Herrnhut Mission College (1869)

Following the example of other mission societies (who themselves emulated the Moravian model), the German Moravian Brethren also opened a missionary training college at Niesky near Herrnhut in 1869 to prepare candidates for ordination. It only accepted members of the Moravian community who were already well educated, mostly at the Moravian Kleinwelka school where Latin, Greek, Hebrew, German, French and English was taught to boys and girls.

The mission training curriculum was much less demanding than at other colleges, with instruction in the mornings and on two afternoons, and a strong emphasis on English as the only foreign language. In 1889, only four new candidates entered, bringing the cohort to 15, and the following year eight candidates were sent into mission and two new students accepted, so the college cohort was very small. But considering the small pool from which the students were drawn, the uptake was enormous.

The Moravian community was much less grounded in Germanness than the Lutherans and had strong sister communities in Ireland and England. This facilitated their entry into the emerging colony of Victoria through the conduit of **Charles La Trobe**, the superintendent of the Port Phillip district since 1839 and first lieutenant-governor of Victoria in 1851. The Moravians also forged a solid working relationship with Scottish Presbyterians in Australia. One of their prominent missionaries, Friedrich **Hagenauer**, became Protector of Aborigines in Victoria, and advised the Queensland Government on mission policy in the 1880s, where Nicolas **Hey** became missionary at Mapoon in 1891.

Factionalism in mission

The confessional differences in the training background of migrant pastors and missionaries rippled through the Lutheran communities in Australia and prevented them from forming a united Lutheran church in Australia until 1966. Their mission efforts, too, were divided by confessional disputes instead of galvanised by a common purpose.

Neither were Lutherans in Australia able to forge a working relationship with the Moravians. A Moravian congregation led by Daniel Schondorf established itself at Bethel in 1854, close to the first Lutheran communities in the Barossa Valley. They invited the nearby Lutheran congregations for their annual mission festivals, but without response. One of the lay members of the Immanuel Synod once asked for clarification whether it was actually 'forbidden to attend the mission festival in Bethel'.[26] It was not exactly forbidden, just not encouraged, in the interest of ecclesiastic conscience, to fraternise with people who had a different point of view. The Immanuel Synod minuted:

> We have received an invitation from Pastor Buck of the Moravian Brethren to be present next Sunday at a Mission Festival in Bethel. Since the point of view of our Church separates us from the Moravian Brethren, the Pastors on the c'ttee were inclined not to accept this invitation, whereas the lay brethren spoke in favour, not, indeed, of the chairman's taking part, but that one of our missionaries should go. Although in the course of the discussion the point of view gradually gained the upper hand, that it could not be wrong to meet the Moravian Brethren halfway in this sphere of common activity, especially since they invited us because of this common interest, yet the voice of the ecclesiastic conscience gained the upper hand, and the invitation was declined.[27]

Actually, the South Australian Lutherans had already formed their own mission society (Hilfsverein) in 1853 to raise money for missionary training and heathen mission and initially directed the funds raised from their mission festivals to Leipzig (presumably because the first four South Australian missionaries came from the Dresden Mission Society, which had been shifted to Leipzig). From 1861, the South Australians began to divide their donations between Leipzig and Hermannsburg. This was just when Hermannsburg was gaining a reputation for its Zulu mission, and its mission festivals were attended by between 10,000 and 20,000 people from all over Europe.[28] Also in that year, John **King** was rescued at Cooper's Creek in Central Australia and the idea of an Australian inland mission quickly gained currency. Gippsland in Victoria, too, was simultaneously colonised in 1862 by the Anglican Church with a mission at Lake Tyers and the Moravian effort in the same year to commence a mission at Mafra (which later took root at **Ramahyuck**).

---

26 Immanuel Synod, Mission Committee Meetings: Kaibels' notes, 1901–14, 25 September 1902, Lutheran Archives Australia (LAA).
27 Immanuel Synod, Mission Committee Minutes, 1895–1901 (translated), 24 October 1900, LAA.
28 *Der Lutherische Kirchenbote*, 2 February 1905, Biographical Collection, Schoknecht Rev. CHM, LAA.

The rush to the interior (Kopperamanna and Killalpaninna, 1866)

The Australian interior was becoming the subject of speculative interest as the new colonies of South Australia and Victoria vied with each other for the untapped potential of the north and offered cash prizes for inland exploration. After the failure of the **Burke** and **Wills** expedition to the Gulf of Carpentaria sponsored by the Victorian Government in 1860, the South Australian Government sponsored another attempt in 1862. As a result of **Stuart**'s successful overland exploration from Adelaide, the Northern Territory was given over to South Australia in 1863. Thomas **Elder** established Beltana station in 1862 and imported camels and Afghan camel drivers as a supply line for this newly tapped interior. A truly grandiose idea was to install the world's latest telecommunication technology right across the continent. Melbourne and Adelaide were already connected to each other by telegraph, but a link to Europe was a daring leap ahead. Massive public works along the south/north axis led to the discovery of gold, so the township of Darwin was officially proclaimed in 1870, and its first Chinese coolies were imported in 1875. The 3,200 km telegraph line, connected to an undersea cable to Java, was completed in 1872, and in 1878 construction began on a north–south railway line (which reached Alice Springs in 1929 and Darwin in 2003). Alfred **Howitt** had found the only surviving member of Burke and Wills party, John King, sustained by Dieri people at Cooper's Creek in September 1861, which gave rise to the idea that this must be a fertile soil for mission.

The Victorian Moravians lodged an application for a mission site with the Victorian Government, but this was declined in 1863, presumably because South Australia had just been granted the administration of the northern territory.[29] Regardless, four Moravian missionaries (**Kramer**, **Meissel**, **Kühn** and **Walder**) arrived from Herrnhut in Germany in November 1864 with the brief to set up an inland mission at Cooper's Creek as an extension of the promising Moravian mission effort already underway in Victoria. Prolonged drought prevented their inland expedition, so they

---

29 Annual Report of the Central Board for Aborigines for 1863, B332/0 1861–1924, Victorian Archives Centre.

attached themselves to various Moravian missions in Victoria until mid-1866, when the call for action came from Melbourne to gather them at Bethel in the Barossa Valley and commence their mission enterprise.[30]

The Moravians already had good credentials with Australian mission, but at the same time South Australian Lutherans also put together a missionary expedition for Cooper's Creek to found the 'first mission in the interior', a much publicised joint initiative of the two Lutheran synods at Light Pass: the South Australian Synod (ELSA)[31] and the Immanuel Synod. They approached Ludwig Harms at the Hermannsburger Missionsgesellschaft (HMG) in early 1863 (the year when the Moravians also lodged their application). Harms agreed to support the venture on the condition that he would have full control. Any surplus funds raised by the mission committee were to be channelled to the HMG to support the training of further missionaries, since a heathen mission was not to accumulate capital. A new mission house had just been completed at Hermannsburg (HMG) and Harms now expected to be able to send out 24 missionaries every second year, so that new mission fields were welcome, and the India mission commenced in 1864. In August 1866, four HMG pastors arrived in South Australia, two destined for the German communities and two for the new mission, Johann Friedrich Goessling and Ernst Homann,[32] accompanied by lay helper Hermann Heinrich Vogelsang, also from the HMG. None of the South Australian mission committee members had ever been in the area near Cooper's Creek. To provide local knowledge, a South Australian lay helper, Ernst Jakob, joined the three newcomers and their triumphal procession left Tanunda on 9 October 1866 and progressed at pilgrim speed, covering 20 km per day.

The two competing mission groups arrived at Cooper's Creek within days of each other, and with the help of the local police constable selected sites within 16 km of each other. They were both unwelcome and had to flee several times from threats of an attack by the Dieri people.

---

30   Jensz, *Moravian Missionaries in the British Colony of Victoria*, p. 167.
31   This was the synod that grew out of the second group of German arrivals in South Australia centred on Pastor Fritzsche at Lobethal near Adelaide and Pastor Meyer at Bethanien in the Barossa Valley. This synod first called itself the Bethanien-Lobethal Synodalverband, then the South Australian Synod, later the Evangelical-Lutheran Synod of Australia (ELSA), which became the United Evangelical Lutheran Church of Australia (UELCA, 1921–66) or VELKA (Vereinigte Evangelische Lutherische Kirche in Australien). It joined the Lutheran Church of Australia at its formation in 1966.
32   Luise Wendtlandt-Homann, *Zugvögel kennen ihre Zeit: Als Missonarsfrau in vier Erdteilen*, Verlag der Ev. Luth Mission Erlangen, Hermannsburg, 1987; 'Luise Wendlandt-Homann, eine Mutter der Deutschen im Ausland', in Die Frau, Wochenbeilage zum *Hannoverscher Kurier*, 16 November 1932.

The Moravians (Kramer, Walder and Meissel) gave up their Kopperamanna station after two years of fear and uncertainty, but the Lutherans regrouped and managed to form a longlasting mission among the Dieri at Cooper's Creek (which until 1875 they also called Hermannsburg but is part of the history of **Killalpaninna**). They also took on the Kopperamanna station left by the Moravians. Homann remained until 1872, and another HMG Pastor, Carl Schoknecht, stayed until 1873.

The cooperation between the two South Australian synods supporting the venture collapsed when the Immanuel Synod sought unification with a Victorian Lutheran synod, which led to a great deal of rankling. The candidates sent from the HMG had all joined the ELSA since the Immanuel Synod was accused of tending towards chiliasm, which was anathema to the HMG dogma. Over the heads of the mission committee, the HMG director Theodor **Harms** recalled the only remaining ordained missionary from Cooper's Creek. Mission superintendent G.A. Heidenreich of Tanunda (also a HMG graduate) wrote to Schoknecht at Cooper's Creek:

> Hold out until the mission festival, then we will see who has the say. Don't go before that or they [Immanuel Synod] will have won the game, as they want to grab all the mission property for themselves ... I have also sent a copy of the circular to W. Harms and given him the necessary details, but mainly that we can no longer have fellowship with Rechner [president of Immanuel Synod] ... Today I am with Oster [president of ELSA] and we are agreed that this mission [Cooper's Creek] should cease, even if W. Harms [HMG] should intervene, for now we are acting from conviction.[33]

After Schoknecht's departure the Cooper's Creek mission was without an ordained missionary, and the government demanded that a qualified teacher must be stationed at the mission. In 1874, the two synods agreed to divide up the mission property between themselves. At Easter 1875, the General Conference of the Immanuel Synod minuted:

---

33   Heidenreich to Carl Schoknecht, 13 August 1873, Biographical Collection, Schoknecht Rev CHM, LAA.

Pastor Rechner informed the gathering that at last a definite decision had been reached concerning both synods with reference to the mission, namely that the two synods go their own separate ways. He added that this separation had not been brought about by us.[34]

The Immanuel Synod obtained help from the Neuendettelsau Mission Society to continue the Cooper's Creek mission at Lake Killalpaninna (which they called Bethesda mission).

The ELSA received the larger part of the Cooper's Creek mission property, including the livestock, and commenced the Hermannsburg mission among the Aranda in 1875, again under HMG direction, with HMG staff and with Heidenreich as mission superintendent. The mission property was to be held in common between the ELSA and the HMG, but in case the mission had to be abandoned, all property would fall to the HMG. This agreement was to lead to immense tensions when the ELSA withdrew from the venture in 1894 over a rift developing with the HMG.

In an effort to gain English-speaking missionaries, the ELSA had begun to collaborate with the American Missouri Synod in 1879 and to send its Australian candidates there for training (until the Concordia College opened in Adelaide in 1890). Missouri provided candidates for the Australian missions without claiming ultimate control over them, unlike the HMG. However, the Missouri Synod took the position on predestination that some men were destined by God to be saved and others to be damned; in 1881, Theodor Harms publicly attacked this position as too close to the Reformed state church from which he had separated.[35] This drew the ELSA into a division over allegiance to either the HMG or Missouri.

The final blow came when in 1890 the HMG, now directed by Egmont **Harms** and Georg **Haccius**, made a controversial rapprochement with the state church to facilitate collaboration on overseas missions by agreeing to mutually admit their members to the Lord's Supper. By now

---

34   Langmeil, Easter 1875, General Conference of the Immanuel Synod, Immanuel Synod, Mission Committee Minutes, 1875–1883, LAA. 'W. Harms' may be a misreading of the handwritten original, since Theodor Harms was the HMG director at the time.
35   Theodor Harms directed the HMG from 1865 to 1885. In 1866, Hanover became a Prussian province and civil marriage and the union church were imposed. Harms distanced the HMG from the state church, refused to use the new liturgy and was stripped of his ministry in 1878. He formed a free church, the Hannoversche evangelisch-lutherische Freikirche. Georg Haccius, *Theodor Harms, sein Leben und sein Wirken. Ein Gedenkbüchlein zu seinem 100. Geburtstag am 19.3.1919*, Hermannsburg Missionshandlung, Hermannsburg, 1919.

over 20 – that is, a quarter of all the Lutheran pastors in Australia – had come from the HMG and the narrow dogmatism of the early HMG had been imported into the Australian Lutheran community. In 1892, most of the ELSA pastors who had come from the HMG favoured severing the ELSA's relationship with the HMG and by 1895 only four ELSA pastors defended the HMG, two of whom were immediately excluded from the ELSA. In effect, the disputes that had arisen from German nation-building had now lost their salience in Germany, but were maintained in the colonies, since they had always been packaged as confessional rather than political issues.

Severing links with the HMG meant that the ELSA withdrew from the Hermannsburg mission in central Australia, which was offered for sale to the Immanuel Synod. In the sales negotiations, the ELSA wanted to claim half of the assets, while the HMG wanted to claim two-thirds. Mission superintendent Heidenreich remained so committed to the HMG that he was also excluded from the ELSA in 1902 along with his son who had just graduated from the HMG. These two then formed a splinter synod called ELSA aaG, meaning 'Evangelisch-Lutherische Synode von Australien auf alter Grundlage' ('along original lines').[36]

The Immanuel Synod acquired Hermannsburg mission and its remaining HMG staff were replaced by the Neuendettelsau graduate Carl **Strehlow**. Carl Strehlow was succeeded in 1922 by another HMG alumni, Friedrich Wilhelm **Albrecht**, who stayed for 35 years, but this time the HMG made no claims on directing the mission.

This rush to the interior was not the only embarrassing competition between German Protestant missions glossed over in their histories. Much the same rifts as occurred in South Australia were repeated in Queensland, and there, too, they led to a splintering of the mission effort.

---

36   This became the Australian district of the Ohio Synod in 1910, which grew to six parishes with seven pastors, including three from the HMG (Heidenreich Jr, Ph. Scherer and W. Roehrs coming via Ohio). In 1926, the ELSA aaG splinter synod finally joined the Lutheran Church of Australia formed in 1921. Weiss index, LAA.

2. PROTESTANTS DIVIDED

The conquest of north Queensland (Cape Bedford, Mari Yamba, Bloomfield, 1885–87)

Even before Queensland became an independent colony in 1859, by 1855 more than a quarter of the new arrivals in Moreton Bay were Germans.[37] During the 1860s, as migration to the new colony buoyed with the help of paid migration agents, Germans migrants flooded into the Moreton Bay region and its hinterland, and the demand for Lutheran pastors could not be met from Germany. The pioneers of the disbanded Zion Hill mission were becoming pioneers of free settlement, and five of them achieved ordination as Lutheran, Presbyterian, Baptist or Methodist pastors after attending J.D. Lang's Australian college established in 1850.[38]

One of the five, Gottfried **Hausmann** (later Godfrey Haussmann), proved to be a true Gossner disciple who attended the interdenominational prayer meetings of Wesleyans, Free Methodists, Congregationalists and Presbyterians. This supra-confessional orientation clashed with the Lutheran confessionalism of many German migrants.[39] Hausmann was ordained in the Presbyterian Church in 1853 and began to instruct and ordain at least five other candidates between 1866 and 1875. This caused a furore among Australian Lutherans, so that one of the pastors ordained by Hausmann was struck off the roll of Lutheran ministers. He then registered as the only minister of the 'Congregational Lutheran Church', the only one of its kind, probably in the world.[40] Hausmann spent a period as migrant pastor in Germantown in Victoria, but was rejected by the congregation because of his 'unorthodox' and 'unconfessional' teachings.[41] Back in Queensland during the 1860s, while its frontier war was in full force, Haussmann tried to uphold the idea of Aboriginal mission, and made two attempts at Beenleigh (**Bethesda**) and **Nerang** with the idea to train

---

37 Philip Holzknecht, 'A priesthood of priests? The German Lutherans in Queensland', in Manfred Jurgensen and Alan Corkhill (eds), *The German Presence in Queensland*, University of Queensland Press, Brisbane, 1988, pp. 155–73.
38 Wagner, Niqué, Hausmann, Gerler and Gericke achieved ordination.
39 Jeanette Nolan, 'Pastor J. G. Haussmann: A Queensland Pioneer, 1838–1901', Honours thesis, University of Queensland, 1964, pp. 106–07.
40 The LAA's Weiss index of Lutheran pastors in Australia records for Christian Berndt: 'As a result of controversy with Pastor Haussmann his name was struck off the roll of Lutheran ministers. He was then registered as a "Congregational Lutheran" minister in Queensland and served the only "Congregational Lutheran Church" in Australia (and most likely the world) at Hillside (Hatton Vale). He was married, but no details are available'. Haussman ordained the Gossner-trained candidates F. Copas (1865), F.W. Burghardt (1866), C. Gaustadt (1869), A.D. Hartwig (1875) and C. Berndt (1876). Weiss index, LAA.
41 Weiss index, LAA.

Aboriginal workers for the plantation-style agriculture that was emerging in Queensland. Hausmann was unable to galvanise the support of his fellow Germans, led by several HMG pastors who distrusted Hausmann's supra-confessional orientation.[42] Hausmann's Bethesda plantation mission ended in 1881. A similar plantation initiative in Mackay undertaken by George Bridgman was also failing. At the instigation of the HMG alumni Gottfried Hellmuth at Beenleigh and Georg Heuer in Mackay, four new HMG candidates arrived in Queensland in 1883 with a view to setting up a Lutheran mission, perhaps at Mackay or Beenleigh, both centres of plantation farming (perhaps to pick up from the abandoned efforts of Hausmann or Bridgeman). But nothing eventuated until both the Victorian Moravians and the South Australian Immanuel Synod were expressing an interest in a north Queensland mission.

In Victoria, the stations at **Ebenezer** (since 1858) and **Ramahyuck** (since 1863) were gaining the Moravians a reputation for success with Aboriginal mission. Their mission president in Australia, Friedrich August Hagenauer, formally a member of the Presbyterian Church, visited Queensland in 1885, where South Sea Islanders were getting imported in the 'black-birding' trade that stained Queensland's international reputation. Hagenauer entered into negotiations with the Queensland Government and convinced it of the likely success of Aboriginal missions that could train Aboriginal labour to replace the imported workforce.[43]

Hagenauer did not find the support offered by the Queensland Government sufficient to risk a mission effort so far north and withdrew from the idea. But the Queensland Government had already progressed the idea of a mission in north Queensland's Daintree rainforest to prevent the unsupervised mixing of Aboriginal people with Chinese and Malay tin miners and plantation workers. A secular 'mission' at **Bloomfield** opened in early 1886 with a government subsidy of £300. The Queensland Government now found itself saddled with an expensive mission that it had to fund itself.

At the same time as Hagenauer publicised the interest of the Moravian church in a north Queensland mission, the Queensland Lutherans attempted to form a local synod, with the result that they formally split

---

42 The only other attempt in Queensland during the 1860s was at Somerset (1867–68). Edward Fuller began itinerant missions at Fraser Island and elsewhere in 1871.
43 Lesley Grope, 'Cedars in the wilderness', *Lutheran Church of Australia Yearbook* 1987, pp. 25–57.

along much the same lines as the South Australian ones. One of the synods formed in 1885 was the Evangelical-Lutheran Synod of Queensland (ELSQ),[44] the other was the United German and Scandinavian Lutheran Synod of Queensland (UGSLSQ),[45] an HMG-leaning synod led by Gottfried Hellmuth, one of the pastors sent from the HMG for German migrants in 1866, and including several Scandinavian pastors who were also HMG trained.

Soon afterwards, in November 1885, the Neuendettelsau graduate Johann Flierl arrived from Cooper's Creek in north Queensland (see Chapter 3) and asked the Lutheran synods to support a north Queensland mission. Since Flierl already had the support of the Immanuel Synod, which was suspected of chiliasm, the UGSLSQ quickly decided to form its own mission instead, at **Mari Yamba** near Proserpine. They gained the use of a reserve on the Andromache River and a government subsidy of £120 per annum, and the mission commenced in 1887. By 1888, the chair of the mission committee, HMG alumni J.F. Gössling, one of the pioneers of the Cooper's Creek mission, announced that he was unable to work with pastor Martin Doblies from Breklum who had now joined the **Mari Yamba** mission. The UGSLSQ disintegrated in 1889 under tensions between the German and Danish members, the latter feeling under-represented in its governance. This meant the failure of Mari Yamba.

However, the Immanuel Synod, at the instigation of Flierl, launched into a mission near Cooktown, at **Cape Bedford** (Hopevale) to which we will return in Chapter 3. In 1887, they also reluctantly took on Bloomfield mission (splitting responsibility for the two mission stations between the Immanuel Synod for Bloomfield and Neuendettelsau for Cape Bedford), and in 1902 the remaining residents of Mari Yamba were relocated to Cape Bedford mission, though many escaped the removal.

When the Moravians began to form mission stations on the west side of Cape York Peninsula beginning with **Mapoon** in 1891 and **Weipa** in 1898, Johann Flierl suspected that the Moravians, acting in unison with the Presbyterian Church, were getting a better deal from the government and gingerly asked Hagenauer for 'advice' in 1898. Hagenauer assured Flierl that 'the English committees were by no means better treated'

---

44 Evangelische Lutherische Synode Queenslands (Evangelical-Lutheran Synod of Queensland) was formed in 1885 and later became part of VELKA and in 1921 part of UELCA, and in 1966 part of the Lutheran Church of Australia. Weiss index, LAA.
45 United German and Scandinavian Lutheran Synod of Queensland, 1885–1921.

than those that might be regarded as foreigners. He explained that the Constitution Acts made no provision for landownership with secure title except through purchase, which was much too expensive for mission societies, so there was no way around the uncertainties of investing in buildings and improvements on insecure land.[46]

Precisely this issue emerged at this time in Western Australia. The Trappists were removing themselves from **Beagle Bay** and its surrounding mission camps, and sought to recoup their investments from the Pallottines who were taking over the Kimberley missions, while the authorities of church and state argued that the property was held in trust for Aboriginal people and did not belong to the Trappists (see Chapter 3).

Conclusion

Political turmoil and poverty in the German states propelled waves of migration, fuelled by the available shipping routes and the active recruitment of German migrants by paid migration agents of the various Australian colonies. After the first community of religious refugees arrived in 1838 under Pastor Kavel, the German ranks in the Australian colonies were quickly swelled with draft-resisters, political refugees, 49ers from America and economic migrants. As Philip Holzknecht observes, their pastors reproduced the diversity in Germany of old-Lutheran, reformed Lutheran, pietist, confessionalist and supra-confessional orientations and formed 'a gaggle of synods' often in close competition and proximity to each other. They disagreed on interpretations of the Augsburg Confession, on the role of lay preachers, on millenarianism, on relations with the Prussian State Church and on transubstantiation, but mostly they had personal clashes cloaked as doctrinal disputes.[47]

---

46   Letter from Hagenauer, Board for Protection of Aborigines, Melbourne, to Flierl, 24 November 1898, filed in Reuther, Georg, 1861–1912, Persönliche Korrespondenz, Vorl. Nr. 4.93/5, 1.6. 35, Archiv de Neuendettelsauer. Hagenauer refers to the Acts establishing the Australian colonies such as the *Victoria Constitution Act 1855* (UK), *South Australia Act 1834* (UK), and the *Constitution Act 1867* (Qld) preparing for the establishment of Queensland.
47   Holzknecht, 'A priesthood of priests'.

Differences emerged immediately among the South Australian Lutherans and between them and the missionaries trained in Dresden, as Christine Lockwood explains.[48] But the HMG features centrally in the rifts that emerged among Australian Lutherans. Its first pastors arrived in 1866, and two of these, Georg Adam Heidenreich in South Australia and Carl Gottfried Hellmuth in Queensland, each formed splinter synods. HMG pastors became involved in the Cooper's Creek mission (1866–74), at Hermannsburg mission (1875–94) and at Mari Yamba (from 1887–93), and all three missions were troubled by confessional splintering that arose from the different confessional training of the pastors.

The profusion of Lutheran mission societies, which led to a range of Lutheran training seminaries, was of course accompanied by the growth of mission societies of other denominations, so the whole picture is even more complex and more dynamic than represented here. This chapter only examined those training seminaries that were not Anglophone and that became active in Australia. Andrew May adds that in Britain the Baptist Bristol Academy has operated since about 1795, the Gosport Missionary seminary of the LMS since 1800, the CMS college at Islington since 1825, and the Welsh Bala College since 1837.[49] The Catholic Church responded with apostolic societies dedicated to mission work, as described in Chapter 1. The picture is also complicated by the rush to the north of white settlement in Australia, which led to interest in the north of Western Australia and north Queensland, the competition between emerging independent colonies prior to Federation in 1901, which led to the inland missions, and emerging colonial ambitions of Germany, to which we turn in Chapter 3.

---

48 Christine Lockwood, 'The Two Kingdoms: Lutheran Missionaries and the British Civilizing Mission in Early South Australia', PhD thesis, University of Adelaide, 2014.
49 Andrew May, *Welsh Missionaries and British Imperialism: The Empire of Clouds in North-east India*, Manchester University Press, Manchester, 2012.

3

Empires of faith

The German acquisition of colonial territories provided new opportunities for its profusion of Protestant mission societies. Even before the German New Guinea Company was properly established at Finschhafen in 1886, pastors from three German Protestant mission societies were already seeking access to the new German territory.[1] Lining up for access to New Guinea were the Rhenisch Mission Society based at Barmen, Pastor Martin Doblies from the Breklum Mission Society and Pastor Johann Flierl from the **Neuendettelsau** Mission Society. George Brown had already established a Methodist mission (1877/78)[2] in the Bismarck Archipelago, a region dominated by Chinese resident merchants from where the German New Guinea Company was importing Malay workers.[3] The Catholic Church sought to checkmate these Protestants with the establishment of the vicariate of Micronesia and Melanesia in 1881, devolved to the French **Missionaries of the Sacred Heart** (MSC). The chess pieces of competitive mission building were already lined up on the draught board of an emerging German empire.

---

1   Susanne Froehlich (ed.), *Als Pioniermissionar in das ferne Neu Guinea: Johann Flierls Lebenserinnerungen*, 2 vols, Harrassowitz Verlag, Wiesbaden, 2015, Vol. 2, p. 14.
2   Helen Gardner, 'Assuming judicial control: George Brown's narrative defence of the "New Britain raid"', in Diane Kirkby and Catharine Coleborne (eds), *Law, History, Colonialism: The Reach of Empire*, Manchester University Press, Manchester, 2001, pp. 156–70.
3   Richard Parkinson, *Thirty Years in the South Seas: Land and People, Customs and Traditions in the Bismarck Archipelago and on the German Solomon Islands*, Sydney University Press, Sydney, 2010.

In Australia, too, the various mission societies were wrestling for spheres of influence in the northward drive of the 1880s. The Catholic Church began to populate its huge diocese of Victoria, so the Spanish Benedictines in Western Australia were now joined in north Queensland by French Missionaries of the Sacred Heart, in the Northern Territory by Austrian Jesuits and in the Kimberley by French Trappists. Gaining control over a vicariate or diocese was a major incentive for the Catholic societies that took on the difficult remote mission task, while Irish Catholicism focused on the more settled region, better able to offer school instruction and parish work in English. The northern extension was framed in the expectation of a 'stepping-stone' policy into the more populous territories to the north of Australia.

The Austrian Jesuits were replaced in 1899 by Missionnaires du Sacré Coeur (MSC), including several German speakers, and the French Trappists were replaced the following year by German Pallottines. This meant that at the beginning of World War I, German speakers strongly dominated the northern mission effort: German Pallottines in the Kimberley, German-speaking MSC in the Northern Territory, and at Cape York German Lutherans on the east coast and Moravians on the west coast. While elsewhere in the world the Great War spelled the end of German missions, in Australia the German Pallottines experienced their greatest period of growth after World War I, a phenomenon worth exploring. This chapter explores the German-speaking mission presence in terms of competing territories of faith grafted onto geopolitical opportunities.

The stepping-stones policy

German Lutherans at Cape Bedford (Hopevale, 1886)

With news of the German acquisition of New Guinea, the Neuendettelsau pastor Johann **Flierl** rushed from **Cooper's Creek** in South Australia to Cooktown in north Queensland to try and catch the next available boat to New Guinea. But the Neuguinea Compagnie (German New Guinea Company) sought initially to keep missionaries at arm's length, and discouraged and delayed Flierl. The representatives of the Queensland Government in the far north were more welcoming. The Queensland Government was dealing with an increasing intermingling of Aboriginal and Asian populations and with a rapidly deteriorating international reputation. The latter was a result of the seemingly uncontrollable importation of indentured and quasi-slave labour from the South Pacific, the Malay archipelago and China for sugar plantations, tin and gold mines and the trepang and pearl-shell fishery. While Flierl was stranded at Cooktown, unable to get a transfer to Finschhafen, the Queensland Government offered him the use of land already reserved near Cooktown, a sailing boat and provisions for missionaries and residents. Flierl must have been aware that the Queensland Government was also in negotiation with the Victorian Moravians over a north Queensland mission. Cooktown seemed poised to become the permanent transfer post to German New Guinea, so Flierl decided to take up the offer of a mission at **Cape Bedford**, six hours walk from Cooktown. The Cape Bedford mission could become a stepping stone to New Guinea and a respite for the future missionaries from tropical New Guinea.[4]

The same 'stepping-stone' policy also drove mission building at the top of the Northern Territory and in the Torres Strait region in the 1880s. As the settler empire was pushing northwards, missions followed in its wake.

French MSC at Thursday Island (1884)

While Flierl and the South Australian Lutherans were focused on the new German territory, the French MSC began to populate their Melanesia vicariate with a focus on British-dominated regions, like the Torres Strait. Thursday Island was becoming the gateway for the British protectorate of Papua, and in 1884 the MSC also shifted its staging point from Sydney to Thursday Island for the conduct of its operations in Papua. Thursday Island served as the point of departure for all Catholic missionaries to British New Guinea and New Britain for nearly a decade (1884–89).[5]

The MSC purchased land at the first land sales on Thursday Island and established the township's first welfare institutions – a school, a hospital, an orphanage and, of course, a convent and a church. These Catholic institutions became an important presence in the polyethnic Thursday Island community, where the Catholic congregation consisted mostly of Filipinos participating in the pearling industry. An MSC priest was stationed at Thursday Island to train catechists for the Papuan mission.[6]

---

4   Froehlich, *Pioniermissionar*, Vol. 2, p. 371.
5   Queensland Heritage Register, '**Our Lady of the Sacred Heart Church**'.
6   The musically talented Fr Joseph Guis was born at Auriol in 1869, and died in 1913.

The Catholic base on Thursday Island now competed with the London Missionary Society (LMS), which had begun in 1871 to establish stepping stones across the Torres Strait and New Guinea. The LMS had made a promising start with the help of South Pacific evangelists at Mer and Erub (Murray and Darnley Islands in the eastern Torres Strait) in 1871, but was unable to effectively supervise these missions and they became part of the Anglican diocese of Carpentaria erected in 1900.

The MSC mirrored the stepping-stone strategy of the LMS that deployed ethnic intermediaries. In 1885, the Yule Island Catholic mission commenced with the assistance of 14 Filipino catechists who married into the local population with the result that the entire population of Yule Island was baptised in 1891. Yule Island, a geographic outrigger of the Torres Strait (now belonging to Papua New Guinea), became a model of success and the centre of MSC operations in Papua and New Guinea – a veritable Catholic fortress in what the Protestants of the LMS considered to be their ecclesiastical territory.[7]

Lutherans in Australia, too, commented with concern on the Catholic incursions into Protestant territory. They firmed up a presence in the Red Centre with a mission at Finke River (Hermannsburg) 'lest it should fall into the hands of Catholics', and Pastor Reuther warned 'Shouldn't we be cross about the Catholics, when, as in New Guinea they are moving into others' land where they should not be'.[8]

Austrian Jesuits at Rapid Creek (1882) and the Daly (1886)

The Jesuit extension to the Northern Territory of South Australia was driven by much the same strategic thinking. The Austrian Jesuits at Sevenhill in South Australia's Clare Valley had wanted to join the northward drive of missions since 1866, when Fr John Hinteroecker arrived at Sevenhill feeling 'destined for work among the Aborigines',

---

[7] James Griffin, '**Verjus**, Henri Stanislas (1860–1892)', *Australian Dictionary of Biography*, National Centre of Biography, The Australian National University, published first in hardcopy 1976; and **Fabila Family** at Yule Island.

[8] Immanuel Synod, Mission Committee Minutes, 14 August 1894, Lutheran Archives Australia (LAA); and Reuther to Kaibel, 26 November 1901, Reuther Boxes, Correspondence Reuther and Kaibel 1900, LAA.

quite against the intentions of his superiors.[9] That year four new missions were formed in Australia, by Lutherans at **Kilallpaninna**, by Moravians at **Kopperamanna**, by the Church Mission Society (CMS) at **Lake Condah** and by a local citizen initiative at **Point Pearce** (aka Point Pierce) on Yorke Peninsula. The first Aboriginal baptisms at Corranderk, **Ramahyuck** and Sevenhill in 1865 and 1866 lent renewed impetus to the mission idea. The Sevenhill superior Fr Anton **Strele** thought that from a base in Darwin the Jesuits could eventually also care for 'the inhabitants of the neighbouring islands who are much more numerous' (presumably a reference to Timor) and that 'we can extend into British New Guinea from there'.[10] Timor was a trade centre and also a point of convergence of different religions on the trepang route to the north Australian coast. Like Yule Island between Australia and New Guinea, it had potential as a fortress of Catholicism. The Jesuit General Superior in Vienna, however, did not want to interfere in any of the 'islands subject to the King of Holland or the King of Portugal'.[11]

The Scottish Fr Duncan **McNab**, a secular priest (i.e. not a member of a Catholic order) with a strong conviction for the need of Catholic mission extension to the far north, softened the ground for a change of heart in the Vatican by explaining the rapid economic development of the Australian north on his visit to Rome in 1878. After negotiations between the South Australian and the Indian governments over the importation of Indian coolies failed in 1881, the South Australian Government was ready to make a financial contribution to a mission that would help train a much-needed labour force. Bishop Dom Rosendo **Salvado** OSB from New Norcia warned Strele that 'all they [the government] really wanted was that the Aborigines should be kept quiet'.[12] Still, in the face of the rapid development of Port Darwin, the Sevenhill Jesuits sought to anticipate 'the ministers of error' (Protestants) and wanted to move quickly lest 'we may be forestalled by Protestant missionaries'.[13] These arguments carried

---

9   G.J. O'Kelly, 'The Jesuit Mission Stations in the Northern Territory 1882–1899', Honours thesis, Monash University, 1967, p. 2.
10 Anthony Strele, 'History of the Mission to the Aborigines in the part of Australia which is called Northern Territory', translated from Latin by F.J. Dennett SJ, ca 1895, Archives of the Society of Jesus, Hawthorn. Presumably Strele as apostolic administrator wrote this history in response to a request, recorded in the Daly River mission diary on 28 October 1895, by the Cardinal in Sydney for a history of the Jesuit mission to be submitted to the Plenary Synod. It is possible that the 'New Guinea' consideration was retrospective, because at the time of writing the Lutherans had already extended into German New Guinea from north Queensland.
11 Strele, 'History of the Mission'.
12 Rosendo to Strele, 21 May 1881, in Strele, 'History of the Mission'.
13 Strele, 'History of the Mission'.

the day. The Darwin bishopric was carved out of the vast and dormant ecclesiastic territory of Benedictine Bishop Salvado for the Austrian Jesuits, who commenced a mission at **Rapid Creek** just outside Port Darwin in 1882 and on the **Daly River** further south in 1886.

On the Daly River, the Jesuits struggled with hunger, hardship, tropical conditions and temptation. Three mission girls were pregnant in 1895 before the Fathers and Brothers were locked up at night behind a clausura fence (see Chapter 6 and **Jesuits in the Northern Territory**). They became so focused on the mission work on the Daly, a region in turmoil after the Coppermine killings, that they neglected the Catholic communities in the townships. As a result, the bishopric was lost to the Jesuits and their superiors lost interest in the northern mission and allowed two successive terrifying floods to wash the Jesuits from the north in 1899.

The MSC in Darwin (1906) and Bathurst Island (1911)

Seven years after the withdrawal of the Austrian Jesuits, the MSC stepped into the Catholic void left in the Northern Territory. The redoubtable Alsatian Fr F.X. **Gsell** arrived in Darwin in 1906 and he, too, considered an island mission as a strategic stepping stone into further territories and hence established **Bathurst Island** mission on the Tiwi Islands in 1911. In this choice of an island location he took his cue from the comments of his Jesuit predecessors, and he also continued their policy of paying compensation to the parents or promised spouses for the marriage rights of their mission girls, for which he became known as 'The Bishop with the 150 wives'.

Carving up the north

The northward thrust of Catholic missions with stepping stones at Thursday Island and Bathurst Island actually represented a bulwark against both Protestant and Muslim influence. In the seventh century, as Continental Europe was peacefully conquered by the small fortified dynamos of agriculture, manufacture, meditation and learning called monasteries, Islam was carried by trade into the East to take root across the Malay peninsula and the Philippines. Centuries of contact with Malay seafarers had exposed the Indigenous people of the far-north Australian coast to Muslim influences. The year that Gsell arrived in Darwin was also the year when the Macassan maritime trade to Australia was prohibited.

With the arrival of missionaries shortly afterwards, much of the cultural repertoire emerging from this long Muslim contact was 'turned in'[14] and only resurfaced decades later under the probing of anthropologists. Perhaps unbeknown to the Christian missionaries, and certainly unacknowledged, a familiarisation with monotheistic beliefs had already been accomplished by this other Abrahamic religion.

The Christians were perhaps too busy competing with each other to pay attention to Muslim influences. Not only did Catholics try to defend the territory of the far north against Protestant influences, they also vied with each other for spheres of influence. When Bishop Salvado was asked for permission for a Jesuit mission in his northern diocese in 1882, he first ascertained that the Jesuits meant Darwin, rather than a location closer to New Norcia. Duncan McNab had recommended Darwin, which was also at a good distance from his own mission attempt in Queensland (at Durundur from 1877). The northward drive of missions in the 1880s into far-north Queensland and the top of the Northern Territory was mirrored a few years later in Western Australia as the Kimberley became subject to a land rush (1882–88) and a revival of the pearling industry (1885/86) brought a surge of Asian workers into the north-west coast.

Carving further into the vast ecclesiastical territory administered by the Benedictines, Fr Duncan McNab gave up his mission in Queensland and instead attempted a mission at Goodenough Bay (**Disaster Bay**) on Dampier Peninsula (1884–86). In January 1887, Matthew Gibney was consecrated as Bishop of Perth and also lent active support to a northern mission in West Australia. Concern over racial mixing was expressed in the 1886 Aborigines Protection Act,[15] which extended the reach of Aboriginal protection legislation over mixed descendants. A few years later, Western Australia's *Constitution Act 1889*[16] required that a minimum of £5,000 be spent each year on Aboriginal people. Here was the promise of some solid government support for a north-western mission for Aboriginal people

---

14 Ian S. McIntosh, 'Missing the revolution! Negotiating disclosure on the pre-Macassans (Bayini) in north-east Arnhem Land', in Martin Thomas and Margo Neale (eds), *Exploring the Legacy of the 1948 Arnhem Land Expedition*, ANU E Press, Canberra, 2011, Chapter 17.
15 *An Act to provide for the better protection and management of the Aboriginal Natives of Western Australia, and to amend the Law relating to certain Contracts with such Aboriginal Natives 1886* (WA).
16 *An Act to confer a Constitution on Western Australia, and to grant a Civil list to Her Majesty 1889* (WA).

of full and mixed descent. In 1889, Propaganda Fide directed the leader of a French Trappist mission that was failing in New Caledonia to Western Australia, where New Norcia was the only mission operating at the time.

The French Trappists in the Kimberley (1892–1900)

The detailed history of the Trappist mission at Beagle Bay has only recently become accessible through Sister Brigida Nailon's translation and publication of much of the correspondence.[17] Bishop Gibney and two Trappists from Sept Fons spent four months scouting Dampier Peninsula for a suitable site, proceeding from Derby to the mission site abandoned by McNab four years earlier, and to Hadley and Hunter's Lombadina station. Young men of the Dampier Peninsula were already working for settlers and maritime entrepreneurs and spoke English, and a tussle emerged between the people of the east and west coast of the peninsula over who should have claim to the mission party and their endless supplies of goods (see Chapter 5 or **Beagle Bay**).

The idea was to build up a monastery with a minimum of 12 monks with a semblance of a monastic lifestyle. The monks offered food for work and were able to attract sufficient interest to build up vegetable and fruit gardens, substantial cattle and sheep flocks and a monastery with three long buildings and several outhouses and workshops. It appears that their annual budget was met to 20 per cent by state government funding, to 10 per cent from donations and the remainder came from the Propaganda Fide and the Trappist Order. The Trappists laid the foundation for language work in the Kimberley with a grammar, a vocabulary and a catechism. Alphonse Tachon recorded the Nyul-Nyul language,[18] while the Spanish Fr Nicholas **Emo** compiled a Yawuru–Spanish dictionary.

Despite all this success, the mission fell apart in 1900. Their first superior already wanted to resign in 1895, but stayed until 1897 and was succeeded by the elderly and reluctant Fr Tachon. Two priests returned to Sept Fons in mid-1899 in protest over the situation at Beagle Bay, and Emo, who became interim caretaker, also commented on the 'confused' and 'uncomfortable' condition at the mission. In particular, the relationship between the two monks stationed at the Disaster Bay outstation, Fr Jean-

---

17 Brigida Nailon, *Emo and San Salvador*, 2 vols, Brigidine Sisters, Echuca, 2005.
18 Fr Marie Bernard to Limburg, 10 December 1900, Australien 1900–1907 B7 d.l. (3), Zentralarchiv der Pallottinerprovinz (ZAPP).

Marie Janny and Br Narcisse Janne, was considered 'special' and 'too natural a mutual attachment'.[19] These descriptions may refer to an actual family relationship between the two, since Jean-Marie Janny was the younger brother of Dom Ambrose Janny, the mission's first superior, and of the prior at Sept Fons, Felix Janny. It is possible that Narcisse Janne was also a brother in the same family. Lending weight to family relations was discouraged among the brethren of a Catholic order, and the spelling of names, read from handwritten sources and across several languages, is often unreliable. On the other hand, it is equally possible that a sexual relationship formed between the two. The resignation of Superior Ambrose Janny at Beagle Bay and of Prior Felix Janny at Sept Fons may express shame about their younger brother Jean-Marie. Emo felt that Jean-Marie was 'accustomed to be free and independent in his nest' at Disaster Bay.[20] Some years later, Jean-Marie Janny moved the Disaster Bay colony to Lombadina and became the last of the Trappists to leave the Kimberley in 1905.

But more than that was amiss on the Beagle Bay Trappist mission. One of the monks took to chasing adults and children with a gun charged with flour or gunpowder, a habit that Emo feared would cause an uproar if it leaked to the press. 'He compromised the good name of the mission' and 'we can say nobody liked him and all complained of him'.[21] Other monks gave away the mission stores and were altogether too friendly with Aboriginal people. Emo as caretaker dismissed the children, stopped the women going into the rooms and locked away the wine and other provisions. With regard to two other monks, Emo wrote, in an 80-page letter defending his actions, that they were 'in imminent danger of losing their vocation' and that 'some scandal may compromise the honour of our holy Order' if they were not sent away immediately. Any more detail 'would be indiscreet to put to paper',[22] but one of these two:

> was always surrounded by young girls and little girls who used to go into his room for tobacco (which is very dear here) because they brought him little lizards for his birds, and he was always going with them in a way that

---

19 Emo to General, 4 July 1899: 'un attachement trop naturel de ces deux pères mutuellement (et ce n'est pas mon seul qui croit le remarquer)'. Nailon, *Emo and San Salvador*, Vol. 1, p. 55. Nailon gives the surname of Br Narcisee as Janne, and later Narcissus Jen, apparently a Latin rendition of the name.
20 Nailon, *Emo*, Vol. 1, p. 91.
21 Emo to Sept Fons, September 1900 and 2 March 1900, in Nailon, *Emo*, Vol. 1, pp. 142, 91.
22 Nailon, *Emo*, Vol. 1, p. 212.

made me anxious. (Sometimes I would see him coming alone in the dark from the garden.) I was afraid in case he was assailed also by some great temptation.[23]

The monks at Beagle Bay responded with anger to Emo's intervention. Jean-Marie 'would rather die than return to Sept Fons', and one of the Australians who had joined the mission as a Brother, and erupted in venereal disease, went into rage at the prospect of being sent to the Trappist mission in Palestine and threatened to go public about the affairs at Beagle Bay.[24] Just weeks before, eight staff were sent to Palestine in April 1900, in March the mission residence and school burned down. Emo claimed that the fire was due to the 'imprudence of a woman who was smoking a pipe too close to the dry bark',[25] but John Harris thinks the Trappists burned down the buildings in anger[26] as Emo was winding down the mission without a clear directive from Sept Fons.

Bishop Gibney was greatly embarrassed by the sudden departure of the Trappist monks. While Emo was sending them away without informing the bishop, Gibney and Fr Tachon in Perth were trying to raise funds for an extension of the mission and to secure the title over the 10,000 acres of mission land. They also commissioned three boats for the mission. According to letters written afterwards in an attempt to explain the tumultuous events at Beagle Bay, the abbott at Sept Fons had instructed Emo in Broome in December 1899 to prepare for a partial withdrawal to turn the Beagle Bay monastery into a grange (without an abbot), but to keep this secret so as not to disadvantage any sale of property. Emo began selling cattle and other property to raise money for the fares of the monks to be sent to El Athroun in Palestine and to Sept Fons in France. When Bishop Gibney finally heard of these repatriation plans, he placed an injunction on the sale of mission cattle and initiated negotiations with the German Pallottines to replace the Trappists.[27] The prior at Sept Fons on his part felt presented with a *fait accompli*. The whole episode was a colossal debacle.

---

23   Emo to Sept Fons, 13 June 1900, in Nailon, *Emo*, Vol. 1, p. 86ff.
24   Emo to Sept Fons, 6 January 1901, in Nailon, *Emo*, Vol. 1.
25   Emo to Sept Fons, 2 March 1900 (received 19 April), in Nailon, *Emo*, Vol. 1, p. 86.
26   John Harris, *One Blood: 200 Years of Aboriginal Encounter with Christianity: A Story of Hope*, Albatross Books, Sutherland, NSW, 1990, p. 444.
27   Emo to Sept Fons, 25 November 1900, 36pp. continued in January 1901 in Nailon, *Emo*, Vol. 1, pp. 148–81.

The handover of Beagle Bay (1900)

Most of the Trappists had left in April 1900, and in August 1900 Bishop Gibney arrived in the north with a rescue party, to get the mission properties ready for inspection by a government surveyor. Gibney described Beagle Bay as being in disrepair and 'abandoned', although it was still inhabited by 147 Christians.[28] Emo in Broome welcomed the bishop's party, including travel writer Daisy Bates, and accompanied them to Beagle Bay and Disaster Bay for a three-month rebuilding program (see Beagle Bay – **The Handover to the Pallottines**). Gibney wanted to secure freehold for 10,000 acres of the 100,000-acre lease to prepare for a handover to the Pallottines.

By this time, the tide of policy had turned against the mission. In 1897, the Western Australian Government over-rode the constitutional requirements of the 1889 Constitution Act by forming its own Aboriginal Department under a Chief Protector of Aborigines, Harry **Prinsep**, and public funding for Beagle Bay mission ceased. The Trappists had spent £11,000 in 10 years and estimated their improvements to be worth £10,000, which was double what was required under the lease conditions.[29] The government surveyor estimated the value of improvements on the lease at £6,000 (still more than was required under the lease conditions). With the shortfall in funding since 1897, the Trappists had run up a debit of £1,471 and wanted to recoup some of their own investment of £3,250. Their asking price was £2,640 for Beagle Bay, and a total of £3,740 including the Broome properties. However, there was a balance of opinion, shared by Gibney, Emo and the government officials, that the value to the mission and its herds had mostly been added by Aboriginal work and was not for the Trappists to sell. The Royal Commissioner of Inquiry into the Condition of Natives in Western Australia, Dr Walter Roth, recapitulated in 1905 that mission land was intended for Aborigines, not for mission societies:

> Your Commissioner recommends that the Lands Department, when issuing the title to the lands in question, will protect the interests of the aborigines, and take care that the property held in trust for them [at Beagle Bay] is not handed over to the Mission.[30]

---

28 '**Trappist mission at Beagle Bay**', *Western Mail* (Perth), 15 December 1900, p. 71, National Library of Australia, Trove.
29 'Trappist mission at Beagle Bay', *Western Mail* (Perth), p. 71.
30 Western Australia, Royal Commission, *Report of the Royal Commission on the Condition of the Natives*, Government Printer, Perth, 1905, p. 30.

It was a risky business for the churches to invest in buildings and improvements on insecure land. State governments were willing to defend the 'interests of the Aborigines' against the churches, but not to fund the actual costs of missions, and neither did they hand over secure title to land, either to the missions or to their Aboriginal residents.

The German Pallottines in the Kimberley (1901)

The German Pallottines welcomed the extension to Australia that was offered to them in consequence of the Trappist withdrawal. The German province of the Pallottines had been erected in 1892 to take advantage of the German acquisition of Cameroon, and most of their effort had been directed there. One of the Cameroon pioneers, the difficult Fr Georg **Walter**, was sent to the Kimberley in 1901 together with two Brothers from Limburg and an English-speaking Pallottine priest, Fr Patrick White. The purchase price negotiated with the Trappists meant that the Pallottine mission at Beagle Bay commenced with a massive debt and became focused on production and income earning. The Pallottines were spending around £900 per year and sent mostly Brothers who could generate income to make up the apostolic twelve demanded by Bishop Gibney, and initially welcomed Jean-Marie Janny at Disaster Bay and Emo in Broome among their numbers.

Relations soon soured between Walter and Emo, who was protective of 'his' properties and influence in Broome. Worse, the 1904 Roth royal commission was much more favourable about Emo's efforts in Broome than about the Pallottine mission at Beagle Bay. In 1906, Emo began working with Bishop Kelly of Geraldton and with the Benedictines, who wanted to extend their efforts northwards, trespassing on the Pallottine territory. The need for a Catholic extension into the east Kimberley was becoming urgent because both Anglicans and Presbyterians were proposing to move into the area.[31] Emo purchased the lugger *San Salvador* with funding from Bishop Kelly and a Broome Filipino entrepreneur, and masterminded the scouting for a new Benedictine mission site. He visited the Cygnet Bay pearling station and Syd Hadley at Sunday Island. Hadley

---

31   Diary of Abbot Fulgentius Torres, 14 June 1906, in Nailon, *Emo*, Vol. 2, p. 25ff. The Anglican Forrest River mission near Wyndham commenced in 1913, and a Presbyterian mission started at Kunmunya in 1912. The diary in 1906 refers only to the Anglican aspirations.

had previously been involved in a mission effort at Forrest River (in which the Anglicans were becoming interested) and his **Sunday Island** station became an officially recognised 'private mission'.

By now Emo was a local protector of Aborigines and legally able to move Aboriginal people. He evacuated 'The Point' in Broome to Cygnet Bay in 1906 to gain some elbow room from Walter in Broome and to await the outcome of the Benedictine deliberations. He then joined the Benedictine Drysdale River mission, which became a fiasco. Emo recorded the Aboriginal deaths resulting from a three-month attempt to choose a mission site, burned his bridges with the Benedictines over the control of the *San Salvador* and towards the end of his life felt implicated in the Aboriginal attack on that mission in 1914. (For more on the debacle at that mission, see Emo – **Drysdale River Benedictine Mission**.)

A separate Geraldton diocese had been erected under Bishop William Bernard Kelly, in 1898, but the Pallottines were seeking an independent Kimberley vicariate. Once the Beagle Bay mission was fortified with Irish nuns and an increased government subsidy for the children removed by police to the mission, Superior Fr Georg Walter left for Europe in 1908 in order to gain the Kimberley vicariate and, failing this, never returned. Walter had been so obstinate that he had come to blows with one of the Brothers (see Chapter 6) and his departure filled the Brothers at Beagle Bay with relief and facilitated a rapprochement between Emo and the Pallottines. In 1910, with a new chief protector and trouble with Hadley and Hunter at Lombadina, the Pallottines were offered **Lombadina** as a second mission station, and invited Emo to take charge.

MSC aspirations

By this time, another German speaker had arrived in the north, the Alsatian Francis Xavier Gsell. Within months of arrival in Darwin in 1906, Gsell was looking for ways of extending his sphere of influence into the 'Pallottine territory' of the Kimberley. The Austrian Jesuits before him had lost the Darwin diocese because they were too focused on Aboriginal mission, and Gsell thought that the same could be said about the German Pallottines, who were just at that time seeking to gain control of the Kimberley vicariate:

> The Pallottines of Beagle Bay, who are better off than us, cry mercy because they get less than £2,000 a year … The Pallottine Fathers have a mission at Beagle Bay, but according to the parishioners of Broome south of Beagle Bay they only care for the blacks, and at that only the blacks who are in the neighbourhood of their monastery. In the regions close to the Northern Territory [around Wyndham] there are hundreds of Catholics, of whom several are very good people and very wealthy. One of those good people came here [to Darwin] and asked me if I couldn't take that province under my wing and send them a preacher occasionally. What do you think, my Reverend Father, if one were to ask Rome to give me the Kimberley, Monsignor Kelly [of the Geraldton diocese] wouldn't be upset and for me it could have several advantages among others that of furnishing me with a bit more work and a few more resources. There is a steamer going there [Wyndham] every six weeks and one could visit them from here two or three times a year, moreover the telegraph covers the whole country and one can correspond rapidly and at a low price. In practice there is a neat solution, one asks for a reunion of the Kimberley with my diocese, or one simply asks Mgr. Kelly for a visiting preacher.[32]

Geraldton was three times further from Wyndham than Darwin, so Gsell did not seriously expect Bishop Kelly to send a visiting preacher from Geraldton to Wyndham. However, Kelly was already making plans for a Benedictine reach into the east Kimberley to forestall Anglican aspirations. Emo's search on the *San Salvador* for a Benedictine mission site began in May 1906, so Gsell's proposal in November 1906 to 'give me the Kimberley' was a timely intervention and quite possibly the reason why Walter's bid for a Pallottine Kimberley vicariate failed.

Gsell resumed his lobbying in March 1908 for an extension of his sphere of influence beyond Darwin. He had heard that the Commonwealth Government was preparing to take over the Northern Territory, and would surely make special provisions for Aboriginal people. 'One has to get ready for this possibility, because it will be a unique occasion which will never again offer itself.' At the same time, Gsell rejected out of hand the proposal of the MSC superior in Kensington to send Sisters to Darwin on the condition that any surplus revenue generated by the Sisters would

---

32 Gsell in Darwin to the General at Issoudun, 12 November 1906 (in French), Correspondance de Mgr. F.-X. Gsell à son cousin éloigné Albin Gsell à Benfeld (1948–1954) conservée chez M et Mme Jean Baumann, private collection.

be directed to Kensington. 'This would not accord with religious life, it would be a farce'. Gsell would rather have no Sisters at all than share power with a mother superior in Sydney.[33]

With a Benedictine mission at Drysdale River, the east Kimberley was now out of reach for the MSC and for the Pallottines. The Benedictine Abbott Torres of New Norcia became Bishop of the Kimberley vicariate in May 1910. The Pallottine superior Georg Walter refused to return to Australia and established himself instead in semi-retirement at his family property of Vogelsburg, a castle and vineyard estate overlooking Würzburg, where he wrote a general history of Australia from the viewpoint of Catholic mission.[34] Gsell turned his attention northward, to the Tiwi Islands, paying heed to the suggestion of his Jesuit predecessors.[35] There he met with another source of resistance – commercial interests. Gsell initially targeted Melville Island and contacted Joe Cooper, manager of the buffalo camp on that island. The unpublished draft of his autobiography is more candid than the published book:

> To make sure, I wrote to the man [Joe Cooper], explaining to him my ideas. He could not legally prevent the establishment of the mission station, but he made no bones about his opinion. There is no suitable place on the island he said, for such a station, and besides, he would rather be without it. That made it clear, and to avoid any trouble, I decided to look somewhere else.[36]

The South Australian Government was also uncooperative and released Bathurst Island for selection as agricultural blocks. Gsell felt 'blackballed by junior officals' and it took some strong-arming from the federal government to reverse this decision and reserve some mission land for Gsell.[37] Gsell finally became Bishop of Darwin in 1938, the second German-speaking bishop in the north after Otto Raible in 1935, despite the anti-German sentiments arising from World War I.

---

33   Gsell in Darwin to the General at Issoudun, 9 March 1908, Chevalier Resource Centre, Kensington (MSC archives).
34   Georg Walter, *Australien: Land, Leute, Mission*, Limburg, 1928.
35   Paddy J. Dalton, 'History of the Jesuits in South Australia 1848–1948', unpublished MS, 1948, p. 52, Archives of the Society of Jesus, Hawthorn.
36   Cited from Gsell's book manuscript by Anthony Caruana, 'Reflections on Hundred Years of MSC Mission Work in the Northern Territory 1904–2004', unpublished MS, 2004, p. 14, MSC archives.
37   F.X. Gsell, *'The Bishop with 150 Wives': Fifty Years as a Missionary*, Angus and Robertson, Sydney, 1956: 42–43.

The decline and rise of the German mission empire

During World War I, anti-German sentiment became so virulent that over 100 townships and scores of families anglicised their names. Many Germans, including German pastors, were interned. On a visit to Australia, the founder of the Missionary Sisters of the Sacred Heart, Fr Hubert Linckens, was denounced for his 'Germanic way of acting'. In the lead-up to the war, about half of all Australian missions had German speakers spread over 12 mission stations, and these were now faced with the need for major reorganisation.[38] The Moravian missions were devolved to English-speaking Presbyterian staff, while Lutherans began to post locally trained, Australian-born staff. The few remaining active German missionaries were not interned but they were suspected of 'instilling German sentiment' and the mission superiors came under close surveillance. **Strehlow**'s management of Hermannsburg came under repeated investigation, but specially targeted were **Bischofs** at Beagle Bay, **Hey** at Mapoon and **Schwarz** at Cape Bedford, all three naturalised British subjects. Schwarz was the only German-born Protestant missionary who held out until World War II.

German-speaking missionaries during World War I

The Herrnhut Moravians had gained an excellent reputation with missions at **Lake Boga** (1850–56), **Ebenezer** (1859–1904), Ramahyuck (1863–1908) and Lake Condah (1867–1913), aided by their collaboration with the Presbyterian Church and the prominent position of Friedrich **Hagenauer** as chief protector.[39] They withdrew from their last Victorian mission in 1913 with the retirement of 73-year-old Heinrich and Marie **Stähle**, whose sons died in Australian military service along with 18 young men from the Lake Condah mission.

The Moravians still had four missions in north Queensland, which they devolved to Presbyterian supervision – **Mapoon** (1891–1919), **Weipa**, (1898–1919), **Aurukun** (1904–13) and Mornington Island (1914–18). Mornington Island and Weipa already had Anglo-Saxon staff. Arthur and Elisabeth Richter from Aurukun were on furlough in 1913 and did not

---

38 In this instance, the propitious number 12 derives from counting in Kramer's itinerant mission and the Kopperamanna outstation.
39 Hagenauer became Chief Inspector for the Board of Protection in 1889.

return from Germany. The last German-speaking Moravian left in the north was Rev. Nicholas **Hey** at Mapoon. He was naturalised and married to an Irish woman, but suffered house searches and harassment. He was forced to retire in 1919 after 28 years of mission service. Embittered by the anti-German sentiments festering during the war, Hey still feared in 1920 that his mail was being intercepted:

> The mail seems to work again but the effects of this terrible war will be felt for years to come. The time has not yet come where I can relate my experiences of the last four years in letters. This is not because of a fear to honour the truth, but because I do not wish to do anything which could damage the purpose of the mission. I have always tried to take as much as possible a neutral position, mindful towards the positive. In that spirit I have upheld and honoured my oath of loyalty as an Australian citizen because only that permitted me to put the lie to those who maintained that a German could not be trusted and believed …
>
> Most German pastors were arrested and interned, many have already been extradited. They will not tolerate German missionaries in the future. I regret not being able to stay in the tropics, but the Presbyterians should continue the mission. They will learn a lot from it. At the moment Mapoon is the only NQ mission without debts.[40]

On the east coast of Cape York Peninsula, Pastor G.H. Schwarz from Neuendettelsau also remained doggedly at his post at Cape Bedford (Hopevale). He also suffered from the anti-German sentiments considered patriotic in wartime Australia. In 1916, he was accused by a neighbour of being an 'educated Hun' and an 'enemy subject' who had an 'intense hatred of the British and everything British', and that he was teaching the Cape Bedford people 'German sentiment and German language'. Schwarz, too, was naturalised and his Australian wife conducted the mission school in English. He had already spent almost 30 years as a missionary, and he stayed on until forced to retire with his internment in 1942, at age 74.

Neuendettelsau financial support for Cape Bedford ended with World War I, and all organisational responsibilities were devolved to second-generation German immigrants. Brisbane Lutherans set up a mission board for north Queensland and New Guinea and obtained some funding from the Iowa Synod. First-generation German speakers rapidly lost their predominance in the Queensland mission effort.

---

40   Hey to Herrnhut, 19 January 1920, Missionsdirektion, Personalakten, Nicolaus Hey, MD825, Archiv der Brüderunität (Herrnhut Archives).

The South Australian mission history was almost entirely German until World War I when three of the five mission stations in that state were Lutheran. **Killalpannina** (Bethesda mission) was officially closed in 1914 and became a privately owned cattle station managed by former missionaries. The Vogelsang family left the Kopperamanna outstation in 1916 (see **Heinrich Vogelsang**, **Theodor Vogelsang**, **Hermann Vogelsang**). Koonibba became staffed with Australian-born personnel (except Gottlieb Blaccs from 1916–18 and T.F. Strelan from Berlin, 1935–47).

All Lutheran schools in South Australia were closed and the government subsidy was withdrawn in 1917 (until 1923).[41] In the Northern Territory, Oskar **Liebler** and his wife returned to Germany in November 1913, but Carl and Frieda Strehlow stayed on at **Hermannsburg** until 1922. There was strong public agitation to close the 'Teuton mission'. Since Germans had become so unpopular during World War I, an Hermannsburger Missionsgesellschaft (HMG) candidate of Polish nationality succeeded Strehlow. Friedrich Wilhelm Albrecht and his wife Minna (née Gevers) arrived in 1926 and stayed for 35 years. At Alice Springs, Ernst Eugen **Kramer** and his wife conducted an itinerant mission until the mid-1930s, and at **Bathurst Island** Fr F.X. Gsell was assisted by Br Lambert Fehrmann while Fr François-Régis Courbon responded to the French military call-up and was replaced with the Australian-born William M. Henschke in 1915.

In Western Australia, the mission effort had by now intensified with the addition of the Drysdale River mission in 1908, a secular government reserve at Moola Bulla in 1911, the Presbyterian Kunmunya mission in 1912 and the Anglican Forrest River mission in 1913. The 'private mission' at **Sunday Island** was taken over by the Australian Inland Mission around this time. At Lombadina and Beagle Bay the German Pallottines came under close surveillance during World War I, and their superior, Fr Joseph Bischofs, was accused of espionage. Bischofs had answered one of the many questionnaires that missionaries often dealt with, and which purported to be from a German migration agency but contained some dubious and apparently unnecessary questions. The government censor intercepted the mission mail, interrogated Bischofs and cleared him of the charge, but nevertheless Bischofs was not permitted to resume his

---

41   M. Lohe, 'A mission is established at Hermannsburg', in Everard Leske, *Hermannsburg: A Vision and a Mission,* Lutheran Publishing House, Adelaide, 1977, p. 31.

position in the sensitive north. To accommodate the concerns of military intelligence, a Redemptorist was placed in charge for the duration of the war, though local intelligence officers did not trust the Irish Fr John Creagh either and regarded him as a 'disloyalist'.[42] (Read more about the military surveillance at **Beagle Bay**.) The remaining German Pallottines were all mature and experienced mission men, and used their home-arrest on the mission to galvanise the whole mission community into building a lasting memorial of their efforts, the now heritage-listed Beagle Bay church with its famous shell-decked altar.

Interwar reorganisation

The loss of the German overseas territories during World War I struck a massive blow to German missions that had taken advantage of the German empire. The Pallottines had lost the Cameroon missions during the war, so the Kimberley missions became all the more important. Rome was willing to sacrifice the Pallottine aspirations for the Kimberley, but the Pallottines in Limburg and in the Kimberley were determined to hold on. After the war, Italian Salesians under Bishop Coppo were posted to take over the Kimberley vicariate. Collaboration with the Pallottine staff on the ground proved difficult. The ageing Fr Wilhelm **Droste**, by now the only remaining Pallottine priest among the Brothers, commented about the Salesians:

> It is simpler to settle in a well-made nest than to found a new station, which is extremely difficult and costly. It is true that the members of the [Salesian] Society were treated [by us] as changelings when one considered all the efforts from the suffering, sacrifice and sweat, which our Brothers have contributed and has turned their hair white. The thought of the material loss to the [Pallottine] Society was devastating.[43]

There was no love lost between the Pallottine Droste and the Salesian Coppo. Coppo objected to Fr Droste's appointment as vicar apostolic. However, Coppo achieved the first two visas for German Pallottines after the war, in 1924. The Salesians 'arrived with a flourish' of reorganisation[44] and, when they withdrew after less than two years, Droste wrote him

---

42 File note 24 June 1918, in Father Bischoff – German Mission Station at Beagle Bay, A367, 1917/50, Barcode 61882, National Archives of Australia (NAA).
43 **Droste diary,** 4 November 1923, in Droste, Wilhelm (Pater), P1 Nr 17, ZAPP, trans. RG.
44 Nailon, *Emo and San Salvador*.

a wonderful but possibly insincere letter of appreciation. Once the restrictions on immigration of Germans were lifted, more Pallottine staff arrived in Australia.

After the withdrawal of the Salesians, the Pallottines could celebrate their Silver Anniversary of the Beagle Bay mission in December 1925, and could finally claim the Kimberley vicariate with the arrival of Fr Otto **Raible** as vicar apostolic in 1928. Raible was naturalised in 1934 and consecrated as Bishop of the Kimberley in 1935. He and a new chief protector, Auber Octavius **Neville**, became embattled like two bulls locking horns. Neville obstructed wherever possible, while Raible extended his sphere of influence with the acquisition of new properties, including Rockhole cattle station practically adjoining the government reserve of Moola Bulla. Raible also broke out of the Kimberley by acquiring a wheat farm at Tardun, and introduced more German staff than ever before, including experts in tropical medicine and languages. Protector Neville greeted Dr Johann **Betz** and Ludwina **Betz-Korte** with reservations about their medical qualifications, and the linguists Fr Ernst **Worms** and Fr Hermann **Nekes** with a curt reminder that photographing and recording Aboriginal people, and entry to reserves, required his permission. (For the Pallottine contribution to science in Australia, see **Nekes** and **Worms**.)

During the 1930s, contact between Aboriginal people of the far north and Japanese pearling crews increased greatly and could lead to violent conflict. The **Caledon Bay massacres** (1932–34) led to competing applications from the CMS and the Methodist Mission Society to establish a mission in east Arnhem Land.[45] Fr Gsell also applied for permission to establish further missions, fearing the imminent collapse of his Tiwi mission under the pressure of such contact. MSC missions were opened at Port Keats in 1935 after Japanese pearlers had been killed there, and at Alice Springs where Ernst Eugen Kramer had recently left his 'tabernacle mission'. The **MSC** was already training Australian staff at its Kensington seminary from 1898, and began to form parishes in the Northern Territory townships at the request of their apostolic delegate in 1929. The Pallottines, on the other hand, still focused on remote mission, true to their name as the Pious Society of Missions (PSM), and still recruited from Germany.

---

45 Gsell in Darwin to NT Administrator and J.A. Carrodus, Acting NT Administrator, 20 September 1935, commenting that the 'recent experience of mission stations in the territory run by the CMS does not inspire confidence in the ability of that organisation to successfully conduct aboriginal institutions' in Port Keats Catholic Mission, Northern Territory (1934–55), A452, 1955/98, NAA.

While the MSC had been very much a transnational organisation since its foundation, the Pallottines organised themselves in 'regions' and 'provinces' that had a much more national character.

By the time of the Golden Jubilee at Beagle Bay mission in June 1940, everything was in great shape for the Pallottines. The mission-hostile Chief Protector Neville had been replaced with a commissioner for Native Affairs, Francis Illingworth Bray, who was much more supportive, and a start had been made towards building up an Indigenous church with a 'convent for native women' at Beagle Bay.

The missions in World War II

Four months later, the 13 German Pallottines who were not naturalised were arrested and interned in Broome. They were released after 11 days of intensive lobbying, and a subsequent public inquiry claimed that the Broome residents welcomed these internments. Bishop Raible wrote a counter-narrative to the Minister for Defence on 17 January 1941:

> I must confess that the sweeping generalisation of this statement has rendered me almost speechless. It ignores the fact that quite a considerable number of white people of Broome expressed to me their dissatisfaction with this high-handed action of the local authorities ... It does not fit in with the fact that from all sections of the community – white and half-caste alike – all sorts of foodstuffs, cool drinks, tobacco and delicacies were sent to the imprisoned fathers and brothers, who indeed declared that as far as food was concerned, they fared much better in jail than on the mission. Even the blacks kept in the same jail had a good time on what was left over. It is common knowledge that dozens of people went to visit them in jail and that, after the release of the missionaries, their church was packed as if it were Christmas Day, and very large numbers of people went to receive the sacraments in thanksgiving ... The police themselves told us that they felt like criminals when they were obliged by their duty to take the missionaries away from those who regarded them as their real fathers and brothers, to whose labours they owe so much.[46]

---

46 D.F. Bourke, *The History of the Catholic Church in Western Australia*, Archdiocese of Perth, Perth, 1979.

Bishop Raible went on the offensive. He issued public statements, claimed child endowment benefits from the federal government in September 1941 and proposed to take on La Grange as a Pallottine mission in 1942. The army objected to the placement of Germans on the coast during World War II so La Grange had to wait.[47]

The more recent German arrivals among the Pallottine staff were not allowed to return to the missions, and were placed under the authority of the bishop in Melbourne. The others returned to the north and laboured under travel prohibitions and intensive surveillance, including army chaplains, mostly MSC, stationed at Broome, Lombadina and Beagle Bay. Any firearms and radios on the missions were confiscated and Deputy War Damage Commissioner W.S. Brown visited Beagle Bay mission in 1943 in military company to check 'whether the federal money [child endowment] was well spent'.[48]

The MSC had by now become Australianised and had the confidence of the military authorities. During World War II, many of them served as army chaplains (see **Missionaries of the Sacred Heart**). One of the MSC Fathers at Bathurst Island raised the alarm over the first Darwin bombing and at least three of the 12 siblings in the Flynn family served as army chaplains at Beagle Bay, Alice Springs, Arltunga, Thursday Island and Melville Island. Frank Flynn, chaplain for the army and Royal Australian Air Force (RAAF) visited all the MSC missions established by Gsell and remained in contact with them from 1942 to 1946, as narrated in his autobiography, without ever mentioning his military affiliation. He also practised ophthalmology at the Darwin hospital and inspired Professor Fred **Hollows**.[49]

World War II brought a much greater disruption to the mission effort than the first war. The whole north was designated a strategically sensitive region. The military bases in north Australia presented direct targets for enemy attacks and National Security Regulations provided for wartime evacuations of civilians. An army garrison of 3,000 mostly US soldiers was stationed at Thursday Island and took over the MSC premises.[50]

---

47   *West Australian*, 20 July 1938, p. 17; La Grange Mission Chronicle 1/1/55–2/6/63, #14284, Archives of the Pallottine Community, Rossmoyne.
48   Beagle Bay Mission, Broome, Western Australia, A885, B77 PT1, NAA.
49   Frank Flynn, *Distant Horizons: Mission Impressions as Published in the Annals of Our Lady of the Sacred Heart*, Sacred Heart Monastery, Kensington, 1947, pp. 19, 20, 26; Caruana, 'Reflections', p. 126.
50   Caruana, 'Reflections', pp. 43, 49.

Hammond Island became a military base and its Sisters, women and children were evacuated to Cooyar in late January 1942.[51] The Hopevale residents were evacuated to Woorabinda in May 1942 with disastrous consequences, Fr Georg Heinrich Schwarz and his son-in-law Victor Behrendorff were interned and a military airstrip was erected at Cape Bedford.[52]

Darwin became 'Fortress Australia' and its southern supply lines were secured through military reinforcements and a brand new 'Spirit of Progress' troop-carrying train to Alice Springs, which also became a military town. The children from 'the Bungalow', an Aboriginal children's home at the former telegraph station on the Todd River at Alice Springs, were evacuated south, and the Little Flower mission, already once removed from Alice Springs to Charles Creek in 1937, was evacuated to an isolated police station near Arltunga in February 1943.

Port Keats became an RAAF radar station and the mission was moved further inland to Wadeye. The Port Keats Sisters and the Bathurst Island convent evacuated just before the first bombing of Darwin on 19 February 1942, after which the whole Northern Territory came under military control and immediate civilian evacuations were ordered. This caused a scramble towards Katherine, and from there further southwards under continued bombing. Bishop Gsell withdrew to Alice Springs along with many Darwin residents. On 22 September 1943, Kalumburu mission, which was used as a refueling station, came under aerial attack, killing the mission superior Fr Thomas Gill and several children.[53] In September 1942, Fr Henschke evacuated Tiwi people to Hawker and Carrieton (near Port Augusta).

Broome, too, became a military station and vehicles and buildings, including the orphanage, were requisitioned.[54] The Broome convent and Aboriginal residents were evacuated to Beagle Bay in February 1942, stretching the mission to its limits (and ending the experiment of

---

51   Luke Taylor, Graeme K. Ward, Graham Henderson, Richard Davis and Lynley A. Wallis, *The Power of Knowledge, the Resonance of Tradition*, Aboriginal Studies Press, Canberra, 1997, pp. 70ff.
52   Dean Gibson, 'War of Hope', NITV, 25 April 2015; Jonathan Richards, '"What a howl there would be if some of our folk were so treated by an enemy": The Evacuation of Aboriginal People from Cape Bedford Mission, 1942', *Aboriginal History* 36 (2013): 67–98.
53   Margaret Zucker, *From Patrons to Partners, A History of the Catholic Church in the Kimberley*, University of Notre Dame Press, Broome, 1994, pp. 112–13.
54   Story of Jimmi Chi in Regina Ganter with Julia Martinez and Gary Lee, *Mixed Relations: Asian-Aboriginal Contact in North Australia*. University of Western Australian Publishing, Crawley, 2006.

a native Sisters convent). Soldiers were also stationed at Lombadina.⁵⁵ After the 3 March 1942 air raids, Broome's civilians rushed south whereas the Sisters at the Derby leprosarium, instead of evacuating by Qantas plane as instructed, went bush with their patients and helpers.⁵⁶

The alternative to being evacuated, or going bush, was to join up. Eighty Bathurst Island men joined 56 Port Craft Company, Royal Australian Engineers, and were stationed at the Larrakeyah barracks, headquarters of the Darwin garrison. Twenty men from Little Flower mission joined the armed forces around September 1942. They became part of a Native Labour Unit, totalling about 150 men stationed at 'the Bungalow'. They were deployed in unloading trains and building roads, such as the Stuart Highway to Darwin.⁵⁷

Military service and contact with black US soldiers raised expectations of citizenship.⁵⁸ The postwar period brought an intensified lobbying for citizen rights, federal payments for Aboriginal people and the liberationist inspirations of the postcolonial movement around the world.

German Pallottines in the Cold War

A rethinking of mission also came from inside the Pallottine Society. By the time of World War II, a controversial movement had arisen among the German Pallottines, inspired by Fr Josef **Kentenich** of Schönstatt, the Pallottine training seminary at Vallendar near Koblenz. The Schönstatt movement harked back to the inspiration of the society's founder Vincent **Pallotti**, to focus on the involvement of the lay apostolate. Under the impact of this movement, the society reverted in 1948 to its original name that made explicit reference to the 'apostolate', Society of the Catholic Apostolate (SAC) instead of PSM. Vincent Pallotti was beatified in January 1950 (an achievement still not equalled by the founder of the MSC, Jules **Chevalier**, despite strenuous efforts by MSC staff, since beatification is even more cumbersome than World Heritage listing with UNESCO, and requires miracles). The Schönstatt idea was to outreach

---

55   Brigida Nailon, *Nothing is Wasted in the Household of God: Vincent Pallotti's Vision in Australia 1901–2001*, Spectrum, Richmond, 2001, p. 153.
56   Zucker, *From Patrons to Partners*, p. 113.
57   Flynn, *Distant Horizons*, p. 77.
58   Robert Hall, *Black Diggers: Aborigines and Torres Strait Islanders in the Second World War*, Allen & Unwin, Sydney, 1989; Kay Saunders, 'Inequalities of sacrifice: Aboriginal and Torres Strait Islander labour in northern Australia during the second world war', *Labour History* 69 (1995): 131–48.

to young people and laity. This youthful and forceful movement very nearly split the German Pallottines. It showed certain similarities with the national socialist youth movement, though the Schönstatt leaders were themselves subject to persecution in the Third Reich. Bishop Raible and some other Pallottine veterans were suspicious of the new movement, and Raible was not invited to the general chapter of the Australian Pallottine Society in late 1952, which 'unanimously' adopted the Schönstatt idea.[59] To give physical presence to the new policy, a Marian shrine to Mother Thrice Admirable, similar to the one in Vallendar, was erected at the Kew headquarters in 1952. By now, a number of Schönstatt priests had arrived who had all been conscripted into the German military during their Pallottine training[60] and most rose to prominence in Australia or Germany.[61] Australian-born candidates were in turn sent to study at Vallendar instead of Rome from 1952.[62]

The new catch-cry of 'Catholic Action' called for the mobilisation of 'The Younger Set' as a lay apostolate.[63] By 1958, Fr Walter Silvester had 17 youth groups active in Kew and trained lay missionaries in the Ver Sacrum Mariana Institute.[64] This Youth Apostolate engaged in fundraising and group activities and participated in Catholic Action groups associated with Bob **Santamaria**'s Social Studies Movement. Amidst concerns of communist infiltration in the Australian labour movement, Santamaria's anti-communist Catholic Action movement split the Australian Labor Party with the formation of the Democratic Labor Party in 1955. The German dimension of this significant historical moment has not been much noticed in Australian historiography.

In the Cold War period, the Catholic Church fostered a worldwide engagement against Communism. The Legionaries of Christ with their lay arm Regnum Christi were establishing themselves in Ireland and

---

59 Raible to General Hoffmann, 22 February 1946, and Kupke to Hügel, 14 December 1952, in Nailon *Nothing is Wasted*, pp. 159, 188.
60 P. Heinrich Menzel, 'Zum Goldenen Jubiläum unserer Kimberley-Mission in Australien', *Pallottis Werk* 1951/1, p. 16.
61 Fr Ludwig Münz became Limburg Provincial (1962–77) and Pallottine General (1977–83), Fr John Jobst became the Bishop of Broome (1958–95), Fr Walter Silvester became the Australian Regional (1958–65), and Fr John Lümmen (1919–2014) became the rector of Rossmoyne training institution and a historian of the Australian Pallottines.
62 Australians who studied at Vallendar were Br Anthony Peile, Fr John Hennessey and Br J. Evans. Nailon, *Nothing is Wasted*, p. 164.
63 Hügel at La Grange to Regional, 25 October 1955, in Nailon, *Nothing is Wasted*, pp. 161–77.
64 Nailon, *Nothing is Wasted*, pp. 167–70.

Mexico.[65] For the Pallottine interest in India, a hotbed of communism, and also within the German Pallottine Province, the Australian Pallottine Region, erected in 1946, was to play a strategic role. Entry to India required a British passport, so the plan was to send Germans to Australia long enough to qualify for naturalisation and to post naturalised or native-born Australians to India.

Communist influence in north Australia also led to the request for Catholic intervention. The new Commissioner for Native Affairs, Stanley G. Middleton, wanted the Catholic Church to commence a mission and school at White Springs sheep and cattle station in 1947 to undermine the Pilbara strikers associated with communist Don **McLeod** who were starting up a school at nearby Yandeyarra. The Port Hedland diocesan parish priest (not a Pallottine) took on the project, which the communist *Workers' Star* described as the 'White Springs Concentration Camp'. There was a firm expectation that the Pallottines would take on White Springs; however, when the lease contract was ready to sign in 1951 at least £9,000 had already been spent, and a debt of £7,000 was outstanding, so the Pallottine Regional refused to sign. Neither the Catholic Church nor the Native Affairs department would ever have contemplated sinking £9,000 into aid for the Aboriginal strikers who strove for self-determination.

The end of the mission era

The forces that ended the mission period were diverse, inexorable and transnational, reflecting a rapidly changing Zeitgeist. There was the postcolonial struggle of colonised peoples around the world of fallen empires. There were the citizenship aspirations of an increasingly mixed and educated Indigenous population who no longer fitted into the protective mission paradigm. There was the government policy of assimilation clawing back control over Aboriginal people from the churches. There was the renewal within the churches themselves. The case of the Kimberley missions illustrates all these forces.

Directives for change also came from the Pallottine society itself. The signposts set by apostolic delegates (official visitations from Germany or Rome) in 1946, 1952 and 1955 were to de-emphasise Aboriginal mission and to focus on parish and urban work instead. The Australian

---

65 *The Legion*, Compass, ABC, June 2014.

Pallottine region therefore placed parish priests in Broome, Derby and Wyndham. Wandering Brook (1944) and La Grange (1955) became the last missions the Pallottines entered into. In the shift of direction towards urban youth, a number of properties outside of the Kimberley were quickly acquired with funding from the German Catholic fundraising organisation **Misereor**: Tardun boarding school (1948), the seminary in Kew (1940), Pallotti House in Strathfield (Sydney, opened as a novitiate in January 1954), premises in Manly (1955), Rivervale (1948–54), the Pallottine mission centre at Riverton including a boys' hostel (1955), Millgrove farm property and apostolic centre in Melbourne (1957), Silverwater (1959) and extensions at Rossmoyne (1959, 1961).[66]

The Western Australian department of education assumed control of Aboriginal education and posted government teachers to the missions, while Catholic education shifted its focus from mission schools on Aboriginal reserves to denominational schools in parishes. Under the banner of assimilation, there was a strong focus on the older boys from the missions, who were generally sent far away from their families if they showed promise. Bishop Raible resisted this change in direction and kept reiterating that not the consent of the department, but the consent of the parents had to be the decisive factor. Raible was as unhappy about separate schools for coloured children as he was about the German direction over the region, and the relationship between his Kimberley vicariate and the Australian Pallottine region was becoming tense.[67]

By the time John Jobst replaced Otto Raible as bishop of the Kimberley in January 1959 there was a general sense that the Kimberley mission was becoming aimless.[68] The flying doctor service, monthly plane services, telephone lines and serviceable off-road trucks had transformed the physical conditions of the once-shielded missions. The new Pallottine staff from Germany arrived with a radically different mindset from the older missionaries. Two of the new German arrivals later explained that as newcomers they had no notion of alternative Aboriginal futures and fully embraced the assimilationist vision. They themselves had left their

---

66   Nailon, *Nothing is Wasted*, passim.
67   Raible to Kearney, 2 June 1957, and Worms to Regional, 29 July 1953, in Nailon, *Nothing is Wasted*, pp. 195, 189.
68   Bourke, *The History of the Catholic Church in Western Australia*.

homes and found it difficult to comprehend the loss and grief experienced by Indigenous youth who were relocated to the south. Full citizenship seemed the self-evident path to liberation and emancipation.[69]

The federal government inserted itself into the force field of Aboriginal management as a third player after it gained powers over Indigenous people in the various states with the 1967 referendum. Instead of funding, the Pallottines were granted a favourable development loan of $250,000 for their Kimberley ventures from the Commonwealth Bank directed by H.C. **Coombs**.[70] With the emerging federal emphasis on self-determination, government funding started to be directed to Aboriginal groups and organisations from the mid-1960s and the deinstitutionalisation of missions intensified under the Whitlam Government elected in 1975. A federal Department of Aboriginal Affairs (DAA) was formed in 1975 and, locked into battle with the Aboriginal affairs departments of the most conservative states, Western Australia and Queensland, began to deal with Indigenous communities directly. Financial assistance became available to Aboriginal communities, subject to self-management, and the DAA began to fund housing on the Kimberley missions, with the result that Aboriginal housing was considered better than that of the missionaries, who saw the DAA interventions as a direct attack on their authority.[71]

The transition from mission leadership to parish work was slow and painful for those Pallottines who had invested a lifetime and felt that their effort was simply not recognised. A number of community histories have since tried to reclaim something of the joint effort of the former missions, and the Catholic diocese newsletter *Kimberley Community Profile* often publishes positive testimonies of Kimberley Aboriginal people that demonstrate the central role the church and its institutions have played in their intellectual formation. Among the students at the Rossmoyne training centre who later rose to prominence were Western Australian AFL premiership footballer Harold Little, Peter Yu who became chair of the Kimberley Land Council, and Steven Albert, also known as actor and musician Baamba, who himself became a strong proponent of Aboriginal education – but on the new paradigm of self-determination (for more on former students see

---

69   P. Omasmeier, 'Australien', *Pallottis Werk* 1955/4; John Luemmen and Brigida Nailon, *Led by the Spirit: Autobiography of Father John Luemmen SAC*, Imprinti Potest Provincial of the Pallottines in Australia, Rossmoyne, WA, 1999, Chapter 4.
70   Nailon, *Nothing is Wasted*, p. 234.
71   Helen MacFarlane and John Foley, Kimberley Mission Review – Analysis and Evaluation of Church and Government involvement in the Catholic Missions of the Kimberley (n.d., ca 1981), p. 16, State Records of Western Australia (SROWA).

Lümmen). Another well-known Rossmoyne student was Jimmy Chi who produced a cheeky take on the mission era with the award-winning 1990 musical *Bran Nue Dae*. One of its central characters, Father Benedictus, was loosely modelled on Fr John Lümmen, but at Lümmen's funeral in Perth in January 2014, a large delegation from Broome, including Albert and Chi, were present to pay their final respects. The last German Pallottine to leave the Kimberley (though not the last Pallottine) was Fr Wendelin Lorenz in 2004, parish priest at Derby for more than 35 years.[72]

Conclusions

Within the emerging political empires, the churches competed with each other to spread their mantle of faith.[73] In the 1880s, German Protestant mission societies, which had for decades been relying on sometimes tenuous contacts with foreign Protestant empires, quickly lined up for access to German New Guinea. At the same time, Protestants and Catholics shared a stepping-stones policy into the Australian north and beyond, following the inexorable settlers who were expanding the reach of the British Empire into north Australia. The geopolitics of New Guinea and north Australia launched the mission project in northern Australia, and this was again characterised by competition between Catholics and Protestants, between different Protestant churches, and between different Catholic societies, similar to the dynamics observed for previous periods in Chapters 1 and 2. There was little awareness that the Australian northward drive also entered into areas of longstanding Muslim influence, but surely Indigenous people noticed the jealousy among missionaries, as they did elsewhere in the world, and kept some knowledge from them or, in the words of Ian McIntosh, 'turned it in'.[74]

---

72 P. Brady, '**Forty faithful years – Derby farewells Father Lorenz in style**', *KCP Magazine*.
73 Patricia Grimshaw and Elizabeth Nelson, 'Empire, "the civilising mission" and Indigenous Christian women in colonial Victoria', *Australian Feminist Studies* 16.36 (2001): 295–309; Diane Kirkby and Catharine Coleborne (eds), *Law, History, Colonialism: The Reach of Empire*, Manchester University Press, Manchester, 2001; Amanda Barry, Joanna Cruickshank and Andrew Brown-May (eds), *Evangelists of Empire?: Missionaries in Colonial History*, Melbourne University Conference series Vol. 18, eScholarship Research Centre in collaboration with the School of Historical Studies and with the assistance of Melbourne University Bookshop, Melbourne, 2008; Norman Etherington (ed.), *Missions and Empire*, Oxford University Press, New York, 2005.
74 Peggy Brock, 'Jealous missionaries on the Pacific northwest coast of Canada', *Journal of Religious History*, 2015; Peggy Brock, 'Negotiating colonialism: The life and times of Arthur Wellington Clah', in Amanda Barry, Joanna Cruickshank and Andrew Brown-May (eds), *Evangelists of Empire? Missionaries in Colonial History*, 2008, pp. 18, 23; Ian McIntosh, 'Missing the revolution'.

German speakers played a prominent role in the Australian mission landscape. As a result of World War I, their prominence declined, together with the short-lived German empire, not only because of the loss of German territories, but also due to virulent anti-German sentiments, and English became the mission language (see Chapter 7). Several German missionaries repatriated and the remainder was subjected to surveillance, but we detect some denominational differences. The German origin of the MSC staff at Bathurst Island was apparently ignored because of the close alliance of the MSC with the military authorities. German Moravians were able to shelter under the umbrella of their alliance with the Presbyterian Church. Lutherans turned to second-generation Germans to staff the missions, with the exception of Strehlow at Hermannsburg and Schwarz at Hopevale.

That the German missionaries who remained in Australia escaped internment during World War I must be due to the realisation that the orderly conduct of remote missions was of greater strategic importance than the risk of Fifth Column activity emanating from these religious. It was enough to set a warning example with the treatment of the Pallottine mission superior Fr Bischofs (see Chapter 6). World War II, on the other hand, was fought much closer to home, and took place after much more contact with Japanese pearlers. The northern missions were severely disrupted with massive relocations and surveillance, and several missionaries were interned – the Pallottines briefly in 1940 and Pastor Schwarz for much longer in 1942. Much of the wartime relocation of Indigenous communities was driven by military strategic considerations, though the evacuation of Hopevale mission is normally explained with reference to missionary Schwarz being German.

The Third Reich tore at the mission movement with new tensions (see Chapter 7 – 'Hitler's men'). For German mission societies, World War II further curtailed the opportunities to place missionaries abroad, particularly in Africa. Herrnhut discontinued mission training in 1941, Basel in 1951, and few mission training institutions (including the HMG at Hermannsburg and the Neuendettelsau Mission Society) were still accepting candidates without a High School Certificate. The trend was towards normal university theology study as the only path to ordination.

Against the worldwide trend of a decline in German mission activity after World War I, the German Pallottines blossomed in Australia.[75] The Catholic Church, a thoroughly transnational enterprise, was able to shelter them from the forces that militated against a strong German presence by placing them under the supervision of staff from other nationalities. The French MSC had already become Australianised by establishing a local training seminary in 1898, and the Pallottines followed suit under the direction of Bishop Raible who lent the Pallottine mission effort a more professional and strategic character. With the acquisition of a wheat farm at Tardun, the Pallottines broke out of the 'Kimberley territory', into which Protestant mission societies had already intruded. Raible's intellectual formation was shaped by the 'Pious Society of Missions', so he resisted the change that was reflected in the society's new name in 1948 away from remote mission towards an urban lay apostolate. However, the forces against paternalistic mission were inexorable, emanating from international shifts in the Zeitgeist, from within the church and also from the aspirations of Indigenous people.

---

75 Marc Spindler, 'Les missions allemandes: leur liquidation et résilience, 1914–2014', Colloque du CREDIC, Neuendettelsau, 2015.

4

The subtle ontology of power

A number of factors facilitated the grafting of missions, with their alien culture and rigid disciplines, onto Indigenous communities. The violence and danger of the frontier society pushed Indigenous people towards missions, but they were also pulled by the material advantages offered by the sheer endless supplies of the missions. Moreover, the interior logic of the missions was decipherable through a shared ontology of power.

Unlike most other settlers, missionaries openly engaged with the supernatural and promised new ways of harnessing and directing preternatural forces. Indigenous people were always interested in new ways of mastering the world they inhabited and often imported new songs, objects and ideas into their cultural registers. Christian prayer, blessings and worship, with altar boys and priests dressed for a carefully orchestrated ceremony, were easily intelligible to peoples already used to staged rituals and incantations in an attempt to influence the supra-material world. Persons who undertook to exert power over the non-material world by deciphering signs and dreams or by casting powerful words were highly respected. Missionaries with the capacity of interpreting the signs of nature, such as comets, and of invoking supernatural help through prayer were in the category of such powerful people. The paper-based information technology from which their knowledge arose was also of great interest. Catholic missionaries had a particularly impressive arsenal of rituals, ideas and objects to exert power over the natural world. They were more likely than Protestants to invoke auspicious numbers and dates, and possessed ritual objects invested with immanent powers.

The missionary convention of referring to each other by symbolic kinship terms (Father, Brother, Sister, Mother) also sits very well with the kinship-based forms of address that traditional societies generally prefer over given names. The missionaries included outsiders in their family of Christ with baptism as a form of adoption signalled by the bestowal of a name.

Local diplomats pursued their own agendas in trying to penetrate and harness this new world of meaning and influence. Baptismal classes and admission to Holy Communion rendered special access to rituals and teaching in a new order that devalued age as a marker of respect. The first baptised candidates on each mission were given a particularly grand welcome to the Christian family, and missionaries staked high hopes on 'first fruit' to work like leavening in the Indigenous society. Finally, mutual cultural incomprehension was softened through Christian men from the Pacific Rim bound into Indigenous society by marriage. Native evangelists, including those imported from the Pacific, played an enormously important role in preparing a fertile soil for missions that is generally underplayed in mission histories that tend to focus on the pioneering missionary figure labouring in isolation.

Divine intervention and wonders

Miracles and wonders accompanied the Catholic missionaries to augur well for their plans. Among Protestants, the appeal to divine intervention is much less common, though a comment by the Moravian Adolf **Hartmann** invoking 'a higher hand' hints at the possibility.[1]

Auspicious numbers

One of the few supernatural staples shared by Catholics and Protestants is the number 12 as an auspicious number of men to launch an institution. Twelve candidates commenced the **Gossner Mission Society** and 12 candidates commenced the **Hermannsburger Missionsgesellschaft** (HMG), 12 men were sent to form **Zion Hill**, Bishop Gibney required

---

1   In a letter to his family in 1870, Hartmann mentioned that the Franco–Prussian war was won by a higher hand for the Prussians (Protestants). Felicity Jensz, 'Everywhere at home, everywhere a stranger: The communities of the Moravian missionary Mary (Polly) Hartmann', in Regina Ganter and Pat Grimshaw (eds), *Reading the Lives of White Mission Women, Journal of Australian Studies* 39.1 (2015): 20–31.

a minimum of 12 staff to conduct the Kimberley mission, the first adults to be baptised at **Beagle Bay** numbered 12, and 12 at Lake **Killalpaninna**, and at New Uniya the Jesuits made room for 12 couples as colonists. Biblical numerology is also woven into an unlikely historical account by Fr Georg Walter, who claimed that the Benedictines wandered in the Western Australian wilderness for 40 days before they settled at New Norcia.[2]

Reading the signs

Dom Salvado, in the quest for a foundation at New Norcia, saw many signs of divine providence. As the food for the working party was running low in 1846, Salvado's dog started hunting and brought back kangaroos. 'Who can fail to see a sign of Divine Providence here?'[3] They drove a flock of sheep through a stretch of land that contained poisonous weeds without losing a single animal, and again Salvado saw the miracle in it. But the key incident in the founding narrative of New Norcia is the story of an icon that Vincent Pallotti, the founder of the Pallottine mission society and later Saint, had given Serra and Salvado as a blessing for the good fortune of the mission. The icon played precisely that role for the Benedictines when a bushfire threatened New Norcia mission during their first harvest. All efforts to keep the fire in check were in vain, until Salvado seized the image of Mother Mary and advanced in prayer against the fire. The wind changed and the fire receded. New Norcia had arrived in the landscape of miracles. Such an incident could not have failed to impress Indigenous people who heard about the strength of conviction with which Salvado invested this ritual object with power over natural forces.

Divine providence was sometimes invoked to explain fortuitous or unfortunate circumstances. In Fr Strele's history, Fr Duncan McNab visited the **Austrian Jesuits** at Sevenhill in 1881 just as they were deliberating on a suitable site for a northern mission, 'led by divine

---

2   Georg Walter, *Australien: Land, Leute, Mission*, Limburg, 1928, p. 119.
3   Rosendo Salvado, *Memorie Storiche dell' Australia, Particolarmente della Missione Benedettina di Nuova Norcia*, S. Congreg. de Propaganda Fide, Rome, 1851; translated E.J. Stormon, *The Salvado Memoirs: Historical Memoirs of Australia and Particularly of the Benedictine Mission of New Norcia and of the Habits and Customs of the Australian Natives*, University of Western Australia Press, Nedlands, 1977, pp. 22, 59.

providence'.⁴ Fr Nicholas **Emo** also felt divine forces at work in times of trouble. In the process of liquidating the Beagle Bay mission assets, against protests from the Trappists, he found a buyer in Broome for the statue of the Blessed Virgin Mary, but by the time he reached Broome this 'rich Japanese lady' had died. 'Evidently there is a superior force that, come what may, prevents the liquidation [of the mission] and which, joined to the piety of our Blacks, has convinced me that God is watching over their lot.' When Bishop Gibney heard about the trouble at Beagle Bay, he announced his visit to the far north, but Emo failed to pick him up and afterwards had much explaining to do. Emo described how he waited for four days at sea to reconnoitre with the passenger ship carrying the bishop, but inexplicably, guided no doubt by an invisible hand, failed to meet the ship.⁵ Some years later on his first voyage out of Broome on the *San Salvador* on 13 May 1906, Emo and Abbot Torres called in at Beagle Bay where the abbot went to visit the missionaries, with whom Emo had a strained relationship at that moment. Emo remained on board to spend his first night on the *San Salvador*, and that night he felt sure that 'the ship is blessed'.⁶

'Divine Providence' might also explain decisions that could meet with criticism. Fr **Gsell**, who became known as the 'Bishop with the 150 wives', attributed his policy of purchasing marriage rights of the mission girls not to the prior Jesuit example, but explained that 'divine providence set us on the right track'.⁷ Divine intervention was also invoked to laud the minimisation of disaster. Soon after his arrival in Darwin, Fr Gsell had an accident in a horse-drawn carriage, which ended up with its four wheels in the air. Gsell noted that this happened on the Feast of our Lady of Miracles, 'and we were quite unhurt'.⁸

Reading such signs is a delicate business. The Catholic missionaries could have read many inauspicious signs telling them to abandon their plans for missions, but chose to ignore them. The 1846 shipwreck of the *Heroine*

---

4   Anthony Strele, 'History of the Mission to the Aborigines in the part of Australia which is called Northern Territory', translated from Latin by F.J. Dennett SJ, ca 1895, Archives of the Society of Jesus, Hawthorn.
5   Emo to Sept Fons, 25 Nov 1900 (36 pages) continued in January 1901, in Brigida Nailon, *Emo and San Salvador*, 2 vols, Brigidine Sisters, Echuca, 2005, Vol. 1, pp. 148–81.
6   Emo to Sept Fons, 25 November 1900, in Nailon, *Emo*.
7   F.X. Gsell (n.d., ca 1925) Report about Bathurst Island Mission, 16 pages, in Bathurst Island Mission Reports 1910–1915, A431, 1951/1294, barcode 66600, National Archives of Australia (NAA).
8   F.X. Gsell, '*The Bishop with 150 Wives': Fifty Years as a Missionary*, Angus and Robertson, Sydney, 1956, p. 19.

4. THE SUBTLE ONTOLOGY OF POWER

with Fr Angelo Confalonieri's party in Torres Strait could have been enough warning against a northern outreach. Similarly, during Bishop Gibney's first exploratory journey around Dampier Peninsula in 1890, the party became bogged in the swamp several times, Fr Ambrose had debilitating attacks of fever and diarrhoea and, just as they were fixing on the mission site at Beagle Bay, Ambrose had a close encounter with a snake and the bishop was retching. Ambrose had serious misgivings about the venture, but Gibney was reading different signs.

The natural environment unleashed its own wonders, which could be loaded with meaning. When the Passionists assembled in Sydney in 1843, planning to head for Moreton Bay, a great and striking comet pointed them to 'the precise location' of their future mission at **Stradbroke Island**, as Fr Vaccari observed. And on the **Daly River** missions, just before Christmas 1895, 'a comet was seen yesterday in the west'.[9] Previous Christmas tidings had been less auspicious. On Saint Nicholas Day of 1895, the Daly River mission community witnessed the frightening phenomenon of a fireball, a rare kind of lighting strike, and two days before Christmas of 1891, 'one of the goats gave birth to a monster with only one eye, and that in the middle of the forehead!'[10] One might wonder what the Indigenous mission residents made of the monster birth.

Propitious dates

Catholics were careful to choose an auspicious date for a beginning. The name day of Salvado appears twice in the selection of a site for New Norcia: on 1 March 1846, at a site called Badji Badji near the Bolgart farmhouse; and on 1 March 1847, when the foundation stone for the first hut was ceremoniously laid on top of a St Benedict medal at the current site. The Jesuits occupied their first site on the Daly River on 1 October 1886, the Feast of the Holy Rosary, and named it the Queen of the Holy Rosary Station. This proved unexpectedly auspicious shortly afterwards when a Tyrolean benefactor in the United States donated $1,000 on the condition that a church should be dedicated to the Holy Rosary.[11] Sacred Heart mission at Serpentine Lagoon was supposed to

---

9   Daly River Mission Diary (DRM), 22 December 1895, Archives of the Society of Jesus, Hawthorn.
10 DRM, 22 December 1891.
11 Anton Strele, Annual Letters from the Jesuit Mission in North Australia 1886–1889, translated by F.J. Dennett SJ, Archives of the Society of Jesus, Hawthorn, 1887.

be formed on the Feast of the Sacred Heart in 1889, but the superior Fr Strele arrived back from Europe too late. In 1891, the Jesuits abandoned Sacred Heart station in favour of St Joseph's mission at New Uniya 'by a just judgement, according to the word of the Lord, on the feast day of St. Francis Xavier' (one of the founders of the Jesuit order).[12]

Since the Catholic calendar is frequently double-booked with feast days, it was not too difficult to find a meaningful date. Bishop Gibney re-erected the **Disaster Bay** mission abandoned by Duncan McNab on 16 July 1890, the day of Our Lady of Mt Carmel, as if the local place name Caromel (as heard by Gibney)[13] had already anticipated it. On the Feast of St Bernard, 20 August 1890, Gibney erected the Beagle Bay mission and dedicated it to St Bernard, principal patron of the Trappists. On the Feast of Assumption of Our Lady, 15 August 1896, the Trappists baptised their first 12 converts and, on the Feast of Assumption, 15 August 1918, the Pallottines dedicated their new church at Beagle Bay. On the Feast of the Sacred Heart in 1911, the first prefabricated cottage at Bathurst Island was ready to be occupied by Gsell. On the feast of Christ the King in 1932, Raible blessed the new church at Lombadina.

Fr Emo was not at liberty to choose an auspicious date on which to take on **Lombadina** mission, previously run as a secular mission – it occurred on 1 January 1911 – but he died in the early hours of 8 March 1915, the Feast of St John of God, an adventurous Spanish martyr, perhaps very similar to himself. The story of his death, too, is surrounded with hints of divine inspiration as it is claimed that Fr Droste at Beagle Bay 'felt an uncanny impulse to go to Lombadina' just as Emo lay dying,[14] although the mission diary reveals that the Indigenous couple temporarily placed in charge of Lombadina sent word to Droste at Beagle Bay.[15]

---

12   The feast day of St Francis Xavier is on 3 December, whereas Strele's 1891 letter describes the duration of the Sacred Heart mission as October 1882 to November 1891. The mission diary has removals beginning in late September. Strele, Annual Letters 1891.

13   Caromel as written by Gibney possibly designates a ritual site, similar to a word Gibney recorded for Beagle Bay, Kirmel, and possibly also related to the Karamala festival observed on the Daly River in the 1890s, also spelled Caramal.

14   John Harris, *One Blood: 200 Years of Aboriginal Encounter with Christianity: A Story of Hope*, Albatross Books, Sutherland, NSW, 1990, p. 445.

15   **Droste diary**, 1–12 March 1915, in Droste, Wilhelm (Pater), P1 Nr 17, Zentralarchiv der Pallottinerprovinz (ZAPP).

4. THE SUBTLE ONTOLOGY OF POWER

Potent rituals

The primary interior purpose of mission was to dispense divine life, or grace. For this task, the rituals of liturgy, prayer, blessings, transubstantiation and the sacraments including the Eucharist (holy communion or the Lord's Supper) were fundamentally important, and missionaries strained to share the inner secrets of these rituals. The outward signs of the rituals were easy enough to decipher. They required appropriate spaces and were held at meaningful times dictated by the hour of the day (evening prayer), the day of the week (Sunday prayer), the week of the year (with events like Pentecost as a fixed point) or the year of emergence of an institution (jubilees). In such rituals, people occupied roles according to their level of initiation, garbed in meaningful attire loaded with symbolism, obeying protocols for progression, behaviour and spatial arrangements with women on one side, men on the other, priests at the front. The requisite ritual objects were themselves invested with immanent signification and were to be treated with respect – the crucifix, the rosary, the Bible, the holy host (prosphoron), the Eucharistic wine, the monstrance and the tabernacle. Besides the Eucharist and baptism, also celebrated by Protestants, the Catholic Church offers the holy sacraments of penance, confirmation, ordination, extreme unction and matrimony. (Although missionaries required a licence from the state to perform legal marriages.) The Catholic cosmology is a conglomerate of mystical and social ideas containing heaven, hell and purgatory, angels, saints and the holy trinity, Mother Mary and the Pope, bishops and cardinals, sins and cardinal sins, blaspheming and blessing, Ten Commandments and house rules. If one tried to systematise this ontology with oral history methods, by interviewing the oldest members of a community, as Pastor Georg **Reuther** did at Killalpaninna, one might face an intellectual quagmire in which the anecdotes are intelligible enough but the overarching ontological structure is elusive.

Baptism

Baptism was the key performance indicator in the quality framework of all mission societies. It was the ritual admittance to the family of Christ, a public declaration of conversion, and therefore the fulfilment of the aim of heathen mission. The standards for admission varied greatly between mission societies, and the Reformed missions became increasingly selective in the nineteenth century, with elaborate instructions to prepare children for baptism and exacting standards for recognition as Christian converts for adults. A monogamous lifestyle became an absolute prerequisite and therefore a great obstacle for Indigenous people. Other provisos might include building a house, avoiding heathen rituals or regularly attending Sunday service and instructional gatherings. Baptism has some intrinsically ecumenical characteristics, easily understood across cultures. It is a public ritual, witnessed by appointed guardians, that revolves around the bestowal of a name to signify belonging. Such a story occurs in one of the contact narratives preserved by the Milingimbi Language Centre in Arnhem Land, the story of 'The Last Visit of the Macassans'. The narrator Djawa tells how in his youth he and his uncle encountered a Macassan captain who was on his last journey to Elcho Island (the 1906/07 season). The captain gave Djawa the Macassan name of Mangalai (a name that occurs in that captain's family), signifying a relationship, and asked him to make his new name public to everyone.[16] One might suspect that this story is not so much about the Macassans visiting for the last time, but about a deep connectedness between Yolngu and Macassans. Precisely such stories were 'turned in' (became hidden) with the arrival of Christian missionaries soon after the Macassan contact period.

There are many early missionary accounts of the individual baptism of Indigenous people (for example, the deathbed baptism of young 'Nanny' at Wellington Valley in July 1839). Such baptisms need not signal conversion to a different faith. The bestowal of a name to signify relationship fitted in very well with Indigenous expectations of the assimilation of strangers, and Indigenous people may have sought to create a fabric of family connections through the acceptance of such names. In Sydney in the 1830s, Bishop Polding observed:

> Oftentimes we have the happiness of seeing fathers bring to us, at Sydney, their children that they may receive a name – it is thus they signify baptism. We grant, without difficulty, this favour whenever a priest resides in the territory which the tribe inhabits, and we give a certificate which is to be presented to the missionary in order that he may watch over the regenerated infant.[17]

---

16   Regina Ganter with Julia Martinez and Gary Lee, *Mixed Relations: Asian–Aboriginal Contact in North Australia*, University of Western Australian Publishing, Crawley, 2006, p. 30.
17   Polding in Sydney to Central Council of the Society for the Propagation of the Faith in Lyons, 10 January 1840, in Osmund Thorpe, *First Catholic Mission to the Australian Aborigines*, Pellegrini & Co., Sydney, 1950, pp. 187–88.

4. THE SUBTLE ONTOLOGY OF POWER

The Fathers on their part also gave a profound meaning to this bestowal of names, so the ritual of baptism created a classical common ground on which the successful meeting of strangers could take place, and involved, as American historian Richard White has suggested, a process of mutual invention.[18]

The first voluntary baptism was the point when a mission became successful. It usually opened the gates to a community and the churches considered it the essential threshold. At Moreton Bay, the early attempts at Zion Hill, Stradbroke Island and **Bethesda** were all considered failures because they did not result in a single baptism. Indeed, the opinion that it was actually impossible to convert Australian Aborigines became widespread even among Lutheran pastors, until the Moravians in Victoria proved otherwise.

In August 1860, on the occasion of the consecration of the mission chapel, the Moravians at **Ebenezer**, a mission formed only in 1859, baptised Nathanael Pepper in the presence of more than 150 people. In 1865, Phillip and Nathanael Pepper, both baptised and married to brides selected by the missionaries, became paid missionary assistants. Ebenezer's early success, unparalleled elsewhere, was much praised and at the same time evoked criticism of those other Australian missions that had less to boast. Pastor Spieseke at Ebenezer tried to deflect: 'the Lord has given us favour in the sight of men, so that I think they sometimes make too much of us and our poor endeavours'.[19] Indeed, the outstanding success of Ebenezer had probably less to do with the capability of its missionaries and more with lucky circumstances, and raises the question of Pepper's motivation, to which Chapter 5 returns.

A degree of denominational competition spawned the break through the baptismal sound barrier. That breakthrough came during the rush to the interior described in Chapter 2. John Green at Corranderk claimed William Barak as the first Victorian Aboriginal convert for the Church of England in 1865, and followed up with two more in 1866. Hard on his heels was the Moravian Friedrich **Hagenauer** with his first fruit James Mathew Fitchet at **Ramahyuck** before a 200-strong gathering in

---

18   Richard White, *The Middle Ground: Indians, Empires, and Republics in the Great Lakes Region, 1650–1815*, Cambridge University Press, Cambridge, 1991.
19   Spieseke, November 1863, Mission Station, Wimmera – Extracts from *Periodical Accounts Relating to the Missions of the Church of the United Brethren*, compiled by C.W. Schooling, ca 1975, MS 9896, State Library of Victoria.

March 1866, on the occasion of the consecration of the church, greatly lauded in the mission newsletters and the local press. In the same year, the Austrian Jesuits at Sevenhill, who planned to enter into heathen mission further north, baptised several Aborigines to assist them in their desire.[20] Meanwhile, Hagenauer at Ramahyuck was able to record another success, with the first two Christian weddings in July 1867, again before a large crowd including 200 white visitors. The publicity surrounding these events was a win-win strategy: for Indigenous persons, being at the centre of a public spectacle was surely some incentive to make a commitment. By 1879, 60 per cent of the mixed-descent residents at the **Lake Condah** Church Mission Society (CMS) mission under the charge of Moravian missionary Stähle were already baptised.[21]

The Lutherans remained more cautious in admitting candidates to baptism. At Cooper's Creek (Killalpaninna), the missionaries said that they hesitated with baptisms because in the course of their work on the Dieri language they found it difficult to adequately translate key religious concepts, like grace and sin. They took care to strike an accommodation between Indigenous and European naming conventions, with a preference for Christian personal names that worked in English and German. Their first 12 candidates were baptised in 1879, including Benjamin Dalkilina and Luise, Benjamin's brother Johannes Pingilina and Clara, Elias Palkilina and Beate, Joseph Diltjilina, Henry Tipilina, Gottfried Yildimirina and Sarah, the disabled Derelina and the young bachelor Diwana, who did not receive a name ending in *lina* because he was not yet *materi* (full-bearded). Later, Pastor Johann Flierl constructed names like Nathanael Nimpilina for a man who had fled from frontier violence in Queensland, or Timotheus Maltilina, a person of mixed descent, with *malti-* expressing gentleness.[22]

Lutheran missionaries were instructed to report the names of the newly baptised and to describe the ceremony in detail,[23] with a view to reporting in the mission newsletters, because then, as now, grassroots fundraising

---

20   G.J. O'Kelly, 'The Jesuit Mission Stations in the Northern Territory 1882–1899', Honours thesis, Monash University, 1967, p. 2.
21   C.A. Meyer at Tanunda, Report to Pastor Herlitz, 8 July 1878, Biographical Collection, Meyer, C.A., Lutheran Archives Australia (LAA).
22   Susanne Froehlich (ed.), *Als Pioniermissionar in das ferne Neu Guinea: Johann Flierls Lebenserinnerungen*, 2 vols, Harrassowitz Verlag, Wiesbaden, 2015, passim.
23   Pastor Rechner to Flierl II, 8 December 1886, Immanuel Synod, Mission Committee, Correspondence book of Pastor GJ Rechner, 1886–1892, LAA.

greatly relied on the reporting of success. The first seven baptisms at **Hermannsburg** took place in 1887 and, by 1893, Hermannsburg registered 25 baptised Christians, mostly from the mission school. They were allowed to choose from a range of suitable baptismal names, so that they could understand their meaning, such as archangel Michael or the 'good Lutheran name' Martin.[24]

The Austrian Jesuits on the Daly, on the other hand, started off by giving local people names like Walpurga, Burgina, Hildegard, Joachim, Dagobert, Waldemar or Kunigunda.[25] Such Germanic names could hardly have been decipherable or even pronounceable to the Indigenous people. Still, they were perhaps an improvement on some of the names deriving from contact with settlers, such as Killingmi or Fanny Taitmiab. That the settlers were 'killing me' or 'tied me up' is entirely credible in the post-Coppermine ethnic violence of the Daly River, and perhaps these women tried to tell a story rather than their name. After a few years, the Jesuits took more care to preserve Indigenous names and integrated them into double names like Anthony Taruak, Margarita Dandam, Teresa Nimbali, Paul Tyedburo or Helena Bayi. They also began to refer to Barramundi as Ngologorog, and to Dummy as Nabba (still a reference to being deaf-mute). Others continued to be called in good European tradition (presumably also arising from settler contact) according to their region of origin, like Pine Creek, Daly and Finiss, or by their function, like Captain. Between 1886 and 1899, the Jesuits on the Daly baptised 197 infants and 78 adults and also performed 78 deathbed baptisms.[26] It would be interesting to examine their baptismal records to recover and document the shifts in their naming policy. I suspect that the early Germanic names were not baptismal names because they derived from the pre-Christian and Nibelungen fables rather than from the Bible.

The 'first fruit' for Queensland Lutherans was claimed by Pastor Ernst Richard Hansche from Neuendettelsau at **Mari Yamba** mission, who baptised an adult man and a child within months of his arrival in

---

24   Everard Leske, *For Faith and Freedom: The Story of Lutherans and Lutheranism in Australia 1838–1996*, Open Book publishers, Adelaide, 1996; Report from O. Liebler in *Kirchen und Missions Zeitung* 47.22 (May 1911): 173; 'Our Australian Mission', in Biographical Collection, Moses Uraiakuraia, LAA.
25   This German name has a striking similarity to 'that mob kuniguni', a place of old women, mentioned in passing by Britta Duelke, *'Same but Different': Vom Umgang mit Vergangenheit Tradition und Geschichte im Alltag einer nordaustralischen Aborigines-Kommune*, Studien zur Kulturkunde 108, Rüdiger Köppe Verlag, Köln, 1998, p. 103.
26   David Strong, *The Australian Dictionary of Jesuit Biography 1848–1998*, Archives of the Society of Jesus, Halstead Press, Rushcutters Bay, NSW, 1999, p. 228.

late 1894. He was severely criticised by his HMG-leaning mission committee because it was 'too soon' and without another pastor present.[27] The committee organised what it considered a proper baptism shortly afterwards, at the Toowoomba mission festival in May 1895, where it presented 13-year-old Magdalena and 15-year-old Maria in the presence of the press to seven pastors and a large crowd including 'numerous English people'. In December 1896, the mission performed three more baptisms, this time in the presence of two Mackay pastors. By the time the Mari Yamba mission closed in 1902, about half the population was baptised.[28] Clearly the response of Indigenous people was not the cause of the eventual failure of this mission.

The 1895/96 success of Mari Yamba reflected poorly on the other missions in Queensland. At **Cape Bedford** (Hopevale) mission only a deathbed baptism in 1892 had so far been performed. Under probing from Neuendettelsau, more girls were baptised in 1896 and 1897, and the first adult baptisms at Cape Bedford took place in 1899. The fate of **Bloomfield** mission was now hanging in the scales, but once the Immanuel Synod received advice in mid-1899 that the first converts would shortly be baptised, the committee decided to continue the mission.[29]

On the other side of Cape York, the Moravian/Presbyterian **Mapoon** mission also recorded success in 1896 with the baptism of Jimmy and Sarah and their child together with two missionary children on the occasion of the consecration of the new church, again a public event. Rev. Nicholas Hey had trouble deciding what to do with Indigenous names. In the case of his first fruit, Hey reflected that Deinditschy was 'Jimmy's real name', also carried by his father, brother and sisters. It also happened to be the name of a bird – although Hey thought that this was possibly incidental and not at all important. Hey decided in favour of Jimmy, a 'nicer sounding' name (to Hey's ears), and as a result of this decision it is very difficult to decipher the life trajectories of the various Jimmys on the Moravian/Presbyterian missions on the western Cape York Peninsula. Chapter 7 will return to the lack of anthropological training of missionaries.

---

27   United German and Scandinavian Lutheran Synod of Queensland, Mission Committee Minute Book, 1887–1903, May 1895, LAA.
28   Leske, *For Faith and Freedom*.
29   Immanuel Synod, Mission Committee Minutes, 1895–1901 (translated), 29 June 1899, LAA.

4. THE SUBTLE ONTOLOGY OF POWER

In the same year as the Moravians at Mapoon and the Lutherans at Cape Bedford recorded their first baptisms, the French Trappists invited the media in August 1896 to witness the baptism of their first 12 young men at Beagle Bay. To the Indigenous or accepted names of the candidates they added their own personal names (Sebastian, Narcisse, Joachim, Joseph, Jacques, etc.). This must have set a strong signal of relatedness between the baptised community and their namesake Fathers and Brothers. In 1897, another 23 gathered for mass baptism, and altogether the Trappists claimed to have baptised over 200 people.[30] This means that the following three years must have seen a veritable rush into this new ceremony with an average of over 50 each year.

By this time, the Moravians at Ramahyuck declared that their mission statement had already been achieved: preaching the gospel, conversion and salvation.[31] Indeed, the 1886 Aborigines Act, which Friedrich Hagenauer had helped to introduce, banished mixed descendants from the Victorian missions and therefore depleted them of residents. Further north it was precisely the mixed descendants, particularly children, who became the focus of missions under the impact of state legislation.

At **Bathurst Island**, Fr Gsell had to content himself with deathbed and infant baptisms for the first 10 years (1911 to the 1920s), 'just spade-work', as he called it, but the 113 baptised children in the mission school 'became the core of the Christian community'.[32] Fr Gsell began to drill down to the system of marriage promise to liberate the girls and their yet unborn babies from future promised husbands, rather than tackle adult polygamy.

Marriage

Polygamy was a major impediment to adult baptism. Missionaries evinced a strong moral disdain for polygamy, and the idea arose early that Indigenous marriage arrangements meant that women were in virtual sexual slavery – Strele at Rapid Creek, Gsell at Bathurst Island and Hey at Mapoon all made comments to this effect. At Beagle Bay, Fr Alphonse

---

30   Nailon, *Emo and San Salvador*, Vol. 2, p. 143, gives the figure as 255, and Sept Fons indicated 200 baptisms. Fr Marie Bernard, Sept Fons to Limburg, 10 December 1900, Australien 1900–1907 B7 d.l. (3), ZAPP.
31   'Mission Work among the Aborigines at Ramahyuck, Victoria, Report for 1894', McCarron Bird & Co. Printers, Melbourne, 1895.
32   Gsell, '*The Bishop with 150 Wives*', p. 73; F. Flynn, '40 ans chez les Aborigènes Australiens – l'évêque aux 150 épouses', *Annales de Notre-Dame du Sacré-Coeur*, December 1960, pp. 266–69.

Tachon asked the advice of Fr Duncan McNab before admitting the first adults, who were all in polygamous relationships, to baptism. In 1896, the Elder Felix Gnodonbor perhaps helped things along by interpreting monogamy as a temporary condition: 'In two months I will turn away again all my wives and will keep only one of them, you will baptize me, for I say it to you, I want to be a Christian'.[33]

But the missionaries were not content with 'turning away again all my other wives', they required a lifelong unbroken commitment to one spouse, and therefore they deeply disturbed Indigenous social relationships. The Jesuits decided in June 1888 that schoolgirls could no longer be given in marriage by the parents without the consent of the missionaries, and the Daly River mission diary is full of troubles caused by wrong marriages. Helena Bayi was the first girl whose marriage rights were purchased from her father in 1892, and while it freed her from a tribal obligation it left her vulnerable to claims from other men (see **Daly River Stories**).

The missionary marriage rules also created their own confusions, as in the case of Johannes **Pingilina**, who tried to live up to expectations but was not considered worthy of a legal divorce when his second wife ran away (see Chapter 5) or in the case of Sebastian at Beagle Bay:

> Sebastiamus was married to a young girl by the Trappists. The young woman, however, refused to live as wife with Sebastiamus and ran away after a short while. When Bishop Gibney visited Disaster Bay mission [1900] he married Sebastiamus to another woman although the first woman was still alive. This second wife died and Pater Nikolaus [Emo] married Sebastiamus to a third woman at Lombadina. When this woman also died Fr. Droste married Sebastiamus a fourth time. This woman also ran away, but was killed last year in a fight at Beagle Bay. The first wife is still alive in Derby. She visited Lombadina last January. Sebastiamus now lives together with a heathen woman who would like to become Christian. The Blacks think that he can't marry her because his first wife is still alive. Neither a written document about the first marriage nor an annulment are extant.
>
> Quaeritur:
>
> Can the missionary Augustius [Spangenberg] baptise the heathen woman and then marry her to Sebastiamus on the assumption that his predecessors also knew about the first marriage?[34]

---

33 Brigida Nailon, *Nothing is Wasted in the Household of God: Vincent Pallotti's Vision in Australia 1901–2001*, Spectrum, Richmond, 2001, p. 154.
34 Note to Raible in Broome, 17 November 1929, in Droste, Wilhelm (Pater), P1 Nr 17, ZAPP.

Indigenous communities sometimes objected to wrong marriages by using the missionary rules, as in the case above and at Bathurst Island.

Like baptism, marriage was a public ceremony that placed the aspirants at the centre of ritual attention, usually with special robing and occasionally covered by a press release, particularly in cases of 'firsts'. It also garnered access to material improvements, such as a place in the inner circle of the mission colony. This status elevation, too, sat well with Indigenous markers of prestige, where more wives flagged greater social stature and being unmarried was an image disadvantage. Like baptism, the sacrament of marriage usually required some preparation. At Ebenezer and the Daly River, the young men were supposed to demonstrate their capacity to support a family by building a cottage or similar structure, and it was meant to last longer than the four months that one such structure held up on the Daly River before it came crashing down.[35] As Deborah Rose observes, it was usually Father Kristen who built, or finished, the cabins to accommodate the Daly River 'colonists' on their garden plots. The endurance, perseverance, discipline and courage required for such an ordeal also resonated with the preparations for initiation. The missionary rules were different, but certainly not undecipherable.[36]

Deathbed baptisms

The threshold standards for adults for admission to the sacraments were demanding, but in the face of death the missionaries were usually ready to put these aside. Any baptism was a soul potentially saved, a small victory for Christ – an increase ceremony.

The Austrian Jesuits on the Daly River missions did not consider deathbed baptism as 'mere spade-work'; for them, any baptism was core business. They were not above dashing off in the middle of night for a deathbed baptism and much regretted if they arrived too late to give the necessary instructions and obtain the proper answers to perform the rite. If they could not baptise someone before death they felt that they had 'let them down'.[37]

---

35   DRM, 4 January 1890.
36   Deborah Bird Rose, 'Signs of life on a barbarous frontier: Intercultural encounters in north Australia', *Humanities Research* 2 (1998): 17–36.
37   DRM, 17 May 1890.

Indigenous people were in general quite willing to take out this free next-world insurance at the last moment. Actually, the black frocks on the Daly became recognised experts in death and dying and were usually notified when somebody was dying. Several people survived their deathbed baptism and, indeed, Fr **Conrath** felt that Catholic baptism could not only save the soul for the next life, but also prolong this life. The mission diary contains entries like 'was near death, and after baptism (if not through baptism) was cured of her sickness in an almost miraculous way'[38] or 'was baptised near death and is now recovering'.[39] The promise of life, and of after-life, was a marvellous gift offered by the missionaries.

Relics and incantations

The Jesuits on the Daly had precious little to defend themselves against the onslaughts of nature and disease, but drew on a wholesome arsenal of instruments of supernatural powers. For healing, the missionaries used smallpox vaccine, snake oil, blessed water from Lourdes and, of course, incantations. They also brought holy oils and relics of saints, obeyed food taboos and appealed to the spirit world to achieve desired outcomes. Once, when the Fathers had feared about the future of the mission and good news finally arrived, Fr Conrath recorded that these positive outcomes 'are rightly attributed to the intercession of St. Joseph, the Patron of this Station'.[40] Special incantations were deployed to combat epidemics. In February 1897, the Jesuits began 'a novena to avert disease from our animals' and nine days later observed with disappointment 'Today is a black day for us – it saw a bull and a cow dead of the same disease, though it is the last day of the novena'.[41] In times of flood, they added a prayer to St John and the *A domo tua* against storms to the Litanies, and to halt the rising waters they exposed the relics of St Nepomuk, protector from floods and drowning, gifted to them by the Archbishop of Prague.[42] Among the icons inscribed with spiritual powers were a black Madonna, a life-size statue of St Ignatius and relics of St Aloysius and St Nepomuk. The relics, together with holy water and incantations of exorcism, were also used when one of the mission girls had a fit:

---

38   DRM, 10 February 1897.
39   DRM, 17 June 1898.
40   DRM, 30 April 1898.
41   DRM, 12 February 1897, 20 February 1897.
42   DRM, 16 May 1891.

> In the evening Helen the Christian girl, became deaf-mute ('nabba'). She seemed not to know what she was doing, made various gesticulations and rushed about the room … she collapsed on the ground … she gave no answer, but simply stayed there with a look of astonishment, her eyes fixed in a strange stare. We used the prayers for private exorcism, the touching with relics, the sprinkling with holy water and giving it to her to drink – and finally she came to herself again and got back the use of speech and hearing. When she was then asked what was the cause of all this, she said it was a devil![43]

Helena Bayi's condition was ascribed to 'obsession or diabolical influx', although seizures called 'nabba' were quite common on the Daly, and her own father carried that name.[44] Their prayers and baptisms promised health and life, but the Jesuit connection with the supernatural was not only capable of healing. The missionaries also demonstrated that disobedience to God's rules could invoke His mortal blow. The death of 'old Bede' was recorded with the comment:

> Nine weeks ago Fr. Conrath told this man [old Bede] not to go to the Karamala which is a pagan festival, threatening him with the punishment of Almighty God if he did go. 'I shall go', said the native, 'let God punish me'.[45]

And so it came to pass: Old Bede died nine weeks later. Indigenous people had their own explanations for such phenomena. They, too, practised distance killing, normally to revenge an unnatural death – 'killing for superstitious reasons', according to the missionaries.[46] Had Fr Conrath really put a death spell on Old Bede?

At St Joseph's (New Uniya 1891–99), a large cross towered over the mission under which the missionaries held speeches and gatherings. Individuals were 'called to the cross' for admonition and interrogation. Aboriginal people were well aware of the image of Jesus nailed to the cross, and feared this massive cross may be used to crucify them as punishment.[47] This fear of the cross is mirrored in many other missionary accounts. Bishop Polding generalised in 1840 about Aborigines (whether at Sydney or Moreton Bay) that 'when I could speak to them on religion I found it

---

43   DRM, 13 November 1891.
44   DRM, 14 November 1891.
45   DRM, 31 June 1898.
46   DRM, 14–17 September 1895.
47   Adolf Kristen SJ, 'Aboriginal Language', 1899, p. 197, MS 1239, Australian Institute of Aboriginal and Torres Strait Islanders (AIATSIS).

very easy to make them comprehend the principal truths of the Catholic faith. The cross, particularly, is for them a subject of serious reflection'.[48] At Bethesda in 1866, one of the leading men demanded an explanation of the image of the crucified Jesus shown in a small illustrated booklet that Pastor Hausmann distributed. Presumably, the message that 'Jesus loves you' was not easily reconciled with such horrific images and a potentially vengeful God.

Double binds

The people at Uniya were also afraid of the cemetery, so close to the main station.[49] Even after accepting baptism, many baulked at having their bodies consecrated according to Christian burial. Sometimes the missionaries were misled as to the whereabouts of the dead or dying so that they would not snatch the corpse and a traditional burial could be performed instead:

> The boy died today at 10am … His father, against our express wish, took the body to the camp of the pagans across the river, and so deprived him of Christian burial.[50]

> News came of the death of Fanny Taitmiab … Fr. Marschner, on Wednesday of last week, judging her to be in danger of death, went with the Holy Oils to the hut where she lived … and said, that he would come back next day and bring her the sacraments … Next day, when about to go there, he heard that she had been taken to another place … He promised tobacco both to the women and to the one who took her there if she were brought back again in the canoe … she was not brought back … and … he heard that she had died last Saturday. Such was her life, and such her death. R.I.P.[51]

One of the Jesuit Fathers, soon after his arrival, interfered with the remains from a tree burial. He opened the bundle, and finding human remains, but not a fully intact corpse as one would expect in a Christian burial, he feared 'malefice'. Instead of giving it a funeral as intended, he quickly and unceremoniously interred the remains.[52] Across a cultural

---

48   Polding in Sydney to Central Council of the Society for the Propagation of the Faith in Lyons, 10 January 1840, in Thorpe, *First Catholic Mission*, pp. 187–88.
49   DRM, 17 April 1895.
50   DRM, 13 January 1893.
51   DRM, 22 February 1897.
52   DRM, 10 May 1900.

divide, it was easy to offend each others' sensibilities, and to get spooked. Their Aboriginal informants often supplied subterfuge stories for fear of punishment, so that misinformation and guesswork often clouded the missionaries' accounts of traditional actions and reactions. Since the missionaries treated abortion as a crime, infanticides and abortions were disguised as stillbirths or mysterious illnesses. (For more on such misinformation, see **Daly River** missions.)

Mission residents were in a cultural double bind. Punishment could easily follow from meeting traditional obligations, while not meeting such expectations could equally incur punishment from the Elders. The case of Mathilda, as narrated in the Daly River mission diary, illustrates this dilemma. When Mathilda came 'of marriageable age' at the mission, the priests forced the issue about her marriage. She refused to give up her promised husband and was therefore 'refused baptism' and 'sent away' together with her father and promised husband.[53] The following year, she was married to Aloysius who was loyal to the Christian missionaries[54] but the promised husband tried to claim Mathilda back:

> Yesterday evening a pagan native tried to take Aloysius' wife Mathilda for himself. He threw a spear at Aloysius and came within an ace of killing him. The man was punished and summarily ejected by Fr. Kristen. The wife [Mathilda], who did not show herself sufficiently on her husband's side, was beaten by him [Aloysius], to her great benefit.[55]

Mathilda subsequently allowed herself to be baptised,[56] but when her baby died she was torn between death threats from the Indigenous society insisting on a proper tree burial and threats of expulsion from the mission if the baby did not get a Christian burial. The Jesuits dismissed her fears as superstitions:

> The funeral was held of a girl who died the day before yesterday – at least the body was given ritual burial. The parents of this child had been filled with superstitious fear, thinking that the body of this infant at the breast must be put up in a tree – if it were buried in the ground, the death of the mother [Mathilda] would follow. The father, Aloysius, rejected this superstition, being warned that otherwise he would lose his garden.[57]

---

53 DRM, 13 April 1891.
54 DRM, 14 January 1892.
55 DRM, 8 September 1892.
56 DRM, 7 May 1893.
57 DRM, 20 November 1895.

Submitting to the Christian rites was a condition of living on the mission and to be expelled from the garden in November, with the onset of the wet and hungry season, would have been a great hardship. The question of her baby's burial confronted young Mathilda with a choice between two sets of intransigent rules.

Indigenous people on missions had much to fear: the wrath of God curses of the missionaries that could result in death, punishment for fulfilling traditional obligations, desecration of burial sites, the cemeteries full of after-life close to the settlement, the use of bones of Saints to achieve intended outcomes, hints of crucifixion, blood-drinking during the Eucharist, and so much talk about death. It is not altogether surprising that bizarre contact cults emerged in an attempt to rebalance the power relationships between people, with the spiritual world and with the material world that the missions were destroying and establishing.

Contact cults

Most missionaries were suspicious of Indigenous ritual gatherings. At Cooper's Creek, Pastor J. Flierl II burned all the boomerangs in 1886 in an effort to eradicate Indigenous culture. (Flierl II was a namesake cousin of the Johann Flierl already mentioned and was later dismissed in disgrace from the Immanuel Synod.) Carl Strehlow at Hermannsburg wrote that 'I have often brought dance singsongs to an end with a stick'.[58] Abstinence from ritual gatherings was a condition for baptism, and at Easter of 1898 Fr Conrath on the Daly even broke up a 250-strong Caramal corroboree (also written as Karamalla) that was usually held in March/April at the Coppermine Landing (aka Paramalmal), which practically the whole mission population was attending.[59] Especially disturbing was the 'diabolical Tyaboi' to which Fr Conrath referred in 1890 and 1893, finding that it involved objectionable rites from which sexually transmitted diseases could be contracted.[60]

---

58 Immanuel Synod, Mission Committee, FRM Box 5, Correspondence Wettengel (transcriptions and translations), LAA.
59 DRM, 10 April 1898.
60 DRM, 20 April 1891.

Tyaboi begins, and the fight of the devil with Christ for the blacks. Benbenyaga (blacks), Chinese garden, Chinese, Coppermines, all mixed up in it – so we have heard from a Christian boy sufficiently grown up to know, and various circumstances prove the evil that is going on.[61]

Anthropologist Deborah Rose adds that the Tyaboi most likely also referred to the Jesuits themselves. She explains that the Tyaboi functioned as a contact cult to incorporate the new, unknown and unpredictable in Indigenous cosmology, and so to tame it. There had been questions raised at the mission about whether Jesus was a Malak-Malak – in other words, whose side he was on. Fr McKillop ventured that the Tyaboi involved human sacrifice.[62] Rose discounts this possibility but suspects that the 'evil spirit' (or Jin-man) to whom sacrifice might be made was God himself, 'the Father who killed his own son', meaning that the concept of human sacrifice was actually introduced by the missionaries themselves. She also points out how closely 'Jin-man' approximates 'Chinaman'. Indigenous lexica elsewhere also paid little heed to the racial differences so highly doted on among settlers, so that in Yolngu languages 'balanda' was used for Asians as well as Europeans.

Tyaboi had disappeared from the Daly by the 1930s, but by this time another contact cult, 'the immoral Gorangara', was observed in the Kimberley. Bishop Raible and Fr Ernst Worms first encountered this near Balgo in 1938, and Worms described it as an immoral, dangerous cult of black magic involving death curses, which was spreading across the Kimberley striking fear into people. His informants refused to translate the curse songs, saying that they had come from elsewhere and were undecipherable. (For more on this contact cult, see Ernst **Worms**.) Worms adjusted his orthography to approximate it to the phenomenon of Kurangara already described by Ronald Berndt in Arnhem Land. Here, too, the cult has been interpreted a revolt against white colonisation.[63] Neither the Pallottines nor the Jesuits entertained the idea that they themselves and their teachings were cast as the devil figure in these ceremonies, or that for non-Christians a ritual curse may not appear all that different from invoking the wrath of God.

---

61   DRM, 17 October 1893.
62   D. Mackillop, 'Anthropological notes on the Aboriginal tribes of the Daly River', *Transactions of the Royal Society of South Australia* 17 (1892–93): 262.
63   Tony Redmond, 'Tracks, texts and shadows: Some intercultural effects of the 1938 Frobenius Expedition to the north-west Kimberley', paper presented at The German Anthropological Tradition in Australia, Nicolas Peterson and Anna Kenny, ANU, 18–19 June 2015.

The power of the word

Just like the curses of contact cults, the missionaries had powerful words spoken in prayers, sermons and admonitions. Fr Conrath on the Daly River predicted the death of Old Bede. Fr Finnegan at Tardun recorded a success of 5 inches of rainfall to his prayers in 1961. The spoken word of missionaries was powerful. The mission superiors pronounced who was able to stay on the mission and who had to leave. But even more powerful was the written word of God. It was contained in the holy book, the supreme ritual object in which knowledge and power was immanent. The Bible seemed vested with all-knowing powers. Anecdotes abound about Indigenous respect for written words, books and papers, and the whole technology of information communication that they represented. Bishop Polding observed:

> Any writing which we entrust to these savages has, in their eyes, something mysterious and sacred, and if they happen to know that the letter or ticket concerns themselves or their children they preserve it with a truly religious care.[64]

The sanctity accorded to the baptismal certificates that Polding refers to is reminiscent of the way in which tjuringas and messagesticks were treated – also material objects on which information is encoded. The meaning embedded in these objects was clearly powerful and could evoke a strong response from those who decoded it. In the case of a baptismal certificate, the decoder would accept the nominee as 'one of us', a fellow Catholic. The missionaries were vaguely aware of the similarity of these media. When Pastor Richter wanted to tell the people assembled near Aurukun in 1910 that they had arrived too early for Christmas, and should come back in a week, they asked for a proper message stick. Richter sent them a piece of cardboard showing the mission address, and instructed the courier to show them seven fingers for seven more sleeps, with the result that 270 people arrived on time for Christmas. Such part-written, part-enacted communication created a middle ground between instrumental attitudes to missions as sources of material benefit, and as grails of knowledge/power with new forms of communication. Senior men (see **Piltawodli**) and young men who felt sidelined by Indigenous hierarchies (see **Aurukun**) were vying for access to this new technology of power.

---

64 Polding in Sydney to Central Council of the Society for the Propagation of the Faith in Lyons, 10 January 1840, in Thorpe, *First Catholic Mission*, pp. 187–88.

4. THE SUBTLE ONTOLOGY OF POWER

Several Indigenous languages refer to writing with synonymous words for the idea and an associated object. In Yolngu languages, which have the longest demonstrated history of contact with writing in Australia, *wukirriwuy*, for example, means both writing and pen, while *darabu* refers both to writing in general and to a particular triangle pattern representing the ensign flags of Dutch-licensed Macassan trepang boats, which have become, with slight variations, patterns representing different dialect groups.[65] Anna Kenny points out a similar instance in the Aranda language and develops from this an interesting reading of the power of paper. She observes that the nickname the Aranda at Hermannsburg used for their missionary Father, *Pepa*, also means paper. His book of law and fundamental truth was also a *pepa*, and local elders were interested in this technology of power and knowledge. According to Kenny, they imparted their secrets for him to write down on paper, in order to produce the Aranda's book of law and fundamental truth, the Aranda's *Pepa*.[66]

At Killalpaninna, too, Pastor Georg Reuther ended up translating Dieri religious texts into German, instead of the other way round. His informant Palkalina narrated in detail the process through which he became a *kunki* to occupy the highest position of honour in his group. Attempting to systematise the knowledge to which he was introduced, Reuther recorded the 17 steps of the three-day procedure and the 13 rules of the *kunki*. Reuther was exposed to an enormous amount of secret knowledge. He was taught how to interpret dreams and how to cast a magic spell on 15 types of objects, including waterholes, yellow ochre, brown ochre, the sun and the rain. Reuther's whole manuscript, some 2,600 pages in dense German handwriting, bound into 13 thesis-sized volumes, reads like he was being recruited, or trained, into Dieri ways of knowing. Reuther struggled with his sanity and finally felt he had to flee from the mission to avoid the lunatic asylum (for more on his struggle with sanity, see Georg **Reuther**).

The knowledge recorded in Reuther's manuscript seems to arise out of a dynamic between Reuther and his informants. Anna Kenny's explanation seems very plausible, that the Elders invested in a new technology to preserve their laws. Just as the missionaries struggled for the right words

---

65 Made by Mambur (or Mick Marambur), Elcho Island 1961, Nr 931 Berndt Collection, Berndt Museum, University of Western Australia.
66 Kenny, Anna, *The Aranda's Pepa: An Introduction to Carl Strehlow's Masterpiece Die Aranda-und Loritja-Stämme in Zentral-Australien (1907–1920)*, ANU Press, Canberra, 2013.

to explain the inner truth of their faith, so the Indigenous informants must also have found it difficult to find the right words to communicate their secrets. It seems like Reuther was instructed in terms that made sense to him. He gained the understanding that there is an all-powerful creator (Mura), to whom believers appeal through the intercession of spirit ancestors (*mura-mura*), who really did once live on earth and have biographies, just like Saints. Chanting sacred texts will help a person in need or great fear. Upon death, the soul rises into the heavens, and there is a beautiful heaven above in the skies. The bad and evil is the realm of the devil. Witchdoctors can save souls and act as intermediaries. Here, Reuther felt compelled to insert one of his rare commentaries. He noted that witchdoctors differ from Western priests in that they are associated not with the benevolent creator, but with the devil. Whether that was the message intended by his informants is doubtful, since the contact cults certainly did not subscribe to that cosmological alignment. Again, we see signs of a mutual invention.

The power of paper in carrying detailed knowledge across vast distances was an amazing technology, also commented by Tony Ballantyne who explores how this technology was taken up by literate indigenous people.[67] A light-hearted anecdote by a Zion Hill missionary relates such an epiphany about the power of books. An axe had gone missing and, while the theft was being discussed, one of the Brethren, who was immersed in a book, stated the name of the thief without looking up. It looked like he was reading the answer from his book. Wunkermany straightaway declared that his pipe was also missing, and could the Brother please check the book about who took it? Pastor Eipper felt that 'a superstition had formed amongst them' 'that out of a book we could know what had happened at a distance, or who had stolen any article'.[68] Wunkermany, who was himself an influential man and communicated with spirits, often knelt down with the missionaries in their prayers, keen to learn more. Presumably for Wunkermany the anecdote was not lighthearted, but a quick-witted attempt to fathom the power of the book.

---

67   Tony Ballantyne has several publications on this theme, for example, 'Paper, pen, and print: The transformation of the Kai Tahu knowledge order', *Comparative Studies in Society and History* 53.2 (2011): 232–60.
68   Christopher Eipper, 'Observations made on a journey to the natives at Toorbal, August 2nd 1841 by the Rev. Christopher Eipper, of the Moreton Bay German Mission – **Journal of the Reverend Christopher Eipper**, Missionary to the Aborigines at Moreton Bay 1841', published in the *Colonial Observer*.

A similar paper miracle forms part of the foundation narrative of the Moravian Ebenezer mission in Victoria in 1859. An epiphany arose dynamically out of a situation where missionary Hagenauer related the published story of Willie Wimmera, a Wimmera boy who was orphaned in a settler attack, was sent to Britain and converted to Christianity.[69] In discussion, this Willie Wimmera of the story was rightly or wrongly identified as the very same boy whom a local settler, who was present at this storytelling, had taken into custody after an attack. These two stories became one and the same, so the written story from England became connected with the lived experiences of some of the young men listening, and also with the mission site in the Wimmera. The words from the book came alive and took physical shape. The dynamic here is again reminiscent of the dynamics of the contact zone described by Richard White in *The Middle Ground*, not a fabrication but a negotiated process of mutual invention.

The Willie Wimmera epiphany led to a hunger for learning to read and write among the young men at Ebenezer. Missionary Hagenauer was shown exactly where this boy's mother had been shot, just metres from where the mission church now stood. The Indigenous diplomats had their own vested interest in seeking an accommodation with the missionaries. Perhaps now the missionaries would understand why it was a meaningful place and corroborees had to be held there, against Hagenauer's instructions.

Conclusions

The project of harnessing the supernatural provided a common ground for missionaries and Indigenous knowledge bearers. The symbolic bestowal of names in ritual baptism, incantations of prayers and the Bible as a ritual object that had to be treated with particular respect were recognisable means of establishing relationships between people and with the material and supernatural worlds. This common ground was, however, loaded with distrust and dismissal of opposing and alternative explanations of cause and effect and of energy-aligning rituals. Armed with sacred objects, incantations and the support of saintly spirits, the Catholic missionaries

---

69   The Willie Wimmera incident has been explored by Jane Lydon, Felicity Jensz, Robert Kenny and the late Bill Edwards.

strained against the 'childish superstitions of the blacks' while Indigenous people often felt that the gospel narratives were untruthful, useless and not for or about them. Translation difficulties compounded the mutual incomprehension. The bizarre contact cults that emerged reshuffled new and old elements of exerting power.

Beginning with mutual incomprehension, but with a shared commitment to metaphysics, it took until after World War II for missionaries and Elders to harness each others' ontologies in the project of inculturation (see Chapter 5) – the forging of a shared understanding that led to the emergence of Indigenous churches, for which the seeds were sown with the first baptisms in each region.

The fastest converters were indisputably the Moravians, who took one year at Ebenezer, four years at Ramahyuck and five years at Mapoon to register the first baptisms. The slowest were no doubt the Lutherans, who took 13 years at Killalpaninna, 16 years at Hermannsburg, a precipitate seven years at Mari Yamba, 10 years at Hopevale and 13 years at Bloomfield to claim 'first fruit'. Catholics claimed instant success on the Daly (Jesuits), early success at Yule Island (Missionaries of the Sacred Heart [MSC]), six years at Beagle Bay (Trappists) and confined themselves to children under Gsell's policy (MSC). While Catholic missionaries were most active in the north and relied greatly on Filipino and other Asian and Pacific intermediaries, the Lutherans had the greatest success with outstanding Indigenous evangelists, as the following chapter explores.

5
Engaging with missionaries

The success of missions in grafting on to local societies crucially depended on individuals seeking an engagement. Not only for language acquisition and translation work did the missionaries need local intermediaries, it was also important to have cultural mediators who had a degree of interest in the missionaries beyond the push-and-pull factors of frontier conditions that drove Indigenous people towards the missions. Such persons interpreted Indigenous society for the missionaries and conveyed the missionary intentions to other members of the Indigenous community. A few of these men (and even fewer women) became active evangelists, and Albrecht's father pioneered the delegation of missionary roles to Indigenous evangelists in Central Australia in the 1920s. Their position was tenuous because they were completely dependent on the missionaries for their social standing within the mission community, while their status in traditional society was undermined by having to abstain from traditional obligations, such as ceremonies and polygamous relationships.

The types of people acting as intermediaries who assisted the missions in taking root differed greatly in different contexts and were driven by a range of motivations. In many cases, such intermediaries came from regions with longstanding contact experience, such as from the Pacific Rim, or from the south to the north of the continent, and were familiar with Christian teaching since childhood. Some Indigenous workers who helped to set up a new mission were delegated by mission-friendly settlers, who themselves often influenced the placement of a mission station near their own farms. Such workers spoke English and were used to dealing with white people, and their proximity to the missionaries elevated their social standing. In some cases, it is impossible to tell the ethnic origins of such intermediaries because the missionaries reported through the lens of religion and distinguished only between Christians and non-Christians.

The degree of external pressure weighing on Indigenous people also manifested in their dealings with missionaries. Under frontier conditions of strong competition for land and resources, and with minimal police presence, many missionaries were threatened, and some were actually attacked. This chapter attempts to tease out from the mission sources the ways in which missionaries and their intermediaries engaged on the ground.

The major source of anecdotes about such interactions are the documents produced by missionaries, and they often trivialise Indigenous people who challenged their authority. Still, occasionally it is possible to glimpse through them the Indigenous humour that gave cheek, or the phenomenon described by Aileen Moreton-Robinson as talkin' up, and expressions of distrust and critical engagement.[1] Disciplining children was usually a sore point, and one where Aboriginal people could become very assertive.

The attempt to convey cultural interpretations across a language barrier certainly left much room for distrust, trivialisation and misunderstanding on both sides, and missionary distrust about Indigenous ceremonies created great tensions. Pastor Carl Strehlow said about the Aranda that 'they are compulsive liars and often give a Christian tint to their stories'.[2] Paul Albrecht observes that Pastors Carl Strehlow and F.W. Albrecht at Hermannsburg had such a fear of syncretism and the danger of worshipping false gods that they themselves never attended any Indigenous ceremonies and disallowed any ceremonies in the mission environment. Meanwhile, initiation and traditional healing were still secretly practised just off the mission. The same clandestine cultural maintenance was reported from Cape York (see **Mapoon**), the Kimberley (see **Lombadina**) and elsewhere (see **La Grange**). Paul Albrecht points out that this kind of schizophrenia hindered the growth of the church.[3]

---

1   Aileen Moreton-Robinson, *Talkin' Up to the White Woman: Aboriginal Women and Feminism*, University of Queensland Press, St Lucia, 2000.
2   Moritz von Leonhardi, 'Über einige religiöse und totemistische Vorstellungen der Aranda und Loritja in Zentralaustralien', *Globus* 91 (1907): 285–90.
3   Paul Albrecht, *From Mission to Church, 1877–2002: Finke River Mission*, Finke River Mission, Hermannsburg, 2002, pp. 73–74.

To examine the importance of local intermediaries and cultural interpreters, and to explore their motivations as far as is possible through mission records, this chapter examines the foundation periods of the German-speaking missions in roughly chronological order.

Quandamooka warriors

In the 1840s, the Moreton Bay missionaries were still indisputably in Indigenous country. The Passionists faced death threats after some children had been taken away from **Stradbroke Island** and a group of islanders demanded that the children be returned on the next steamer.[4] These were 'an orphan boy' and the son and daughter of a leading Stradbroke Island man who brought the children to the missionaries in June 1843, presumably expecting that they would be schooled and fed like the children at **Zion Hill**. However, Archbishop **Polding** had no confidence in his Austrian brethren and no resources to start a school on the island and instead took these children to Sydney. According to Polding, the children were returned after about five weeks.[5] The Quandamooka also drew on their experience with Zion Hill in their negotiations about working for the missionaries and stipulated that if they worked a garden then they would claim the proceeds as theirs. The Passionists did not attempt a garden, nor a school, nor did they give away food, nor learn a local language. The Quandamooka quickly lost interest in them and moved elsewhere. When asked about praying to God, their diplomatic response was: 'We have not yet spoken to Him, for He has not yet spoken to us; but we expect to see and speak to Him after death'.[6]

Fr Vaccari's intransigence left him deserted by his three brethren and he then struggled on alone for another year, apparently supported by a caretaker. When he was without food or money, a man called 'Canary'

---

4   R. Windeyer (Chair), Parliamentary Committee on the Condition of the Aborigines, 1845, Q. 572.9 P.A. 1, Mitchell Library.
5   Windeyer, Parliamentary Committee, 1845. In September 1845, Polding had two Stradbroke Island boys by the name of Smith living in the residence – presumably John and Albert, the sons of Dick Smith and 'Neli', who underwent the first recorded Catholic baptisms in Queensland. Victor Gray, *Catholicism in Queensland: Fifty Years of Progress*, Roberts and Russell, Brisbane, 1910, p. 52.
6   Vaccari at Dunwich to Polding, 19 December 1843, in Osmund Thorpe, *First Catholic Mission to the Australian Aborigines*, Pellegrini & Co., Sydney, 1950, p. 213.

threatened him.⁷ Vaccari, evidently beside himself, wrote to Captain Wickham to request police protection. Had not the Irish priest in Brisbane who had arrived in Australia together with Vaccari suppressed that letter, the most likely police response would have been a contingent of Native Police, which would have meant a violent response. In July 1847, Vaccari bolted from Stradbroke Island under mysterious circumstances, and reappeared under a false identity in a Franciscan monastery in Lima. (For signs of mental strain on Vaccari, see **Stradbroke Island** mission.) The Passionist missionaries on Stradbroke Island did not establish good relationships and were threatened with violence at least twice. They either lacked cultural intermediaries to build bridges to the Stradbroke Island Indigenous groups, or did not take them seriously enough to write about them.

The Zion Hill Brothers

The records of Zion Hill mission suggest a very different story. There the missionaries were taken around by self-appointed guides who were their adopted brothers, like Pastor **Eipper**'s brother Dunkley (possibly a Turrbal man) and Brother Wagner's brother Anbaybury from the Bunya Mountains. Being brothers meant that the wives of these men were responsible for providing food. In early August 1841, Eipper and Wagner were taken to an initiation ceremony in Deception Bay. They travelled north along 'roads and paths' and their guides showed the two missionaries where to camp, where to bury provisions and how much food to distribute at each camp. At Bribie Island, they were accommodated in 'the largest huts we ever have seen, twenty feet in length'.⁸ The missionaries felt there was some degree of competition between people from the Bunya Mountains, from Toorbul and from Bribie Island about the location of a future mission station.

---

7 '**Local Intelligence**', *The Moreton Bay Courier*, 24 April 1847, p. 2, National Library of Australia, Trove (henceforth Trove); and **Classified Advertising**, *The Moreton Bay Courier* (Brisbane), 1 May 1847, p. 1, Trove.

8 Ray Evans has also commented on the large buildings and well-built roads that early white visitors found in the Moreton Bay region. C. Eipper, 'Observations made on a journey to the natives at Toorbal, August 2nd 1841 by the Rev. Christopher Eipper, of the Moreton Bay German Mission – Journal of the Reverend Christopher Eipper, Missionary to the Aborigines at Moreton Bay 1841', published in the *Colonial Observer*, (henceforth **Eipper journal**, 1841); Raymond Evans, 'The mogwi take mi-an-jin: Race relations and the Moreton Bay penal settlement 1824–42', in Evans, *Fighting Words: Writing about Race*, University of Queensland Press, St Lucia, 1992.

5. ENGAGING WITH MISSIONARIES

The ceremony also served as a forum for diplomatic talks and disputes. During a fight, which the two missionaries felt called on to calm, an old woman threw a spear at Eipper. Presumably, Indigenous people did not expect the missionaries to get involved in personal affairs about which they knew nothing. They wanted the missionaries to come to their country to set out gardens so they could eat, and bring firearms so they could defend themselves. Being shown where to 'sit down' was no licence to become involved in community affairs.

On this same journey, a total eclipse of the moon occurred that lasted for two hours during the night. Eipper and Wunkermany began to vie for command of the situation through rituals for which both demanded the silence of the other. Eipper wrote:

> We had our evening worship during this eclipse, and told them to be silent while we spoke to God, which was much better than to scold the Devil, who had no power over those who belong to the Lord Jesus Christ.[9]

According to these cosmological battle-lines, one either belonged to the Lord Jesus Christ or one belonged to the devil. The missionaries were told to be silent while Wunkermany spoke to the spirit who was taking hold of the moon. Wunkermany opprobriated the spirit(s) and called out the name of every male in his group three times. The key terms of the explanation were lost in translation, so that the place to which 'souls' depart after death became 'England', and the ancestral spirits that needed to be appeased became the 'devil'. The missionaries felt amused by the Aboriginal rites: 'we could not keep our gravity'. Pastor Eipper's attempt to convey an alternative ontology was equally unsuccessful: 'This was, they said, what the white man believed, but it was not for the black man'.[10] The next evening the men made jokes about the whole affair, perhaps to cope with the fear they had experienced, which could only have been amplified by the unconvincing missionary interventions and doubts, or as pay back for the ridicule. The missionaries did not take Indigenous cosmology seriously and, conversely, they themselves were not treated as knowledgeable males to be taken seriously – during the initiation ceremony they were placed with the women and children. Afterwards, the women insisted on staying on for a while but the missionaries were impatient to leave and travelled home in two separate groups. Brother Wagner, after a

---
9   Eipper journal, 1841.
10 Eipper journal, 1841.

detour to the Bunya mountains, was so keen to get back to the mission that he covered 'upwards of fifty miles' in one day. Pastor Eipper with sore feet and Wunkermany with a cut on his ankle, as if in sympathy pain, dragged on behind. Wunkermany, who had shown himself as a ritual leader during the lunar eclipse, attached himself to the ritual leader among the missionaries and evinced a particular interest in the power of the written word. His companions did not quite share Wunkermany's respect for the missionaries and made both him and the missionaries the butt of jokes. For example, Eipper's companions, downcast and hungry because on the homeward journey the group was without women to provide for them, cheered themselves with up a practical joke:

> All at once they desired Mr. E[ipper] to look into his book, and to find out if Mr. W[agner] with the other party had killed a kangaroo; and when Mr. E[ipper] knowing what they meant, told them hat he had no book with him, one of them untied Mr. E[ipper]'s bundle and taking out his New Testament, opened it, saying, "Mr. Wagner large kangaroo", after which he shut and replaced it.[11]

Meanwhile at Toorbul, Wagner was getting berated by his brother Anbaybury about the way in which the missionary presumed that he should always be in the dominant position:

> He said one day to Mr. W[agner] that when he [Anbaybury] was at Zion's Hill, he did everything for Mr. W[agner] – fetch wood and water, bark, prepare clay, chop wood, work the ground with the hoe, etc. Now, as Mr. W[agner] had come to his abode, he ought to do the same for him [Anbaybury]. Mr. W[agner] told him it was quite right that he had done so, for he had paid him well; but he ought to consider that he (Mr W.) was a missionary and Anbaybury a black fellow. Now, as he had come to him to Toorbal to visit him, it was a shame that he, as his brother, had never come to fetch wood or water for him, nor had he built a hut to live in it. When he heard this, he changed his tone, and said, he would have done all for Mr. W[agner] if he had come to the place where his tribe had their camp.[12]

Though spoken as seemingly lighthearted banter, the missionary's assumption of superiority was questioned.

---

11 Eipper journal, 1841.
12 Eipper journal, 1841.

A year later, in 1842, Eipper and the colonist Hartenstein again ventured north with Wunkermany and his two wives, who complained bitterly about all the luggage they were supposed to carry as provisions to last for a journey to Humpy Bong (old camp). At the Pine River camp, a group from Durundur (already a pastoral station) joined them, and Eipper took the opportunity to hold school with up to 21 children for a few days. A school for children was perhaps not what Indigenous people most needed just then. Around this time, the Aboriginal camp at Yorke's Hollow was destroyed by two soldiers who were refused access to Aboriginal women.[13] In 1844, Hartenstein and Hausmann were attacked at Burpengary in the attempt to set up a mission, from which Hausmann sustained a lifelong injury. The Yorke's Hollow people were finally displaced with the arrival in January 1849 of the 550 pious Protestant dissenters recruited by J.D. Lang who camped in 'Fortitude Valley' 'armed to the teeth'.[14] What happened to Wunkermany, Anbaybury and Dunkley, the men who had taken Lang's missionaries under their wing, is uncertain. The seeds of this early contact germinated much later, in what appeared like a chance encounter.

The sons at Bethesda

Twenty-five years later, in January 1866, several grown and bearded men who were visiting Beenleigh for a ceremony came up to Pastor Hausmann at **Bethesda** and introduced themselves as his former pupils from Zion Hill: 'Father, don't you know us?' This meeting revitalised Hausmann's mission project, now inspired by the success reported from **Ebenezer** in Victoria. Hausmann (now with anglicised spelling, either Haussman or Haussmann) had the support of recently arrived younger **Gossner** candidates, including his own son. He attempted to turn his sugarcane property into an industrial mission, combining two purposes and ministering without public funding. One of his former Zion Hill pupils, Kingkame (or Kingkema) brought his family for daily devotions and paid work to Bethesda. At the prayer meetings, Yugambeh listeners encouraged Hausmann with questions and promises to reform themselves.[15] On

---

13   November 1842, Eipper and Hartenstein, John Dunmore Lang Papers, 1837–67, A2240 Vol. 20, item 82, Mitchell Library.
14   Raymond Evans, *A History of Queensland*, Cambridge University Press, Port Melbourne, 2007, p. 62.
15   Hausmann, *Australischer Christenbote*, February 1867, in M. Lohe, 'Pastor Haussmann and Mission Work from 1866', unpublished MS, 1964, Lutheran Archives Australia (LAA).

Sundays, they received clean clothes to attend Hausmann's two-hour service held in German and sat 'quite still and with great devotion' and afterwards praised him: 'Father, you have preached mightily'.[16] Kingkame expressed the wish to become a Christian and mediated the establishment of an outrigger industrial mission at **Nerang Creek** in 1869. By now, the whole Moreton Bay region was awash with new settlers protected by Native Police.

An Aboriginal called Jack addressed Hausmann as 'Papo'.[17] He attended reading and writing instructions from October to December 1867 and held out promise as Hausmann's first fruit. In January, Jack left with a catechism, promising to evangelise among his own people, but there is no further mention of him.[18] This may be the same man as **Bilinba**,[19] also called Bilin Bilin, Jackey Jackey, Kawae Kawae and John Logan, whose 1875 breastplate identified him as 'King of the Logan and Pimpama'.[20] Steele describes him as a highly respected Yugambeh man who insisted on payment for Aboriginal labour, and who tried to resist the displacement from Aboriginal land. He also assisted early explorers and settlers in the Logan district. Aboriginal history has it that 'Bilinba charged Lutheran Missionary Haussman [sic] … 5/- per week to sit and discuss religion with the tribe. The tribe cleared 10 acres of land at the rate of 1 pound per acre'.[21] This seems like a local diplomat who strategically inserted himself in the cultural encounter. The catechism he took with him, either under a cloud of misunderstanding or under false pretences (like so much ethnographic collecting),[22] may have been useful for such a cultural interpreter, though perhaps not in the way intended by Hausmann. Bilinba eventually moved to Deebing Creek mission, where he died in 1901.

---

16 Hausmann, *Australischer Christenbote*, July 1869, in Lohe, 'Pastor Haussmann and Mission Work from 1866'.
17 It is tempting to read 'Papo' as a typing error for the German 'Papa'. However, the Aranda at Hermannsburg called Carl Strehlow 'Pepa', which means both 'paper' and 'law' and refers to his evangelical position of power. Anna Kenny, *The Aranda's Pepa: An Introduction to Carl Strehlow's Masterpiece Die Aranda-und Loritja-Stämme in Zentral-Australien (1907–1920)*, ANU Press, Canberra, 2013.
18 Hausmann reported only in the Victorian Lutheran newsletter *Australischer Christenbote*.
19 Karen Laughton, '**Frontier Relations in the Logan District**', n.d., German Missionaries in Australia, Griffith University.
20 Robyn Buchanan, *Logan: Rich in History, Young in Spirit. A Comprehensive History*, Logan City Council, Logan, 1999, pp. 12, 65; J.G. Steele, *Aboriginal Pathways in Southeast Queensland and the Richmond River*, University of Queensland Press, St Lucia, 1983, p. 81.
21 Steele, *Aboriginal Pathways*, p. 81.
22 Susan Cochrane and Max Quanchi (eds), *Hunting the Collectors: Pacific Collections in Australian Museums, Art Galleries and Archives*, Cambridge Scholars Publishing, Newcastle upon Tyne, 2014.

The hopes of such Indigenous diplomats that a mission on their land could secure their survival were largely frustrated, because the missions were usually disbanded when settlement overtook them, and those that survived the 1890s began to be used by governments as repositories for removed children from elsewhere. Nor would missionaries help a local tribe to assert themselves over neighbouring Indigenous people. Such a misunderstanding about the role of missions ended the Jesuit mission in Darwin.

Showdown at Rapid Creek

When the Austrian Jesuits commenced a mission at Rapid Creek (Darwin) in 1882, the Larrakia and Woolner people were already used to white people. They paid lip-service to the expectations of the missionaries, who wanted everyone to stay on the mission year-round and to keep the children at school. They informed the missionaries if they were planning to leave ('obtained permission') and left the children behind, and the children absconded a few days later to join their parents. Upon their return to the mission, the children would be taken back into the school and the parents would be excluded from the mission for a week. 'They accept the penalty without complaining.'[23] The missionaries felt they were in charge, while the Larrakia felt that by permitting the use of their land they had a legitimate claim on the supplies and stores of the missionaries.

This perception was ruptured in May 1887 when some visiting Alligator River people, who camped on the Rapid Creek, had run out of food and the missionaries gave them a bag of flour. This caused a dispute between the Alligator River people and the Larrakia and Woolner. The argument became increasingly heated and was finally battled out on the beach. Five were injured and one of the Alligator River men died later from his wounds. When the locals returned to the mission ground, the Elder in charge was ordered off the mission.

> He thought the order was a joke, but when he realized that it was meant seriously he went. He soon returned, though, leading a great crowd of natives painted for war and armed with stone-pointed spears.[24]

---

23 Strele 1887 in Anton Strele, Annual Letters from the Jesuit Mission in North Australia 1886–1889, translated by F. Dennett SJ, Archives of the Society of Jesus, Hawthorn.
24 Strele 1887, Annual Letters.

The fighting group retreated when they were 'ordered off'. The report does not specify how just one Father and one Brother persuaded the armed and angry warriors to retreat. Years later, there was a passing mention of Brother Scharmer's reputation with the shotgun, a reputation that may well have been established at this moment. It was a pyrrhic victory for the Jesuits. After this incident, none of the locals dared to stay the night at the mission for fear of a renewed attack and gradually the Jesuits realised that Rapid Creek mission never recovered from this blow.[25] The Jesuits trivialised the whole affair as a tribal fight, without realising that they had not only offended the dignity of the leading men, but also completely shattered the expectations of the locals.

Daly River interventions

When the Jesuits came to the Daly River in 1886, the local Woolwonga, Woolner, Malak-Malak, Maranunngu, Djerait, Ponga-Ponga and Dilk people were under extreme pressure from settler violence, dispossession and degradation of their land. They were interested in the material and security advantages of the mission, and several groups invited the missionaries to form a station on their country. When two mission stations were abandoned to be amalgamated at the third site of New Uniya, the abandoned mission property at Serpentine Lagoon was demolished by people from Komorkye, who 'were discontented because they did not get flour which, they said, had been promised them, and so they had inflicted various kinds of damage on the Station of the Sacred Heart, and had threatened more to come'.[26] The Komorkye people clearly felt betrayed. A mission on the other side of the river, outside of their country, was no good to them.

Several adult men tried to impart Indigenous ethics to the missionaries, much like Bilinba at Beenleigh, but to little avail. Charlie Yingi once led a group of children off the mission in protest against punishment. On the question of physical punishment for adults, the Jesuits and the people of the Daly were often in agreement. Adulterous women were punished by their husbands and vice versa. But Aboriginal people did not tolerate the physical punishment of children. If young adults felt unjustly punished,

---

25 Paddy J. Dalton, 'History of the Jesuits in South Australia 1848–1948', unpublished MS, 1948, p. 6, Archives of the Society of Jesus, Hawthorn.
26 Daly River Mission Diary (DRM), 27 January 1893, Archives of the Society of Jesus, Hawthorn.

they generally left the mission in protest for a period, often in company with several others showing solidarity (see also Chapter 7, 'Discipline and punishment').

Charlie Yingi also tried to teach the missionaries that if he expended energy on their behalf then they owed him some sustenance:

> Charlie and the other Leo got back from their journey quite worn out; why they were so worn out we do not know – what they said was that they had contracted this weakness in our service, and they demanded food in compensation. We did not agree.[27]

This man, referred to in the press as 'long-legged Charlie', had some years before been accused of the Coppermine murder – another issue around Indigenous ethics – but not convicted. He was assisted at court by a Chinese interpreter. The strong Chinese presence on the Daly River formed another layer of cultural interaction, but little of this penetrated into the mission environment, so that non-Indigenous cultural intermediaries did not play a strong role on these Jesuit missions. The Catholic Filipino Engracio family joined the mission community for 10 months in 1897 and 1898, working for board and lodging, and Chinese work gangs from the Coppermine performed some major irrigation work that made it possible to tend large gardens. Chinese interaction with Aboriginal people was considered highly controversial. In order to diffuse the animosities, the Coppermine Chinese hosted the missionaries for a dinner, and the Chinese boat captain supplying the mission introduced himself as being very familiar with Jesuit missionaries in China. Still, all diplomatic approaches failed under the strain of disputes over women (see **Daly River – Daly River Stories**).

Another Elder who tried to influence the missionaries was old deaf and mute Nabba, who was closely connected with the mission. In one instance, he was enraged because some Woolwonga men had stolen his fish. Nabba demanded that Fr **Kristen** 'shoot the thieves'. Again, the missionary sense of justice did not measure up to local expectations. The Woolwonga were themselves in great distress and targeted by settler violence, and as a reprimand one of the Woolwonga men was 'summoned to the cross' and given a public admonition:

---

27   DRM, 2 January 1893.

> It seemed a good occasion to point out to them what they would come to if they did not have the refuge we gave them at the foot of the Cross of Christ. If they did not listen to us, we would go away, and their destruction would follow. He understood, and perhaps the boys standing by did also; indeed it was a strong and stringent argument for their conversion to protect themselves from the anger of God who sent among them bad white men.[28]

It is unlikely that this public reprimand made much sense to the 'boys' standing by. How could all of them now be in trouble when the thieves were Woolwonga men? Fr Kirsten's threat sounds like another curse that eventually came true. Both W.E.H. Stanner and D.B. Rose describe the desolate state on the Daly River after the mission period.[29]

Even among the Elders who sought an entente with the missionaries, there was considerable resistance to the Christian teachings. Fr **Conrath** recorded the response from an Elder after a long instruction on the need for baptism for the salvation of the soul: 'Very good. Now I am saved. For a long time I was not sure of my salvation. When I am at the point of death you will give me baptism'. This diplomatic compromise, holding on to culture in this life and planning for salvation for the next life, was not what the Jesuits intended. Another Elder announced that he had now taken a third wife, recorded as Oshinni, and Conrath reproached him 'You already have one too many, why do you take a third?' to which the man countered, 'One of them might die. What name will you give my new wife?' The man invoked the death-and-dying discourse so characteristic of Jesuit philosophy, and in effect confronted Conrath with the new family arrangements, demanding their recognition with a name for the new wife. Conrath ignored this request and instead told the man, 'Probably you will die first, and then, by and by Oshinni will die'. Some time later, that same man asked for some clothes and Conrath promised to give him some 'by and by', to which the man replied, 'That is not good. Give it today. By and by I die and then I need no more clothing'.[30] The old man used Conrath's own words to contradict him, just like in other instances Christian rules of marriage were invoked to oppose wrong marriages.

---

28   DRM, 26 March 1888.
29   Deborah Bird Rose, 'Signs of life on a barbarous frontier: Intercultural encounters in North Australia', *Humanities Research* 2 (1998): 17–36.
30   Dalton, 'History of the Jesuits', p. 42.

Some of the younger boys on the Daly seemed particularly promising. Johnny was the son of the first adult Christian at the mission and prayed with his father Zachary Pambari in his dying hours. Johnny told the missionaries 'how Zachary at the end made the sign of the Cross and said "Banunga Kandolan" i.e. I am going to heaven'.[31] This was considered a breakthrough and Johnny was asked to repeat this story many times. He was selected to accompany Fr McKillop on a southern fundraising tour. When Johnny heard of this plan he ran away, but eventually he did accompany Fr McKillop. It appears that, altogether, three boys from the mission attended a Jesuit school. Johnny returned two years later to a triumphal welcome home.[32] However, neither of these boys fulfilled the hopes that the missionaries vested in them.

The insistence on monogamous couples and severance from Indigenous obligations created many tensions. The missionary's punishment for adultery was either eviction or demotion from 'colonist' to resident, with the result that, as far as can be ascertained from the diaries, nobody actually had the use of a private garden long enough to enjoy its fruits and to experience for themselves the benefits of settled agriculture, which the missionaries found clearly superior to hunting and gathering (see **Daly River Stories**). After 20 years of Jesuit mission work, in 1899 only five families, consisting of 29 Christians, lived at the mission.

During the mission period, the Daly River people were under tremendous pressure from settlement and became very protective of their land boundaries. The mission stations, however, were relocated several times with little practical regard for such tribal differences. Possibly because of this misalignment, no Indigenous person appears in the Jesuit diaries as rising to influence on the Daly River missions. Though the ritualised spiritualism of the Jesuits had many resonances with Indigenous cultural practices, a sustainable middle ground was not created. Half a century after the Jesuits' departure, a former mission resident summed up the promise of Christianisation as a chimera. He felt that Jesus was always on the team of the white people and, after all the effort invested on every side, 'only the Aborigines had nothing. … That is the dreaming for all you lot'.[33]

---

31 DRM, 4 July 1892, 9 July 1892.
32 DRM, 24 November 1894.
33 Rose, 'Signs of Life on a barbarous frontier', p. 36, note 32.

The Ebenezer catechists

Displacement and frontier conflict also seemed to play a role in the case of Ebenezer, the Moravian mission in the Wimmera (Victoria), which recorded an early spectacular conversion success that became a beacon of hope for other mission efforts in Australia. The question must be asked why some of the Indigenous men were so helpful in establishing this mission, as Felicity Jensz points out.[34] The Indigenous men who were most engaged in establishing Ebenezer were Daniel Boney, Corny, Timothy Talliho and three males who referred to each other as brothers and began to construct bark huts at the mission: **Nathanael Pepper**, 'a lively lad about 17 years of age';[35] the older Charley (later Phillip Pepper), who spoke English well; and Tommy Light.

Daniel Boney, who was the first to appear at the mission for instruction, and Tommy Light, who died at the mission in 1862, are both also mentioned as helpers at the **Lake Boga** Moravian mission in 1855 near Ganawarra station,[36] owned by the mission friend Archibald Macarthur Campbell. By the time Ebenezer mission was established, Campbell had moved to the Wimmera, and again a location close to his sheep station was recommended to the missionaries. (Perhaps because Rev. Alexander James Campbell was a member of the Presbyterian mission committee.) It seems that these Aboriginal men came with Campbell from Lake Boga to the Wimmera, and that they had their own baggage of a difficult history – the missionaries knew that one of them, Tommy Light, had killed a man.[37] Reverend Hagenauer was moreover aware that, in retaliation for the murder of white men, police had killed two innocent Aboriginal men near Ganawarra in February 1854, to which he publicly expressed his outrage.[38] Perhaps Hagenauer knew who the real perpetrators were.

---

34   Felicity Jensz, *Moravian Missionaries in the British Colony of Victoria, Australia, 1848–1908: Influential Strangers*, Brill, Leiden, 2010, p. 119.
35   J.F.W. Spieseke, 6 February 1860, 14 February 1860, Mission Station, Wimmera – Extracts from *Periodical Accounts Relating to the Missions of the Church of the United Brethren*, compiled by C.W. Schooling ca 1975, MS 9896, State Library of Victoria (henceforth Mission Station, Wimmera, *Periodical Accounts*).
36   Robert Kenny refers to Ganawarra; however, the newspapers of the day and Jensz spell the property as Gannawarra.
37   Spieseke, April 1862, Mission Station, Wimmera, *Periodical Accounts*.
38   *Missionsblatt*, August 1854, in Jensz, *German Moravian Missionaries in the British Colony of Victoria*, 2010, p. 85.

Hagenauer did offer a safe haven for men who could expect traditional revenge. For example, he took in a man who had been expelled from his people further south-west, to which the locals objected so strongly that they prepared for an attack in late 1859.[39] On that occasion, Hagenauer sheltered in his cabin to pray until the nearby station owner Ellerman appeared on the scene with Nathanael Pepper and some other young men. According to Hagenauer, they also prayed, with the result that 'the "extraordinary ferment" on the mission subsided'.[40] It is possible that these rescuers prayed, but it is very unlikely that farmer Ellerman came unarmed, so that Hagenauer's account perhaps overestimates the role of prayer in this event. This missionary cosmology, in which words, even unspoken words, could be so powerful, quickly became interesting to Nathanael Pepper. His baptism elevated this young man to a special position at the mission. He began to conduct services in the vernacular and drew large crowds by preaching and psalm singing. One of the hymns, translated by Pastor J.F.W. Spieseke, was:

Winya wallo neango mamamorek!	How near is my great Father!
Kakum bangung yereru.	His Spirit came in me
Wurruwin parrin!	Make plain the way!
Kaledia!	Great thy glory![41]

Pastor Spieseke understood this as a Christian hymn, although it had a 'very monotonous melody'.[42] Actually, it follows a decidedly traditional rhythm, and invokes the supreme being 'Mahmamorack', the all-father described by Spieseke as pre-existing in Aboriginal mythology.[43] It seems that Nathanael had an amazing ability to blend local and imported rituals and traditions as if they belonged together. His celebrated conversion experience was a reflection on Jesus in the garden of Gethsemane. Pepper

---

39   Spieseke, 14 February 1860, Mission Station, Wimmera, *Periodical Accounts*.
40   Spieseke, 14 February 1860, Mission Station, Wimmera, *Periodical Accounts*.
41   Extract from the Australian Christian Messenger for the Evangelical Lutheran Church in Australia (*Australischer Christenbote für die Evangelisch Lutherische Kirche in Australien*), published by Matthias Goethe, Lutheran Minister in Melbourne, May 1861 in Queensland. Legislative Assembly, *Report from the Select Committee on the Native Police Force and the Condition of the Aborigines Generally*, Fairfax and Belbridge, Brisbane, 1861, Appendix, p. 79, aiatsis.gov.au/sites/default/files/catalogue_resources/92123.pdf (accessed 10 July 2017).
42   Victorian Association in Aid of Moravian Missions to the Aborigines of Australia, *Further Facts relating to the Moravian Missions in Australia. Sixth Paper*, Fergusson & Moore, Melbourne, 1867, pp. 7–17, MS, State Library of Victoria, handle.slv.vic.gov.au/10381/173013 (accessed 12 January 2018).
43   Victorian Association in Aid of Moravian Missions to the Aborigines of Australia, *Further Facts*, p. 15.

verbalised how the narrative of the sacrifice of Christ for the salvation of all mankind had direct personal relevance 'for me'. The local relevance of these gospel narratives was precisely what mattered. Soon afterwards, Corny, Talliho and Mark claimed the Willie Wimmera story as a local narrative, making the same bridge between a story from far away and the local. This, too, was rewarded with much missionary attention and amazement. These two anecdotes are the bedrock of the Ebenezer mission founding narrative.

Others soon requested baptism. Tommy Light was refused (because he was known to have killed a man), but Daniel (Boney), Phillip Pepper (Charley), Timothy (Talliho) and Matthew were baptised. Nathanael Pepper again became the centre of attention with the first Christian wedding on the mission, and was taken to meetings including one with the Governor in June 1862 to help advance the case for an inland mission. In 1865, Nathanael and Phillip, who had also been allocated a wife, became paid missionary assistants, so the rewards of engagement with the missionary cosmology were very visible. Of this group of early converts, Daniel Boney left Ebenezer in 1866 to help the Moravians form a mission at Cooper's Creek, but died along the way. Nathanael Pepper became an instrumental catechist at Ramahyuck. Only Phillip Pepper stayed at Ebenezer, where he became a central figure.

If Tommy Light and Daniel Boney came from Lake Boga with their white employer, and Tommy, Nathanael and Phillip called themselves 'brothers', then it is by no means clear that these were all local people from the Wimmera. Corny and Nathanael Pepper have been described as local Wotjoballuk boys, but there is no reference to the parents of the others who appeared as helpers in the establishment of Ebenezer mission. From Hagenauer's comments, it appears that Tommy Light had killed a white man at Lake Boga and an innocent Aboriginal man was killed in his place, so that it made much sense for him to shelter at the mission, and for his 'brothers' to help construct an alternative future.

Brother Pingilina

The loss of Daniel Boney meant that the Moravian missionaries appeared without an Indigenous helper at Lake Kopperamanna in 1866, where they received a hostile reception just like their Lutheran brethren at Lake

Killalpaninna. These two Cooper's Creek missions, too, were located near a mission-friendly pastoral station in a region undergoing rapid development.

The Birdsville track from the Channel country to the railhead for Port Augusta was getting developed with the help of government bores to water the cattle, such as the one at Kopperamanna. To cross the flood-prone Cooper's Creek at Kopperamanna, drovers and travellers often required ferry assistance, which the Lutheran missionaries were to provide as a source of income. To service the infrastructure requirements of remote stations, camels and Afghan cameleers were getting imported, and a postal network began to stretch across the inland stations. Victoria, meanwhile, was coping with up to 17,000 illicit Chinese goldminers flooding in via the South Australian port of Robe to avoid the Victorian poll tax. All across South Australia, Indigenous people were coming under extreme pressure. The Dieri at first drove both mission parties away, and it took 13 years for the 'first fruit' to come forward at Cooper's Creek in 1879.

One of Pastor C.A. Meyer's 12 'first fruit' was Johannes **Pingilina**, a top shearer, who was particularly valued for his linguistic ability and became an important assistant for Pastor Meyer. In 1878, he and his wife Clara lived in the colony next door to Pastor Johann Flierl. Their daughter Maria was born in 1880 and Emma in 1884. Baby Emma died when an influenza epidemic swept over the mission in 1885.[44] In June 1886, Pingilina accompanied Pastor **Meyer** to **Cape Bedford** (Hopevale) and began to learn Guugu-Yimidhirr. In May 1887, he accompanied the Meyers to their new position at **Bloomfield** mission with yet another language, Kuku Yalanji. Here he began to court a Bama woman who worked in the mission kitchen. When she refused him, he found it intolerable to continue working in the same household. Within a few months, Pingilina returned to Cape Bedford mission, where he apparently collaborated with Pastor Schwarz in a translation of the Lord's Prayer into Guugu-Yimidhirr.[45] He also met up with Pastor Johann Flierl visiting from Simbang in late 1887, and met Rosie, a Cooktown woman, with whom he began to plan for a second marriage. Meanwhile, Meyer felt that he could not progress his

---

[44] Of the first 12 baptised Flierl mentioned ten by name: Gottfried and Sarah Yildimirina, Benjamin and Luise Dalkilina, Joseph Diltjilina and wife, Elias and Beate Palkilina, the young bachelor Diwana, the lame Henry Tipilina. Susanne Froehlich (ed.), *Als Pioniermissionar in das ferne Neu Guinea: Johann Flierls Lebenserinnerungen*. 2 vols, Harrassowitz Verlag, Wiesbaden, 2015, Vol. 1, p. 222.
[45] John Haviland and Leslie Haviland, 'How much food will there be in heaven? Lutherans and Aborigines around Cooktown to 1900', *Aboriginal History* 4.2 (1980), p. 133.

mission work at Bloomfield without Pingilina, and under pressure from the mission committee Pingilina returned to Bloomfield in early 1888, on the condition that he would receive wages, like the other mission assistants. Pingilina wrote to the committee affirming his commitment to the faith, describing the responsibilities he shouldered in the engagement with the local people who were dismissive of the gospel, and asked about his wages, since he was about to get married. Meyer proposed £5 per year 'held in trust'.

Nine months after his wedding with Rosie, Pingilina wanted to take his wife to Simbang to join **Flierl**. This proposal caused a storm of protest from the Queensland Government in mid-1889. Pingilina was constantly confronted with the impossibility of being a black evangelist: his wages, if any, would be 'held in trust', he could not travel freely, let alone leave the country with his Aboriginal wife. Meyer began to find Pingilina difficult: 'full of pride' and 'wanting to be respected by all whites'.[46] Pingilina had not been allocated an official role in the mission. He was neither an assistant missionary nor a lay helper, neither part of the Indigenous community on the Bloomfield nor white like the other missionary staff, and he was struggling with this indeterminate identity: 'I don't know what I am. I am just me'.[47]

By February 1891, Rosie had left Pingilina, and he now wanted to go home and see his daughter Maria at Killalpaninna whom he had not seen for four years. Perhaps he had also received word of Maria's illness. In August 1891, Pingilina asked about a divorce and Meyer obtained legal advice. Pingilina's marriage had been the first Aboriginal marriage for the Anglican pastor in Cooktown, and the local lawyer was also astounded and gave a dismissive response, remarking that it was unlikely that Pingilina's wife would 'legally pursue him' if he removed himself to South Australia. Again Pingilina was not taken seriously. When the Meyers left Bloomfield to return to South Australia in 1892, Pingilina was not permitted to accompany them, since Pastor **Hörlein** now required his help. (We will return to Hörlein at Bloomfield below.)

---

46 Meyer to Rechner, 7 August 1891, Immanuel Synod, Bloomfield Mission Correspondence (henceforth Bloomfield correspondence), LAA.
47 Johannes Pingilina at Bloomfield to Rechner in South Australia, via Hergott Springs, 29 April 1890, Bloomfield correspondence, LAA.

After six years in north Queensland, Pingilina arrived back in Adelaide in February 1893, his box and spears arriving three months later. His 15-year-old daughter Maria died in the home of Pastor Georg **Reuther** in 1895. Pingilina remained a faithful supporter of the missionaries. During his time at Killalpaninna, he became Reuther's main ethnographic informant. In October 1901, the mission committee delegated him and Moses Tjalkabota to the Blazes Well outstation of Hermannsburg mission and, in November 1901, Pingilina married Katherina from the Finke River (Hermannsburg) in a group wedding at Killalpaninna. Like the European missionaries themselves, Pingilina was willing to give up home and family for the mission work, and to observe their marriage rules and arrangements. In his letters in Dieri, he addressed Pastor Rechner as 'older brother' and signed off as 'younger brother'. But to gain recognition as a missionary Brother, he lacked the one basic qualification that was always unspoken.

Moses of Hermannsburg

At Hermannsburg, too, the Lutheran missionaries enjoyed the support of a few key individuals. Around the turn of the century, the missionaries still attempted to include adults in their school classes, and it is easy to imagine such a classroom becoming a contest of authority and face-saving. For example, Pastor Nikolaus **Wettengel**, who was at Hermannsburg from 1901 to 1906, found that whenever he corrected the answers of one old man in his class, this man always turned the tables and blamed Wettengel for the wrong answer. Another young man, who wished to raise a question, insisted that the missionary should look at him straight in the face or else the 'question wouldn't come out'. Evidently, the requirement to 'look me in the eyes' to give an honest answer was being turned back on the missionary. The question was whether Mary and Joseph had enough blankets when they escaped from Jerusalem.[48] This question effectively undermines the Christian message of the Christmas story (no room at the inn) and turns attention to the material conditions of the Indigenous mission community. Such anecdotes hint at the struggle for dignity of the adults under instruction.

---

48   Leske, Everard, *For Faith and Freedom: The Story of Lutherans and Lutheranism in Australia 1838–1996*, Open Book publishers, Adelaide, 1996, p. 27.

Very gradually, Indigenous catechists were able to bridge such tension. Timotheus Maltilina and Moses **Tjalkabota** were already trusted drovers in the 1890s, taking cattle to market and working with lay helper J. Rüdiger in the transfer of cattle to Killalpaninna.[49] Timotheus, who was of mixed descent, moved with his family to Blazes Well in 1901.[50] Moses Tjalkabota married an Aranda woman in 1903 and his droving career ended in 1905, when he became blind. During a dispute between the two pastors at Hermannsburg in 1903, Wettengel highly praised Moses as an example of successful conversion, whereas Carl **Strehlow** remarked that Moses was surely not 'the only shining light of Christian example' and could even be called a 'whorer'.[51] Strehlow's spiteful comments, only months before Moses' Christian marriage, were meant to injure Wettengel rather than Moses. When Strehlow began to translate the New Testament into Aranda in 1913, he relied greatly on Moses Tjalkabota, Nathaniel Rauwirarka and Jacobus. Eventually Moses became a trusted evangelist at the mission. Pastor Oskar **Liebler** (at Hermannsburg 1910–13) thought that during baptismal classes the candidates were learning more from Moses than from himself. 'Blind Moses was the mouth of God for them, amplified by my presence and interventions.' Liebler hastened to add that in Australia it was impossible to have independent native evangelists like in India, because there was far too much family pressure so that an 'Australian Black' could never exert enough authority.[52]

But Moses proved him wrong. After Strehlow's death in September 1922, the mission was without pastor for three years and, during this time, Moses continued to hold Sunday services and baptismal instruction.[53] Pastor F.W. Albrecht, who arrived in 1926, found Moses 'very handy'.

---

49   Immanuel Synod, Mission Committee Minute Book, 1895–1901 (translated), 27 November 1895, 13 April 1897, LAA.
50   At Blazes Well, two of Maltilina's sons were run over by a dray and one of them died. Immanuel Synod, Mission Committee Minute Book, 1895–1901 (translated), December 1901, LAA. Timotheus chose his baptismal name and Flierl composed the surname from 'malti', 'meaning calm or soft, with the ending '-lina' for grown up men. Timotheus married a Wonkanguru (Salt Creek) girl who had accompanied Flierl on his first mission journey and whom Flierl baptised in the name of Anna. These two later moved to Lowbank where Timotheus worked as a horse breaker. Froehlich, *Als Pioniermissionar*, Vol. 1, p. 272.
51   Correspondence in relation to a letter Wettengel to Kaibel 16 July 1903, Immanuel Synod, FRM Box 5, Correspondence Wettengel (transcriptions and translations), LAA.
52   'Daß ein schwarzer Christ hier selbständig den Gehilfen, etwa in dem Sinne der indischen eingebornen Gehilfen, machen könnte ist deshalb leider ausgeschlossen, weil gegen Verwandte zu viel Nachsicht geübt würde und leider der Schwarze sich höchst selten, was nötig ist, aufzutreten traut.' Report from O. Liebler in *Kirchen- und Missionszeitung* 47.22 (May 1911): 173.
53   Leske, *For Faith and Freedom*.

Moses was still holding the confirmation classes with 10 children, of whom three could read. Moses, who could recite long passages from the Bible by memory, 'patiently reads out to them'.[54] Moses sometimes delivered the Sunday sermon and taught Albrecht Aranda.

Moses also taught Albrecht much more besides. Albrecht's mission diary relates a dramatic incident at Hermannsburg in 1927. Some boys had run away, were retrieved and locked up at the mission dormitory. One of them, Reinhardt, yelled for half an hour in protest until Pastors Albrecht and Schaber 'both went there and I gave him a good hiding' after which Reinhardt fell silent. But now 'the whole camp erupted in a wild death howling, they said I'd killed him'. The adults rushed to the dormitory, demanded the key and approached Albrecht 'with threatening fists, I was never to touch their children again'. The evangelist Jacobus was allowed entry to the dormitory to examine Reinhardt. Moses tried to calm the situation by asking Albrecht to promise never to deal out more than three strikes to a child, 'but I refused'. Albrecht tried to disperse the adults, telling them to come back the next day, but they stood their ground. 'They threatened and scolded me as I left, but I didn't give in.'[55]

Such different attitudes about the appropriate treatment of children created a vast gulf between missionaries and Indigenous people, a gulf that could be bridged by local intermediaries like Moses. The Lutheran missions in New Guinea were already relying on native evangelists (and began to train indigenous pastors in 1939). Albrecht at Hermannsburg was the first to adopt this model in Australia.[56] In July 1926, Albrecht sent Moses and Thomas to evangelise in Henbury.[57] After that, with Albrecht's encouragement, four Indigenous evangelists (presumably Moses, Martin, Thomas and Timotheus, who was paid double the mission stock-workers' rate at 10 shillings a week) began to travel to contact people outside the mission's reach.[58] Moses walked, rode and hitchhiked to Horseshoe Bend, Jay Creek, Alice Springs, Arltunga and many other places.[59] After Pastor E. **Kramer** withdrew from Alice Springs in 1934, Moses and Martin held

---

54 F.W. Albrecht, 24 April 1926, 'My Mission Diary at Hermannsburg 1926–1927', LAA.
55 Albrecht mission diary, 28 March 1927.
56 Barbara Henson, *A Straight-out Man – F.W. Albrecht and Central Australian Aborigines*, Melbourne University Press, Carlton, Vic., 1992, p. 67.
57 Albrecht mission diary, 27 April, 13 July, 23 August 1926.
58 Leske, *For Faith and Freedom*, 1996.
59 Paul Albrecht, '**Tjalkabota**, Moses (1869–1954)', *Australian Dictionary of Biography*, National Centre of Biography, The Australian National University (henceforth *ADB*), published first in hardcopy 2005.

services on the banks of the Todd River. Moses subsequently transferred to Jay Creek between Alice Springs and Hermannsburg, where he still conducted Christian outreach in the early 1950s.[60] When Albrecht himself moved to Alice Springs in 1952 and began to visit the outlying stations, he was able to build on the prior work of Moses and Martin.[61]

Like Pepper at Ebenezer, Moses, who was born at Ntaria (later the name of the Hermannsburg mission), invoked traditional references to render the gospel decipherable, and he met much the same dismissal from traditonalists as Pingilina encountered at Bloomfield. Moses reported a dialogue with a man called Njetjaka, who argued:

> I [Njetjaka] am the tjurunga called Ilbangura and I have the songs and decorations. Look, at the uncreated home of the kangaroo at Krenka, we have many more tjurunga, and more powerful ceremonies. I [Moses] said, 'You men are unbelievers'. They said, 'We have another one that we believe in. You at Ntaria believe in one God, but we have another one'.[62]

Under Albrecht's direction, outstations with cash stores such as Haasts Bluff were established under the supervision of such evangelists as Alexander, Titus, Epaphras and Eugen. Eventually, a few women were also given this role, like Daphne Puntjina at Areyonga who worked alongside Leo Tjukintja who was later ordained. When the Haasts Bluff station was transferred to Papunya in 1958, it was supervised by Obed Raggett (ordained in 1979), who married a Papunya woman and quickly became a fluent speaker.[63] This was the beginning of an Indigenous church, the ultimate goal of mission.

Cape York stories

Returning now to the north Queensland missions of the 1890s in which Pingilina assisted the Lutherans, a few anecdotes of interactions survive from there that shed light on the mutual misunderstandings and other teething problems of newly arrived missionaries.

---

60 Paul Albrecht, *From Mission to Church*, p. 19.
61 Paul Albrecht, *From Mission to Church*, p. 31.
62 Albrecht, 'Tjalkabota, Moses (1869–1954)', *ADB*.
63 Paul Albrecht, *From Mission to Church*, p. 30.

Georg **Pfalzer** arrived at Cape Bedford in 1886 from Neuendettelsau still unordained at age 20. He shared with Pingilina the task of instructing 30 school children while Pingilina helped Pfalzer learn Guugu-Yimidhirr. Once the Meyers and Pingilina left for Bloomfield to administer that mission on behalf of the Immanuel Synod, Pfalzer was left in charge at Cape Bedford on behalf of the Neuendettelsau Mission Society, assisted by the Jamaican skipper Christopher Wallace and South Australian lay helper Johann Biar. With self-deprecation, Pfalzer complained about the affairs at the mission: 'One of us can't sing at all [Pfalzer]. The other cannot sing in German [Wallace]. And the third can only sing if someone leads [Biar]!'[64] The unassuming Pfalzer was keenly aware of his lack of singing talent and claimed that he was usually asked to ring the bell or hold the torch while the others were singing.[65]

Pfalzer also had a keen sense of the ironies inherent in his interactions with Aboriginal people. On his way to a public meeting in Cooktown, where he intended to deliver a prepared speech in favour of a total day-and-night curfew on Aborigines in the town, his canoe inexplicably tipped over landing all his papers and himself in the water. Pfalzer suspected that his Guugu-Yimidhirr boatmen engineered this accident to prevent him from attending the meeting because they disagreed with his position. He also mentioned that it was not unusual for someone to interrupt his sermons if these went on for too long, with the suggestion 'do you want us to chop some wood, or dig the garden?' or more bluntly, 'are we getting something to eat now?'[66]

Cape Bedford was not the only place where Indigenous people understood their attendance at religious service and instruction as a service rendered deserving of remuneration. John Haviland discussed the question raised by Aboriginal people about 'How much food will there be in heaven?' as the decisive issue concerning the benefit of becoming Christian.[67] Sermons that went on for too long, or were too repetitive, might also be cut short, as Pastor Hausmann found at Bethesda with a reminder that he had already told them all this before, and they did remember – in other words, no need to repeat all the old stories.

---

64 *Kirchliche Mitteilungen*, 7 (1887), p. 55.
65 Froehlich, *Pioniermissionar*, Vol. 1, p. 117.
66 Howard J. Pohlner, *Gangurru*, Lutheran Church of Australia, Adelaide, 1986, p. 40.
67 Haviland and Haviland, 'How much food will there be in heaven?', p. 133.

Pastor Georg Heinrich Schwarz arrived at Cape Bedford (Hopevale) in September 1887 from Bavaria and had already heard all about cannibal natives. The Guugu-Yimidhirr 'looked fierce' and made little attempt to settle his nerves; on the contrary, one commented that since Schwarz was 'so good', he must also be good to eat, and another traced the sections of human flesh that were good to eat on Schwarz's back, running shivers through Schwarz's spine.[68] Presumably this man was showing Schwarz where the kidney fat was located. Apart from the sensationalising function that such narratives played in missionary reporting, it must be presumed that they have some truth value, and also played a function in the self-representation of Guugu-Yimidhirr: that they were far from harmless, a people to be taken seriously and respected.

As the sixth of nine children on a Hessian farm, Schwarz was used to hard work and masculinist assertion. He arrived barely 20 years old but already with a facial growth that earned him respect.[69] Schwarz tried to teach the Guugu-Yimidhirr his proper name, 'but all that comes out is wux'.[70] Therefore his surname, meaning 'black', was translated as 'Muni' and became his badge. With the advantage of this name, and a fully grown beard, Muni appeared as a man to be taken seriously. In June 1900, he organised a theatrical foot-march of 25 men from Cape Bedford to Cooktown to lobby for funding while the newly appointed Northern Protector of Aborigines, Dr Walter **Roth**, visited Cooktown. It would surely have been easier to travel by boat, but the foot-march did not fail to make an impression and achieved funding for a government teacher. Schwarz ended up marrying the teacher and, during his 55 years at Hopevale, Muni became a celebrated father of the Guugu-Yimidhirr. He had the beard of an Elder and was 'black' by name, but this mission also had the help of a Jamacian skipper, a Dieri evangelist, and eventually local men appointed as the supervisors of outstations.

At nearby Bloomfield, Johann Sebastian **Hörlein** had a much harder time. He also arrived at age 20, in July 1891, also straight from Neuendettelsau, but compared to Schwarz his was a clean-shaven baby face, and Hörlein arrived with a strong sense for German correctness. In Cooktown, he was advised to wait a few days before proceeding to Bloomfield because

---

68   Pohlner, *Gangurru*, p. 43; Gordon Rose, 'The Heart of a Man: A biography of missionary G.H. Schwarz', *Yearbook of the Lutheran Church of Australia*, 1978, p. 48.
69   John Haviland with Roger Hart, *Old Man Fog and the Last Aborigines of Barrow Point*, Crawford House Publishing, Bathurst, 1998, p. 89.
70   Georg Schwarz, *Kirchliche Mitteilungen* 12 (1887): 92.

floods had just washed away bridges, but instead of wasting any precious time Hörlein decided to pay a visit to Pastor Schwarz at Cape Bedford. He engaged two Indigenous guides and his narrative of that journey is inadvertently droll because Hörlein's sense of cultural superiority kept getting challenged. Riding ahead out of Cooktown, Hörlein and an unnamed companion were annoyed because their Aboriginal guides, who were following on foot, made no effort to catch up to the horse riders:

> We had taken along two blacks as guides. But after only 12 miles we had lost the way. The blacks, who knew the way, had let us ride ahead and strolled behind at their own pace. We made a rest stop and waited for them. When they came up to us we asked them 'is this the right way?' and they replied, "depends which way you want to go". 'Well, we want to go the right way, of course, you're supposed to show it to us, we don't know it.' 'Well, the right way was six miles back.'[71]

The neophyte Hörlein, with more confidence in his own bush skills than in those of his local guides, kept riding ahead of them in semicircles so they had to track him, and the day's ride became a two-day trek during which Hörlein became totally dependent on his guides to gather drinking water in palm leaves. Eventually he noticed that his guides followed pathways marked by incisions in trees and were much more skilled than he was to survive in the bush.

At his own mission on the Bloomfield River, Pastor Hörlein thought it below his dignity to teach little children to read ('das ABC beizubringen'). A lay teacher had to be engaged, but Hörlein's iron-fisted rule drove the lay assistants away. After Pingilina's departure, no other Indigenous intermediary stepped forward and the mission was closed in 1901 under a cloud of scandal (see **Bloomfield River** mission) whereas at Hopevale outstations were formed under Indigenous leadership.

The Lutherans at Bloomfield and Cape Bedford had the initial assistance of Pingilina from the south, where missions had been established a generation earlier. In the other northern missions, workers were imported from the Pacific for the maritime industries, and Indigenous people participating in that industry with a longer exposure to white employers played a similar facilitating role.

---

71   Hörlein to friends of the mission, 10 August 1891, Bloomfield correspondence, LAA.

Big men at Mapoon

Mapoon was selected as a mission site because it had become a recruiting harbour for the trepang industry. It was already a place of intercultural encounter and presumably mixed family formation, and it took only five years to claim the first adult converts in 1896. South Sea Islander Harry Price (possibly from Tahiti) became Pastor Hey's paid assistant from around 1897 until his death in 1901. Price had a colourful past, including visits to Sydney, London and the United States on an American whaling boat; pearling in Western Australia and at Thursday Island; and finally as overseer at Frank **Jardine**'s Bertiehaugh station at the tip of Cape York, where Jardine had allocated him a wife, who accompanied Price to Mapoon. Harry Price was not fluent in the local language but led a prayer group for young men.

At around the same time as Harry Price, Jimmy Deinditschy from the Pennefather River (near Weipa) took on a leading role at Mapoon. Jimmy and his wife Sarah, like the Peppers at Ebenezer, became trusted evangelist helpers. At their baptism in 1896, Jimmy delivered an engaging speech before a large crowd including 400 children, where one 'could have heard a needle drop'. An older man, Oki, followed up with another speech, and also wanted to be admitted for baptism, but was refused because he had two wives.[72]

Jimmy led the Sunday prayer service and oversaw a married couples' outstation at a distance from the mission consisting of six houses for 12 adults. He also helped to set up Weipa mission on the Embley River in 1898. He spent his winters at his home on the Pennefather River (near where Weipa mission was formed in 1898), and a number of young men from that area married Mapoon mission girls, forming a strong attachment between the two sites. After 1897, Mapoon became a repository for mixed-descent girls removed from their families by police under Queensland's *Aboriginals Protection and Restriction of the Sale of Opium Act 1897*.

Not much is recorded about Jimmy or Sarah's background. Sarah was literate and Jimmy was a boat skipper. Either or both of them could have been of mixed descent and fighting for a new way of imagining Aboriginality, or a way of engaging with the new age that was descending

---

72   N. Hey, 30 October 1896, North Australia, North Queensland, microfilm, MF 186, Australian Institute of Aboriginal and Torres Strait Islanders (AIATSIS).

over Cape York with the massive engulfment of pearling and its Asian workforce.[73] In 1900, Jimmy came under pressure to accept a second wife resulting from the death of a relative. Sarah disagreed with this plan and informed missionary Hey, who subjected Jimmy to a public shaming and gathered the congregation to 'pray the devil out of Mapoon'.[74] After this, Jimmy avoided his Pennefather River people, and fades out of the mission record. Presumably he lost face with both sides. Still, Jimmy certainly leavened the grounds for a new mission at Weipa.

Another assistant at Mapoon, who was Hey's 'right-hand man' for nearly 30 years, was referred to as 'Mamoos'. (Mamus was a form of address for a local leader in Torres Strait.) He may have had some mixed Torres Strait and Pacific Islander lineage and was married to a baptised woman of mixed descent, Lena (or Lina), book-keeper for the outstation. Mamoos was appointed as assistant in 1906 with a public ceremony, and in 1907 became skipper of the fourth sailing boat on the mission to organise fishing, turtle hunting and trepang collecting, which was now an important income source for the mission. He became a key figure on the mission, preaching in the local language, and he also wrote sermons in English and collaborated with Hey on language work. He was always 'bright and happy' and Hey was full of praise for him.

Other Pacific Islanders also assisted Hey around the same time as Mamoos. Dick Kemp from the New Hebrides oversaw another outstation, where he conducted daily blessings, and this group built their own church in 1910. Batavia River outstation was supervised by a Samoan from 1911 to about 1921, and Jack Charger oversaw the trepang fishery and lived on his own farm at an outstation with his wife from Mapoon, who helped him to prepare sermons.

It was much the same at Aurukun and Weipa. Richter's first assistant, another Jimmy, died of dengue fever within the first year and was replaced by Tom Solomon, who captained the mission boat. For a period in 1905, Solomon was in charge of the mission assisted by James, also a South Sea Islander. At Weipa, Peter Bee assisted, and the mission received its first white assistant after 10 years, about which Pastor Brown commented:

---

73   Ganter, *Pearl-Shellers*.
74   Hey, Annual Report for Mapoon for 1900, MF 186, AIATSIS.

an event which marks an epoch in the history of our station, viz, the passing of the Kanaka assistant by the advent of a duly recognised white assistant, who can be an assistant indeed, and not a mere overseer requiring himself constant supervision.[75]

This is a remarkable misjudgement of the important role of such cultural intermediaries. The context of this dismissive comment were the upheavals caused by Peter Bee's sexual transgressions (see Chapter 7), but the Cape York missions were crucially dependent on South Sea Island assistants. Though much is made of the Indigenous first fruit at Mapoon, Hey and his colleagues relied to a very great extent on imported men, already exposed to Christian teaching in the Pacific, and they were aided by the already cosmopolitan nature of the trepang recruiting port.

Mixed relations of Beagle Bay

In 1896, when the first baptisms took place at Mapoon, the Trappists at **Beagle Bay**, too, celebrated their first baptism, only four years after their arrival. They had the advantage of a man described only as 'Knife' who had assisted Fr Duncan McNab at Goodenough Bay, where McNab had enjoyed the help of a group of Filipinos. 'Knife' now lived at Boolgin homestead and kept up a positive image of missionaries as friends and providers.

Another key intermediary was Felix Gnodonbor, who helped Fr Alphonse to learn Nyul-Nyul and translated key concepts. Very soon Father Alphonse was able to preach in Nyul-Nyul to an attentive congregation at Sunday mass, but if he went so far as to denounce some Indigenous custom, an Elder might stand up and begin to argue vigorously.[76] The fact that Gnodonbor spoke Nyul-Nyul rather than Bardi suggests that he may have come from the Disaster Bay area on the east coast of Dampierland, like 'Knife'. The Trappists valued Gnodonbor's knowledge, and he in turn became instrumental in the acceptance of the Christian missionaries at Beagle Bay. He remained at Beagle Bay mission with his wife Madeleine until 1931.[77] Two of Felix Gnodonbor's nieces, Leonie Widgie and Fidelis Elizabeth Victor, became early converts, and one of

---

75   Brown, Annual Report for Weipa for 1909, MF 186, AIATSIS.
76   '**The Trappist Mission At Beagle Bay**', *The West Australian*, 3 November 1896, p. 2.
77   Brigida Nailon, *Nothing is Wasted in the Household of God: Vincent Pallotti's Vision in Australia 1901–2001*, Spectrum, Richmond, 2001, p. 153.

Felix's granddaughters, Magdalene Williams, later helped to found Balgo and LaGrange missions.[78] His nephew Remi was among the first to be baptised in August 1896, a ceremony witnessed by a visiting journalist who described the evening rosary, the daily school for children and the instructions for adults, and the Aboriginal altar boys dressed in red serving at the daily morning mass.[79]

Gnodonbor himself was baptised the following year, 1897, in the name of Felix like the prior at Sept Fons, whose two brothers were in the Kimberley. This baptismal name therefore connected Gnodonbor to the highest Trappist authority in Sept Fons (Fr Felix Janny), to the superior of the Kimberley mission (Fr Ambrose Janny) and to the supervisor of Disaster Bay (Fr Jean-Marie Janny).

The godfather at the baptism of Felix Gnodonbor was 28-year-old Thomas **Puertollano**, another key cultural intermediary for the Trappists. This Catholic Filipino had arrived in Australia as a protégé of the Filipino–Spanish nationalist Filomeno Rodriguez in 1891, and became skipper of the mission's *Jessie* when the Trappists acquired the Lombadina lease in 1892. Puertollano helped to build the Broome church for Fr Emo and helped the Trappists to establish a grange at Disaster Bay in March 1897. In February 1898, Puertollano married Aboriginal–Irish woman Agnes Guilwil O'Bryan from Beagle Bay and the couple became instrumental in the Disaster Bay outstation. In 1901, after Fr Jean Marie Janny returned to Disaster Bay, Agnes and Thomas Puertollano were providing food three times a day for 35 Indigenous people.

Some time between 1902 and 1904, the Disaster Bay station was moved to the former Hadley and Hunter pearling station at Lombadina, where the Puertollanos now took over part of the lease and provided for Fr Jean-Marie Janny. Once Janny, the last Trappist in the Kimberley, left, the government objected to an Asian being in charge of a mission settlement and declared Lombadina a government 'feeding station' under the supervision of Hadley and Hunter, who were running a 'private mission' at Sunday Island. In 1911, as a result of Hunter's conviction for 'cohabiting with native women', Fr Emo was placed in charge of Lombadina, and the Puertollanos gave up their house to him. In 1913, they were pushed out of Lombadina under the threat of legal action for employing Aborigines.

---

78 Brigida Nailon, *Emo and San Salvador*, 2 vols, Brigidine Sisters, Echuca, 2005, Vol. 1, p. 273.
79 'The Trappist mission at Beagle Bay', *The West Australian*, p. 2.

Despite Fr Emo's active support, Puertollano had still not been able to achieve naturalisation, and therefore could not register a lugger in his name. Puertollano's new house became the mission convent and he sold his substantial cattle herd and opened a bakery in Broome.

The Puertollano story shows how at odds the racialised policy of the state government was with the Catholic Church, with the two institutions looking through the very different lenses of religion and race. An Aboriginal–Filipino Catholic family was just what the church needed to extend its mission, and about the last thing the state government wanted to support.

Nicholas Emo and the Kimberley Filipinos

Fr Nicholas **Emo** (1849–1915) was not steeped in the Trappist tradition like his fellow monks. He had many years of mission experience in South America and only joined the Trappist order so that he could come to Australia to missionise among the 'wild blacks'. As the only Spanish speaker among the Trappists arriving in the Kimberley, Emo was stationed in Broome in 1895 to minister to the Catholic community there and off the missions, consisting almost exclusively of Filipinos engaged in pearling. Being stationed in the township of Broome instead of at the remote Beagle Bay mission must have seemed like a setback, but eventually a stint at Drysdale River fulfilled his romantic ambition of encountering 'wild blacks'.

Emo's attitude to race relations was inspired by the Spanish conquistadores' policy of intermarriage – the opposite of the British insistence on maintaining racial boundaries. In Broome he very quickly engaged a Filipino catechist and his mixed-descent Aboriginal wife to set up a school, and he worked closely with the Catholic Filipinos of the entire Kimberley area. [80] Several Aboriginal/Latino families had settled along the tidal creeks and coves of Dampier Peninsula including John Andriasin from Manado (Kupang), Severo Acosta (or Seveiro da Costa), the Filipino Damasco

---

80 'The Trappist mission at Beagle Bay', *The West Australian*, p. 2.

Maagina (or Don Damaso Maagna Trinidad) and Joseph Marcelina from Chile.[81] The latter (Joe Marsalino) with his wife Margarita, offered shelter to Br August **Sixt** who was expelled from Beagle Bay mission in 1909.[82]

Not feeling bound by any particular Order, Fr Emo performed a diplomatic tightrope walk in his collaboration with the Trappists, the Pallottines, the Benedictines, the Irish Bishop Gibney in Perth and Bishop Kelly in Geraldton. He was unafraid to burn bridges to pursue his own policy and he championed the cause of mixed marriages even against the increasing resistance of the Pallottines and the government after the turn of the century. The Catholic Filipino and mixed Aboriginal community in Broome embraced him. In the wake of the revolution against the Spanish in 1897, the Broome Filipino community grew rapidly and included both Catholics and Muslims. This political turmoil affected Emo's work in Broome when his church was burnt down, and political refugees, who needed to forge new identities, joined the community. In a stocktake of his congregation at Broome in 1896, Emo mysteriously described one of his parishioners: 'This is Leandro Loredo, husband of Matilda (Aboriginal) living at the Point but nobody knows (but me) the true name'.[83]

Emo had two protégés of Filipino descent, Martin Sibosado and Sebastian Damaso, who became core members of the mission community. They accompanied Emo on his peregrinations from 'The Point' in Broome to Cygnet Bay, Drysdale River and Lombadina. Damaso became a Cistercian novice, but the sudden withdrawal of the Trappists ended his aspirations of joining the Order; however, he remained a faithful mission supporter. A poignant line from the Beagle Bay mission diary in 1916 records that while preparing a new patch of land for a garden, Damaso found an old human bone at Namogon and 'sang the Miserere softly to himself' while reburying it.[84]

Emo acquired the *San Salvador* with the help of his Filipino congregation and staffed it with Filipinos and members of the mixed Filipino–Aboriginal community. The people who reappear in Emo's references are Catalino

---

81 Mary Durack, *The Rock and the Sand*, Corgi, London, 1971, p. 190.
82 V. Kopf PSM Provinzial und Visitat, 2. 3. 1909, in Sixt, August (Br – Ex), P1 Nr 28, Zentralarchiv der Pallottinerprovinz (ZAPP).
83 Entry No. 157 in Emo, Broome Census Book of 1896, in Nailon, *Emo and San Salvador*, Vol. 2, p. 175. Elsewhere, Nailon refers to Matilde as Timorese, and to Leandro as coming from Luzon. Their 12-month-old baby Alexander Maria Loredo died 7 November 1906 and their adopted daughter was from Broome. The couple 'served Emo' for eight years at the Point. Nailon, *Emo*, Vol. 2, pp. 28, 88.
84 **Droste diary**, 10 December 1916, ZAPP.

Torres and (part Aboriginal) Lorenza, Leandro Loredo and (Timorese/Aboriginal) Matilde, the Puertollanos and Sebastian. In the period of absence of missionaries, such as at Beagle Bay from the departure of the Trappists to the arrival of the Pallottines, or at Lombadina between the departure of Janny and the arrival of Emo, it was these Filipinos who carried on the work.[85] As much as the Moravians at Mapoon and the London Missionary Society (LMS) in Torres Strait relied on Pacific Islanders, the Catholic missionaries in the Kimberley and Thursday Island leaned on Filipino helpers. The missions at Cygnet Bay, Drysdale River, Disaster Bay and Lombadina were grafted onto the close bond between Emo and his Catholic Filipino supporters.

Bathurst Island melting pot

The same may be said about the establishment of the Missionnaires du Sacré Coeur (MSC) in the Northern Territory. Most accounts of Fr Gsell's arrival at Bathurst Island in 1911 read as if he came north all by himself. But Gsell was very aware of the importance of Filipino lay helpers in grafting on to an Indigenous society. He had just spent six years at Yule Island mission that was set up with the assistance of 14 Filipino catechists.[86] Gsell expressed regret that government policy did not permit him to import Filipino assistants. However, at Thursday Island, Filipinos were already getting trained as catechists for the Papuan mission, and it seems that Gsell recruited some of these to Darwin, perhaps during his visit to the MSC Sisters at Thursday Island in June 1907.[87] The evidence for this assumption is that in 1908 Gsell mentioned that a Filipino family was looking after his laundry in Darwin and that one of his assistants in Darwin and at Bathurst Island was Alfonso Aboliro. Aboliro, a sailor, was born in Laiti in 1874, arrived in Australia in 1897 and married Mary Elisabeth, who was born on Thursday Island, in 1869.[88]

---

85   Emo to Sept Fons, 6 January 1901, in Nailon, *Emo and San Salvador*, Vol. 2, p. 212.
86   James Griffin, '**Verjus**, Henri Stanislas (1860–1892)', *ADB*, published first in hardcopy 1976; and **Fabila Family at Yule Island**.
87   Gsell foreshadows this visit in his letter to the MSC Provincial at Kensington of 12 November 1906, Chevalier Resource Centre, Kensington (MSC Archives).
88   Both were resident at Bathurst Island when they registered as aliens in 1916. Alien Registration of Alfonso Aboliro, 24 October 1916, MT269/1, barcode 6561190, National Archives of Australia (NAA); Alien Registration of Mary Aboliro, 26 October 1916, MT269/1, barcode 6561191, NAA. Thanks to Julia Martinez for this information.

5. ENGAGING WITH MISSIONARIES

Gsell arrived on Bathurst Island in 1911 with four Filipino men on a Jolly Company pearling lugger. An arrival narrative in French by Fr Frank Flynn MSC suggests that they constructed a 'hut from branches',[89] but Gsell mentions that they brought with them a prefabricated house from Darwin. It was erected by Br Lambert and two men described only as 'one-eyed Boolak and hunchback Tokoopa'.[90] These names sound a little like bullock and cooper and perhaps these men, both incapacitated, had previously been working at Joe Cooper's bullock camp on Melville Island, and may have been Tiwi or Iwadja or of mixed descent. The (unnamed) Filipinos remained on the island and 'helped Fr. Gsell build the mission'.[91] Alfonso Aboliro captained the mission boat and remained a lay helper at the mission until about 1950, residing with his family in a separate house.

Gsell was certainly not alone among natives. The French assistant missionary Fr Regis Courbon arrived, if not with Gsell, then within days to be present for the completion of the first residence. By the time Fr Henschke arrived in 1915, the **Bathurst Island** mission had a church and 'a couple of other houses for the Manila men'.[92]

Tiwi Islanders had much exposure to Asians in the Macassan trepang fleets and the pearling boats operating from Darwin offered alternative sources of barter, food and entertainment. The Tiwi avoided the mission, so the Northern Territory administration ensured the mission's successful launch by removing mixed-descent children from the Daly River to Bathurst Island, according to an observation by the visiting Russian Queenslander Leandro Illin.[93] In other words, Catholic Filipinos and the mixed-descent children from a former Catholic mission region provided the fertile soil for a successful mission on Bathurst Island.

After the introduction of the White Australia Policy in 1901, the presence of Asian men on missions became increasingly problematised. Sometimes the role of Filipino assistants was simply not apprehended, as in the case of

---

89   F. Flynn, '40 ans chez les Aborigènes Australiens – l'évêque aux 150 épouses', *Annales de Notre-Dame du Sacré-Coeur*, December 1960, pp. 266–69.
90   F.X. Gsell, *'The Bishop with 150 Wives': Fifty Years as a Missionary*, Angus and Robertson, Sydney, 1956, pp. 46–50.
91   Anthony Caruana, 'Reflections on hundred years of MSC mission work in the Northern Territory 1904–2004', unpublished MS, 2004, p. 14, MSC Archives.
92   Caruana, 'Reflections', p. 14.
93   Illin toured the Northern Territory in 1911 as an expert advisor to the federal government with a view to turning the Daly River into a Russian expatriate community. His 92-page report refers to these removals in passing. Elena Govor, *My Dark Brother: The Story of the Illins, a Russian–Aboriginal Family*, University of New South Wales Press, Sydney, 2000, p. 126ff.

Daisy Bates who accompanied Bishop Gibney to the Kimberley missions in 1900 and helped to work the gardens along with what she considered 'native women'.[94] In fact, she mentions by name Catholic women of mixed descent with Filipino husbands, like Agnes, Matilde and Lorenza, who were themselves products and beacons of a new age (see **Emo**). It is ironic that Bates later claimed to know so much about racial mixing.[95]

The role of Filipino lay helpers in facilitating Catholic missions in the Torres Strait, in the Northern Territory and in the Kimberley cannot be underestimated and deserves acknowledgement. With their marriage bonds and mixed families, they formed an intermediate social stratum between the foreign missionaries and the local population.

Postwar syncretic approaches

The Lutheran missions did not have these strong intermediate cultural layers of imported workers. They took much longer to achieve baptisms and to find 'native evangelists', but, when they did, such men became outstanding beacons of strength and intercultural communication.

Pastor Paul Albrecht, with over 40 years of experience at Hermannsburg, acknowledges the importance of these cultural mediators: 'Understandably ... effective Christian instruction leading to baptism could only take place when evangelists could be found to live and work on these [mission] stations'.[96] Indigenous congregations were formed after World War II, under the leadership of evangelists like the Pitjantjatara man Pastor Peter Bulla at Aileron, congregations led at Ti Tree, Aningie and Napperby by Josef Kentiltja and Gustav Malbungka, Pastor Davey Ingkamala at Utopia, Alcoota and Amaroo, and Pastor Paulus Wiljuka. Two evangelists were ordained at Hermannsburg in November 1964, Conrad Raberaba and Peter Bulla, followed by Cyril Motna in May 1969 and Paulus Wiljuka and Colin Malbungka in November 1971. Tensions arose over the remuneration of such pastors, since Lutheran pastors are usually remunerated by their own congregations, and over the standing of these

---

94   Elizabeth Salter, *Daisy Bates*, Angus and Robertson, Sydney, 1971, p. 81.
95   Since Bob Reece's biography of her, Bates has been much remembered for her dictum 'the only good half-caste is a dead one', published in '**Aboriginal reserves and women patrols**', *Sunday Times* (Perth, WA), 2 October 1921, p. 18, Trove; Bob Reece, *Daisy Bates: Grand Dame of the Desert*. Vol. 3, National Library of Australia, Canberra, 2007, p. 90.
96   Albrecht, *From Mission to Church*, p. 32.

pastors in the Lutheran Church. The general synod of the Lutheran Church Australia (LCA) resolved in 1972 that the aim of mission to establish an Indigenous church had already been achieved, and preparations should be made to hand over the 'major portion of the work' to Aboriginal people by the centennial year of 1977.[97]

The outstation policy at Hopevale also paid off with strong Indigenous leadership. Wayarego outstation near the McIvor River only had a missionary from 1928 to 1932, and was disbanded in 1936 due to soil exhaustion. It housed the families of Fred Deeral, Pearson, Baru, Gibson, McLean, King and others, and such people instigated the return to Hopevale from Woorabinda after the war and continued to visit and support Pastor Schwarz in retirement at Cooktown. One of the Wayarego residents, Simon King, who had been removed by police as a 12-year-old from the goldmining town of Maytown in 1922, became an active evangelist and revived the old Bloomfield mission in December 1957 as Wujal-Wujal, working under the direction of Hopevale Pastor Bernard Frederick Hartwig. At Bloomfield, King preached in Kuku Yalanji (Gugyalanji) and 'went off every morning with lunch and bag of books to bring the message of God to the older folk'. Pastor Prenzler also records that King 'cured a crippled woman through prayer'. King attended the dedication of the Kuku Yalanji New Testament at Pentecost in 1985 and was buried at Hopevale in December 1986.[98]

As mentioned above, the Lutheran missions in New Guinea gave a much greater role much earlier to native evangelists. Neuendettelsau graduates opened a training seminary to prepare nationals for ordination in 1939. From that college the first New Guinean ordained priest in Australia, Nawoh Mellombo, came to minister at Hopevale and Wujal-Wujal in March 1979.[99] The Christian energies are now flowing the other way round, with priests from the Pacific Rim, Africa, China and other former mission fields holding Australian pulpits.

The Pallottine training centre in Rossmoyne (Perth) was also assimilationist, and it, too, produced notable identities (see **Lümmen**). One of its buildings is named after Edith Little, a staunch supporter of Fr Lümmen. Her funeral on 8 December 1975 was attended by 450 people, including

---

97 Albrecht, *From Mission to Church*, pp. 33ff.
98 Description by Pastor Martin Prenzler, in Johann Flierl II file at LAA.
99 Traugott Farnbacher and Christian Weber (eds), *Ein Zentrum für Weltmission – Neuendettelsau – Einführung, Zeittafeln, Dokumente, Namen, 1842–2002*, Missionswerk der Evangelisch-Lutherischen Kirche in Bayern, Neuendettelsau, 2004, p. 35.

Mum Shirl from Redfern, Department of Native Welfare officers and representatives of the Catholic Church in Perth. Lümmen considered Little 'the co-founder, inspirator, soul and backbone of the Pallottine Centre ... let us work and pray that Edith Little may become the first canonised Aboriginal saint in heaven'.[100] High hopes indeed, but the Catholics still stopped short of ordaining Indigenous priests.

The Kimberley Pallottines embraced the concept of inculturation under pressure first from the state government and then from the federal Department of Aboriginal Affairs (DAA). This approach was pioneered by Fr Werner Kriener and Fr Peter Willis (who later left the Pallottines). The Australian Bishops Conference of 1978 agreed to a five-year period of enculturation of the liturgy, which meant that mass could be held in a local language or a mixture of languages. Inculturation built on a shared commitment to metaphysics, where Elders and missionaries were able to harness each others' ontologies, rituals and symbols to make room for the growth of an Indigenous church.

Fr Werner Kriener encouraged the merging of cultural symbolism. He witnessed and documented initiation ceremonies, and invited Indigenous creative participation in Christian rituals. The uptake from artists, performers and faithful was resounding. The Halls Creek artist Mangmang produced a carved sculpture of the pregnant Madonna drawing on the style of the *wandjina* figures typical for the Kimberley region. For Pentecostal celebrations in 1984, about 200 people travelled 250 km from Balgo to meet up with people from the Kimberley at Rockhole near Halls Creek. In a rocky cave, an area was cleared of grass and bushes to prepare a sandy ground for the performances. The men gathered early in the morning, around 6 am, to get painted and prepare for mass and then seated themselves on the prepared ceremonial ground. They had painted crosses and symbols of the Holy Spirit onto their bodies. The Balgo dancers wore their traditional pointed headgear, but with a cross painted on it, which they used for the dance during the holy mass, when transubstantiation transforms the altar wine into the blood of Christ. Parts of their body and headgear decorations were made from flower petals traditionally affixed with human blood. These symbolic affinities involving blood were like a closing of the loop of earlier mutual suspicion.

---

100 John Luemmen and Brigida Nailon, *Led by the Spirit: Autobiography of Father John Luemmen SAC*, Imprinti Potest Provincial of the Pallottines in Australia, Rossmoyne, WA, 1999, pp. 63, 64.

Dance groups accompanied the various priests to the altar, which consisted of an ordinary table decorated with paintings. The background was decorated with religious images painted especially for this occasion using chalk, ochre and red sandstone, with doves representing the Holy Spirit entering the community. One painting showed an Indigenous man with spear, peace doves, the Holy Spirit and the cross of Christ. Another represented the landscape and its hills, with a symbolic Mother and Child at the centre, captioned as 'Yadanilu bilirgu' (Spirit, come here) and subtitled 'Welcome'.

Finally, there was also room for a bit of lampooning. Two young dancers, also adorned with crosses, were given the stage and impersonated an old Father with a walking stick. Looking through his albums in Limburg, the late Father Kriener, already hard of hearing to the point of deafness and unable to respond to questions, explained 'Such dances serve to tell stories and to remember and commemorate. Important new developments are woven into the dances and thus recorded for the community'. Kriener treasured the mail he received from his former flock, even if it was just a quick 'Happy Birthday, Father!' from Mary Minga.

In the Kimberley, Kriener performed baptisms in the open air, sitting on the ground. For the baptism of 13 adults and 19 youths at Halls Creek in 1987, Kriener brought a large shell for holy water from the church. Other times, the baptismal font might be a nicely decorated plastic bucket, such as at Ringers Soak, where he baptised 'the whole tribe' with the candidates wearing a white headband. The white headband perhaps stood in for the everlasting flower tiara worn by German baptismal girls along with a white dress outfit including gloves, handbag, candle, candle font, shoes and stockings. As in Germany, the ceremony was followed with a good feed for everyone.

The Easter Passion Play at Turkey Creek was preceded by eight days of fasting, as there is always a fast when a close relation dies, and the resurrection of Christ was accompanied by a cleansing smoke ritual, as in a traditional funeral. The symbolic body of Jesus was dug out from the ground and laid onto a tree as in a traditional tree burial. Queenie McKenzie, the Warmun Elder leading the women's dance troupe, played a leading role in the dance representation of the Stations of the Cross. The whole ceremony had to commence in the early hours of the morning because the Halls Creek Easter horseraces started at 10 am – another allowance made for the sake of cultural accommodation.

No doubt the high point in Fr Kriener's Kimberley experience was the Papal visit to Alice Springs in November 1986. Kriener and his congregation from Red Hill, Ringers Soak and Warmun, including Queenie MacKenzie and her by now famous dance troupe, were accommodated in the Catholic school at Alice Springs, decorated with the Australian Aboriginal flag, where they intoned Yawuru hymns. When the Pope finally arrived, Bishop Jobst had managed to occupy a prominent position with good view while Fr Kriener was hidden in the throng with the Kimberley people. However, John Paul II slowly wound his way through the thick crowd and personally greeted Fr Kriener, asking how the Pallottines in the Kimberley were faring, whereas the bishop watching from on high missed out on a close encounter.[101]

Conclusions

Examining the motivations and roles of local intermediaries in the earliest mission period in each region, by carefully focusing the lens of mission records, we find some functionalist attitudes as well as genuine curiosity among Aboriginal people who stepped forward to the missionaries, and begin to sense the fundamental importance of cultural mediation.

A number of the anecdotes show Aboriginal men struggling for dignity next to missionaries assuming cultural superiority. Resistance strategies ranged from gentle humour, to contradicting the missionary, to sabotage and instilling fear, and many missionaries were faced with violence (to which we return in Chapter 6).

To recapitulate, the Zion Hill missionaries were of interest to Indigenous people primarily because of their supplies, including firearms, in the hope of such a station on one's own land. Later, Hausmann at Bethesda still misinterpreted the attention shown as interest in religion and conversion, whereas the Rapid Creek setting shows the rift in mutual expectations when some of the supplies were given to outsiders.

The case of Ebenezer and its early band of young male sympathisers suggests that Indigenous diplomats may also have had personal reasons for seeking the shelter of a completely new social order if they were in difficulties with their own people or with police. Moreover, preaching

---

101 Interviews with Fr Werner Kriener at the Limburg monastery, 2011–13.

became a new source of prestige, and young Nathanael Pepper was allocated a wife and a cash wage, both of which also increased his standing at Ebenezer. The expectation that a wife would be allocated brought many younger Aboriginal men into missions. Pingilina, too, expected the missionaries to make sure that he had a wife and he also spread the news of such opportunities to other Aboriginal men. Getting supplies, a house, a spouse, an education and, perhaps, a wage were the surreptitious employer provisions in an unstipulated career progression for Indigenous people willing to engage with missionaries.

Another cluster of interest was the power of knowledge that the missionaries were displaying through books, reading and writing, as the anecdotes preserved from Ebenezer and Zion Hill suggest very strongly. In hindsight, it seems that the Zion Hill Lutherans trivialised precisely the man who showed the most interest in their spiritual powers when they described Wunkermany as speaking to the devil and as harbouring a superstition about books. What emerges is that in the early mission phase an earnest effort to embrace the missionary teaching could bring Aboriginal men into a situation where they were neither taken seriously by the missionaries nor by their Indigenous compatriots, and Pingilina's letters illustrate the identity loss that might result. Pastor Albrecht in Central Australia, too, was initially dismissive of the cultural counsel that people like Moses could offer, but eventually delegated evangelising responsibilities and so fostered the growth of an Indigenous church.

Where reliance on cultural mediators is concerned, social geography rather than denominational differences explain the different strategies of missionaries. In the centre and south of the Australian continent, the Muslim cameleers and Chinese pastoral and mining workers could not play this role for the Christian missionaries, so they relied more on Indigenous evangelists and took longer for first conversions, but in the polyethnic far north Catholics, Moravians and Lutherans resorted to an intermediate layer of imported workers to facilitate the growth of missions. Men from the marine industry assisted at Mapoon, at Cape Bedford, in the Kimberley missions and at Bathurst Island. Due to the geopolitics of empires, Filipinos played this facilitating role for the Catholic missions whereas Pacific Islanders were involved in Protestant missions.

However, the Pacific Island evangelists of the LMS, who forged the growth of an Indigenous church through intermarriage in the Torres Strait, became targets of government intervention as early as the 1870s, and later the far-reaching impact of the White Australia policy made it increasingly difficult for such cultural intermediaries, like Puertellano, to conduct self-directed work. Eventually, the missionaries had to either adapt to local expectations, interpretations and rituals to involve locals, or quit.

The cultural rifts were too large to be bridged in the first generation of contact – with a few extraordinary exceptions such as the Peppers at Ebenezer, Pingilina at Cooper's Creek and Moses at Hermannsburg – but, generally, cultural interpreters with a longer personal history of exposure to whites were required to prepare the ground for a mission. Indigenous churches and congregations did not really take off until after World War II, when Indigenous evangelists raised on missions were placed in charge of outreach and outstations, and missionaries were ready to embrace local adaptations of their rituals, liturgies, interpretations and allusions. Yet the Catholic accommodation with polygamy, subincision, circumcision and magic remained uneasy. Missionaries reported battling against child marriage, forced marriage and infanticide,[102] and these are still the humanitarian issues that organisations like World Vision, CARE and others successfully flag to promote development aid.

---

102 Margaret Zucker, *From Patrons to Partners: A History of the Catholic Church in the Kimberley 1884–1984*, University of Notre Dame Press, Broome, 1994, p. 178.

6
The trials of missionary life

Having explored the likely motivations of Indigenous people to seek an encounter with missionaries, we now ask the same question about the missionaries themselves. Beyond the strategic considerations of the various Churches explored in the earlier chapters, each individual made up their own mind about accepting the call into mission service, and few of them had Australia at the top of their list of desired destinations. What awaited them in Australia and why did they go?

The missionary adventurer

Like the mail-outs of development organisations today, mission publications aimed at generating donations and arousing interest, particularly from young people in Europe. The large mission societies active in Australia had regular newsletters and publishing houses that released autobiographies and mission histories often commissioned for jubilees. These emphasised the small triumphs achieved on various missions and exoticised the encounter with foreign worlds. The lure of adventure was surely a factor in recruiting young men into denominational development aid.

In this type of literature, the founding of missions is cloaked in myths of individual enterprise, often a sole missionary striking out into the unknown. References to living 'like a hermit' and 'going alone' on closer inspection mean, at best, the absence of other white people, and sometimes occlude the guidance of a local settler or his staff. First encounters with threatening 'wild blacks' are savoured, sometimes years later and with a twinkle in the eye (see **Schwarz**).

Mission life on the ground was of course much more mundane. In most mission locations, there was already a core of people with contact experience and a basic grasp of English. Exceptions were at Cooper's Creek, where the intended cultural intermediary of one of the parties died along the way and, at Drysdale River, where there was no pregiven 'middle ground' other than Fr Emo with his Filipino assistants. Even the Dampierland men were afraid to go to the Drysdale River, and a number of Aboriginal people were killed in the search for a suitable mission site in that area (see Nicholas **Emo**).

The lonely pioneer missionary figure arriving in the wilderness is particularly pronounced in the founding narratives of Mapoon, Hopevale and Bathurst Island, all places with long histories of contact. At **Mapoon**, Rev. Nicholas Hey refers to the night-time howling of the Indigenous people on the night of their arrival and omits to mention that he and Rev. John Ward arrived under police protection in a harbour long frequented by recruiters for the marine industries where English was spoken.

At Hopevale (**Cape Bedford**), the Aboriginal community annually celebrates Muni Day, named after the day of arrival of their missionary Georg Schwarz in September 1887. Pastor Johann Flierl established the mission a year earlier, but Schwarz stayed for 55 years and actually had a striking resemblance to Flierl, both featuring the same impressive beard, and possessing similar stature and facial features. When Schwarz first came to north Queensland he arrived two days earlier than expected at Cooktown, so that there was nobody to meet him. The story goes that with typical initiative, Schwarz hired a boat to take him to Cape Bedford mission, but was accidentally dropped at a beach just short of the Cape, and spent the night in a cave at the place that was later to become a mission site. In fact, Schwarz was accompanied by his colleague Pastor Georg Bamler, destined for the New Guinea mission, and the missionary in charge of Hopevale at the time, Pastor Georg Pfalzer, wrote that when he came to Cooktown to pick up Schwarz and Bamler, he found that the pair had checked into the most expensive hotel in town.[1] The most peculiar feature of this foundation narrative is that it is mirrored in the

---

1   Pfalzer to Deinzer, 20 September 1887, cited in Howard J. Pohlner, *Gangurru*, Lutheran Church of Australia, Adelaide, 1986, p. 40.

founding narrative of Simbang mission that Johann Flierl founded in New Guinea shortly after setting up Hopevale: there, too, we have the lonely missionary spending his first night in a cave.² Presumably these narrative displacements (Flierl/Schwarz, Hopevale/Simbang) are an effect of oral history.

Another strong founding myth surrounds the Missionaries of the Sacred Heart (MSC) activities in the north. The Catholic mission staff surrounding Fr F.X. **Gsell** almost disappear from the mission histories of the MSC in the Northern Territory. This has something to do with the high staff turnover around the fixture of Fr Gsell. Moreover, at Issoudun, the difficulty of recovering the life stories of the MSC staff was explained with reference to the motto of their founding father Jules Chevalier, that missionaries should 'embrace being unknown and to count for nothing' ('aime á être inconnu et compter pour rien').³ It is also an effect of the purpose of most of the mission's history, reproduced for the 2006 centennial celebrations of Gsell's arrival in Darwin and, in 2011, of his arrival at Bathurst Island.

Gsell's autobiography and a book written by one of his lay assistants, Pat Ritchie, *North of the Never Never*, compete with each other for outback adventure and Aboriginal encounter stories, and tell some of the same stories in significantly different ways (see **Bathurst Island**). Pat Ritchie's book includes the dubious image of a 'giant turtle with her hatchlings' and is clearly aimed at an audience for whom the outback is exotic and unknown.⁴ In Ritchie's narrative, humanitarian intervention and adventure, or anthroposophy and machismo, become powerfully entwined.

Missionaries were often faced with violence, not only witnessing violent encounters, but also exposed to threats directed against them personally, and sometimes they resorted to firearms. Even Nikolaus Wettengel, who was at Hermannsburg when it was well established (1901–06), felt threatened enough to keep a rifle in the house, because of talk that 'the

---

2   Susanne Froehlich, pers. comm. 2012.
3   Interview with Frère Bailly, Issoudun, October 2014.
4   The book, *North of the Never Never*, was written in collaboration with Henry B. Raine, and published by Angus & Robertson in Sydney, 1934, and by the Catholic press Burns, Oates and Washbourne in London in 1935. It was also translated into French.

whites should get out of the area'.⁵ Attacks by Aboriginal people were averted at **Stradbroke Island**, **Rapid Creek**, Uniya (**Daly River**), **Ebenezer**, Cooper's Creek (**Killalpaninna**) and Lake Condah. A few missionaries were actually attacked, like Eipper and Hausmann in separate incidents at Moreton Bay (see **Zion Hill**), the Benedictine staff at Drysdale River in September 1913 (see Emo) and the Presbyterian staff at Mornington Island in October 1918, where Pastor Robert Hall was killed (see **Hey**). Remarkably, these locations of actual violence do not coincide with the most colourful accounts of adventurous 'first contact' mentioned above. As if in role reversal, the more 'middle ground' contact sites have become the scene of adventure narrative, and the raw cultural encounters resulting in violence (like Drysdale River) have become obscured. Characteristic of fantasies, the potential for transgressions, but not actual violence, were the stuff of an interesting story.⁶

The typical missionary career

Many of the German-speaking missionaries were from rural or working-class backgrounds, and they typically arrived at a very young age, freshly graduated from a mission college. A mission placement was their first step out into the world, and some lengthy travelogues of the journey to Australia survive.

Niel Gunson observed a dynamic of upward mobility of missionaries in Papua and New Guinea arising from the immersion in a settler society.⁷ For non–Anglo-Saxon missionaries in Australia, this pattern is not so evident. Nicolas Hey at Mapoon enjoyed close relations with the government resident, but in a clearly filial role, and the Catholic Bishop Salvado and the Moravian Rev. Friedrich **Hagenauer** exerted a prominent influence on state legislation regarding Aboriginal people and served in secular capacities as protectors, but generally the non-Anglican mission societies sought to maintain independence and distance from the British colonial state apparatus. Of around 180 German-speaking missionaries and helpers in Australia, only a few occupied positions where they

---

5   Immanuel Synod, FRM Box 5, Correspondence Wettengel (transcriptions and translations) (henceforth Correspondence Wettengel), 19 September 1903, Lutheran Archives Australia (LAA).
6   Susanne Zantop, *Colonial Fantasies: Conquest, Family and Nation in Precolonial Germany, 1770–1870*, Duke University Press, Durham, NC, 1997.
7   Cf. also Niel Gunson, *Messengers of Grace: Evangelical Missionaries in the South Seas 1797–1860*, Oxford University Press, Melbourne, 1978.

6. THE TRIALS OF MISSIONARY LIFE

superintended more than one mission at a time (the Moravians Hey and Hagenauer, and the Pallottines Walter, Droste and Bischofs), and only three German-speaking Catholics achieved episcopal status (Gsell, Raible, Jobst). A few missionaries gained a longlasting reputation while the remainder had at best a period as mission superior, or remained subordinate as Protestant lay helpers or Catholic Brothers.

Wages

Protestant missionaries were subject to the micromanagement of a mission committee and were completely dependent on organisations chronically short of funds. The annual wage of an ordained Lutheran missionary in the late nineteenth and early twentieth century was usually set at £25 for an assistant and £50 for a missionary in charge, with perhaps a small allowance for a married man or one with extra responsibilities such as station management and many children (e.g. **Reuther**). A lay assistant could expect around £15 to £20 per annum. These were survival rates and not the foundation for a career. In comparison, a government schoolteacher drew around £300.

Real inequalities were introduced when public service staff and religious collaborated on the same mission. At the end of the mission period, when the Northern Territory missions were forced to adopt a proper budget system and began to factor in wages, their budgets blew out and it became abundantly clear that the religious mission staff had been massively subsidising the public purse (see **Bathurst Island – Postwar Changes**). Catholic Sisters, Brothers and Fathers did not draw a wage but had more reliable institutions to support them in old age (see below).

Employer provisions

Mission staff were instructed to 'live together in love and faith'. If that idyllic concept collapsed, there was hardly any back-up provision. For someone who left their service or was dismissed there was no severance package and no legal redress. Staff might even have to struggle to have their personal possessions sent after them (**Siebert**), or be required to pay for the fares of their spouses out of pocket (**Wettengel**). The Catholic Pallottine Society was a legal entity that could be taken to court, whereas the Protestant mission societies were associations of indistinct legal character and there were no employment contracts. When Bloomfield mission was given up, the mission committee minuted:

> The Committee is also convinced that there can be no talk of its being obliged to see to the future maintenance of the two missionaries, and that whatever the Committee could and would do for them, would depend entirely on its good will.[8]

Goodwill was shown to the family of Johann **Flierl**, for whom a residence was made available in Tanunda on Flierl's retirement, but there was no legal obligation. At the time of Pastor Reuther's death in 1914, after 18 years of mission service and 8 years of independent farming, and including a Tanunda property inherited from his father-in-law, his whole estate was valued at £3,000. The financial disclosure of Fr **Schwarz** of Hopevale at the time of his interment in World War II shows that he and his wife owned two cottages in Cooktown, one of which was furnished and often accommodated Mary Schwarz during illness, and may have been part of Mary's inheritance from her Cooktown parents. Their joint savings were close to £300, representing about 10 per cent of his lifetime earnings. Their other assets were valued at £400, but Schwarz was still servicing several loans.[9] It hardly amounts to a resounding pecuniary attainment for 55 years of service. As Pastor Wettengel wrote, 'if I had aspired to wealth, I would have stayed at home'.[10]

The Protestant missionaries had been far removed from the lap of their natural families and estates in Germany, but they could not rely on retirement provisions, and leave provisions were more liberal for mission superiors than other staff. Hey's furlough worked out to 28 months in 28 years. Johann Flierl had one year's leave after his first 10 years, and two years leave a decade later. Protestant mission superiors generally could expect a year-long furlough after 10 years of service, but not reliably so. Pastor W.H. Schwarz at Hermannsburg had to hold out for 12 years without furlough. Pastor Georg Schwarz at Hopevale was granted his first furlough after 13 years, but was recalled before he could leave for Germany with his new wife in 1901 and finally took furlough in 1922. Pastor Poland, who was not a mission superior, waited 17 years for his first furlough. Most of the Protestant lay helpers were recruited from the

---

8   Immanuel Synod, Mission Commitee Minutes, May 1900, LAA.
9   Schwarz, Report on Prisoner of War, MP1104/2, Q490, National Archives Australia.
10   Wettengel to Kaibel, 18 November 1901, Correspondence Wettengel, LAA.

southern Australian migrant communities, and, of these, only Hermann **Vogelsang** is recorded with a three-month furlough at Tanunda in 1905 after 40 years of service at Bethesda (Killalpaninna).

The Pallottines tried to afford at least one home visit for their Kimberley priests, and sometimes the Fathers saved the return fare by acting as the priest on a migrant ship (e.g. Hügel in 1961). The Catholic Brothers, however, usually did not return to Australia once they were repatriated to Germany (except **Wollseifer**), and we will return to their retirement provisions below.

Housing

Accommodation was free and basic rations were also allocated, but living conditions on the missions were often primitive, particularly in the first years of each mission, not only for mission residents but also for staff. The missionaries themselves had to build or at least mastermind and supervise the building of their accommodation, and supplies of material were difficult to organise. Usually a beginning was made by the men, and the wives (or Catholic Sisters) were introduced later, once habitable accommodation could be provided. Lydia Günther sat down and wept when she arrived at **Wellington Valley** and was shown her new home, the mission house that had been unoccupied for six years. Whether it was in the 1840s or the 1940s, arriving in a new mission location was always uncomfortable. At the **Tardun** farm, the first Pallottine Brothers battled with heat, insects, snakes and rain seeping through the roof. The first Pallottines at **Rockhole** station found only the large open verandah of the station home inhabitable. The two mud-walled and unventilated rooms were only usable as chapel and storeroom.[11]

The mission house was normally the first substantial structure on a mission, and defined its centre. If possible, it became flanked with a church and a school. It often served as visitor accommodation and school building, and if an assistant missionary arrived it might have to be shared between two families. The mission house was not private property, and did not offer a private sphere. It was a household on public display, modelling standards of housewifery for the 'colony'.

---

11   The Brothers arrived at Rockhole Station in 1934. Alphonse Bleischwitz, 'Geschichte der australischen Mission', MS, B7d,r (18)d, Zentralarchiv der Pallottinerprovinz (ZAPP).

At **Beagle Bay**, the 'colony' for residents consisted of mudbrick single-roomed houses, and some such cottages were also occupied by the Pallotine Brothers lucky enough to get a room of their own. Eventually the staff residences at Beagle Bay ended up in worse condition than those of the mission residents, who were able to access federal building initiatives, and in 1975 the government health inspector condemned most of the buildings. By 1980, it was found that in the Kimberley the 'standard of living quarters for missionaries in all of the missions is far below that of Aboriginal and public service housing'.[12]

The living conditions of the early Kimberley parish priests in the townships were hardly better than those on the remote missions. Daisy Bates described Emo's Broome residence, later occupied by other Pallottines, as a shack. Fr Francis **Hügel** in Derby (1951–54) lived in a galvanised iron lean-to at the back of the church, which was also built from galvanised iron. Little wonder that some of the early Brethren embarked on extensive building programs. Fr White's construction endeavours in Broome set the Kimberley mission budget back by years, and Fr Walter retreated very soon from Beagle Bay to Broome, and from Broome to his palatial family residence in Würzburg. Other Catholic mission superiors also embarked quickly on extensive overseas or southern voyages to raise funds, while many Protestants withdrew their families and themselves from remote mission for health reasons, which was the only honourable exit.

Health

Service in mission was speckled with hardships, illness and trauma, including many accidents involved in building, maintaining and extending the missions. The narratives of the Pallottine Brothers include falling off horses and camels, getting attacked by bulls, accidents during well-digging and handling explosives, boating accidents (**Spangenberg**, **Herholz**, **Contemprée**) and getting caught up in cyclones on land and sea.

While introduced diseases decimated Indigenous people, conversely the Europeans were hard hit by the tropical diseases to which they had no resistance, like malaria and dengue fever. Pastor John Ward died of fever

---

12   Helen MacFarlane and John Foley, 'Kimberley Mission Review – Analysis and Evaluation of Church and Government involvement in the Catholic Missions of the Kimberley', ca 1981, p. 116, MS, State Records of Western Australia (SROWA).

6. THE TRIALS OF MISSIONARY LIFE

four years after arriving in Mapoon, and the remaining staff also suffered from malaria, as did the Richters at **Aurukun**. Malaria also affected the staff on the eastern Cape York, on the Daly River, at Bathurst Island and in the Kimberley, and two Pallottine Brothers contracted Hansen's disease, a tropical form of leprosy (**Ratajski** and **Hanke**). In the dry centre, it was 'sandy blight' (trachoma) that afflicted the eyes of many newcomers (e.g. Wendlandt, Wettengel, Strehlow).

The Protestant missionaries had even more trouble than the Catholic Brethren because they were also responsible for their children and wives, and many of them blamed themselves for the illness and death of their family members.

The health risks were enormous, especially for child-bearing women. Young Mary Handt had no midwife for her first childbirth at **Wellington Valley** and became deranged with fear and pain. Twenty-six-year-old Amalie Bogisch died at Ebenezer within a few years of her arrival. At Cape Bedford mission, the five-month-old baby of Pastor **Poland** died in April 1892 as a direct result of a shortage of food.[13] At **Bloomfield**, Mrs Jesnowki died of consumption, Pastor **Bogner** left in 1894 because his wife suffered from malaria, but Pastor **Hörlein** stayed on. Hörlein's wife died from malaria in 1900, and he never forgave himself for bringing his wife into such a difficult and dangerous place. At **Hermannsburg** Pastor **Kempe** buried first a child and then his wife before he gave up in 1891, after his two confreres had already taken their family to the safety of South Australia. At Killapaninna, Br Rüdiger buried his daughter in July 1892 and in 1900 he had to take his ailing wife south and came back to the mission by himself. Three-month-old Edwin Reuther died while Pastor Reuther was away for five weeks in October 1894, and Reuther, like Hörlein, never forgave himself and began to battle depression. Some of the pastors took to drink (Meyer, Flierl II) and Hörlein began to take opiates.

In terms of mental health, the letters of the Pallottines Br **Zach** and Br **Herholz** are interesting, Fr Vaccari's flight from Stradbroke Island is intriguing and Fr Nicholas Emo, too, eventually succumbed to self-doubt, depression and psychological self-flagellation. Pastor Reuther was candid about his 'head trouble', as he called it, and Hörlein's letters express

---

13 Wilhelm Poland, *Loose Leaves: Reminiscences of a Pioneer North Queensland Missionary*, Lutheran Publishing House, Adelaide, 1988.

all the signs of clinical depression. However, a mental health assessment of mission work is impossible, because of the discretion exercised in the sources, the carefully screened access to them and also because living descendants of missionaries resent an allegation of suicide.

Daily life and rhythm

The mission bell dictated the daily life rhythm of a mission. Not only the Indigenous residents, but the missionaries themselves were regimented by this pulse of activities. The Trappists at Beagle Bay rose at 2 am and retired at 8 pm. They chanted into the night at 3 am, 4.30 am, and again at 2 pm, and performed the Salve and Angelus at noon and 6 pm. In between, they held Mass at 4 am, read in Chapter at 10.30 am and performed night prayers around 6 pm. Their physical work was four hours in the morning and 3.5 hours in the afternoon. At least that is how they reported it. Even if they performed only a fraction of what they reported, it bespeaks an amazing discipline and expectations that seem beyond human capacity in a daily rhythm that scarcely leaves time to be spent alone.

Most extant daily mission schedules show an early rise at 5 am, and morning blessings. Kühn at **Point Pearce** held church services twice daily. Hey at Mapoon began each day with a religious service, led mid-week prayer meetings and on Sundays he held two services and Sunday school.[14] At Hermannsburg, Pastor Wettengel complained that he was supposed to act as a missionary to 50 Aboriginal children and as parish priest for the German staff, and that it took him three days to prepare a separate sermon in German.[15]

Paperwork

Mission management also involved an endless stream of paperwork. Writing was part of the lifeline of a mission. There were mission diaries; records of births, deaths and marriages; correspondence with committees, government departments and colleagues; supply orders and entries for mission newsletters to write. On the Protestant missions, all financial and staffing decisions had to go through a mission committee. Missionaries reported to their mission committee and to the state government,

---

14   J.N. Hey, *A Brief History of the Presbyterian Church's Mission Enterprise among the Australian Aborigines*, New Press, Sydney, 1931, p. 26.
15   Wettengel to Kaibel, 18 November 1901, Correspondence Wettengel, LAA.

estimating the number of residents, number of Christians, number of schoolchildren, reporting progress and land improvements. The Mari Yamba missionary was asked to submit quarterly reports in two languages to his mission committee. Hagenauer in Victoria reported to three or four supervising bodies in different periods, Hörlein at Bloomfield recorded each meal doled out and members of work gangs allocated each day to justify the government subsidy. Schwarz at Hopevale was criticised for not reporting enough, and complained that 'I can barely write five lines without being called away for this or that'.[16]

Contribution to science

Pastor Hey at Mapoon complained in 1896 that 'not a month passes where we don't send 30 to 40 letters, often [answering] requests for beetles, plants, and so on'.[17] There was much call from scientists for detailed information and, if possible, specimens. At Beagle Bay, one of the French Trappists collected live birds, and one of the Pallottines sent crates of prepared birds to Limburg. The emerging science of anthropology leant heavily on the collaboration of missionaries for detailed information to support or refine various theories.[18] The armchair anthropologist Moritz von Leonhardi sent the Neuendettelsau missionaries a 'much abbreviated' questionnaire of 30 open-ended questions, such as 'Are there any fables about stellar bodies? Are the stellar formations named? Are stellar bodies considered sentient?' Pastor Reuther answered one of these questions with a 14-page essay on dreams, which was filed away with his other correspondence in Neuendettelsau instead of getting passed on to Leonhardi.[19]

---

16   Schwarz to Neuendettelsau, 21 August 1893, reprinted in Traungott Farnbacher and Christian Weber (eds), *Ein Zentrum fuer Weltmission – Neuendettelsau – Einführung, Zeittafeln, Dokumente, Namen 1842–2002*, Missonswerk der Evangelisch-Lutherischen Kirche in Bayern, Neuendettelsau, 2002.
17   Hey to Roemig, 3 April 1896, North Australia, North Queensland, microfilm, MF 186, Australian Institute of Aboriginal and Torres Strait Islanders (AIATSIS).
18   Leonhardi to Neuendettelsau, 1 May 1899, filed in 1.6. 35 Reuther, Georg, 1861–1912, Pers. Korresp. Vorl. Nr. 4.93/5, Archiv de Neuendettelsau.
19   Reuther, 1.6. 35 Reuther, Georg, 1861–1912, Pers. Korresp. Vorl. Nr. 4.93/5, Archiv de Neuendettelsau.

In many cases, the exchange with scientists backfired for the missionaries, such as when Carl Strehlow was drawn into a dispute with Baldwin Spencer over religious ideas among the Aranda.[20] Fr **Bischofs** at Beagle Bay naively filled in an overblown questionnaire for a body that claimed to be a German migration society just before World War I, and was accused of espionage. Fr Emo's drawings of rock art at Drysdale River are ascribed to the ornithologist Gerard Hill, and in several cases the work of missionaries was published under the name of an armchair scientist. Under the impact of scientific interest, missionaries began ethnographic and botanical collections, such as Reuther's vast collection acquired by the South Australian Museum. Ethnographic museum collections in Australia and Europe drew strongly on contributions from missionaries, and the mission houses at Issoudun, Limburg, Herrnhut, Neuendettelsau and Hermannsburg had extensive botanical and ethnographic collections. Several edited volumes have examined the contribution of missionaries to science.[21]

Communal life

Missionaries had very little private sphere, and a minimum of private property or capital with which to improve the communal facilities provided for them. The remote mission workers had to rely on each other for economic, social and emotional support and, if one of them became ill, they were a drain on everyone else. In these small and isolated communities friction easily arose, whether over working hours (Bloomfield), over mission policy (Hermannsburg) or over personal incompatibilities. There was serious discord at Hermannsburg between Wettengel and Strehlow, at Killalpaninna between Reuther and Siebert, at Bloomfield between Hörlein and, first, Meyer and then Mack, and at Wellington Valley between Watson and, first, Handt and then Günther.

---

20   Walter Veit, 'Social anthropology versus cultural anthropology: Baldwin Walter Spencer and Carl Friedrich Theodor Strehlow in Central Australia', in Walter Veit (ed.), *The Struggle for Souls and Science: Constructing the Fifth Continent: German Missionaries and Scientists in Australia*, Occasional Paper No. 3, Strehlow Research Centre, Alice Springs, 2004, pp. 92–110; Anna Kenny, *The Aranda's Pepa: An introduction to Carl Strehlow's Masterpiece Die Aranda- und Loritja-Stämme in Zentral-Australien (1907–1920)*, ANU Press, Canberra, 2013.
21   Reinhard Wendt, *Sammeln, Vernetzen, Auswerten: Missionare und ihr Beitrag zum Wandel europäischer Weltsicht*, Gunter Narr Verlag, Tübingen, 2001; Walter Veit (ed.), *The Struggle for Souls and Science – Constructing the Fifth Continent: German Missionaries and Scientists in Australia*, Occasional Paper No. 3, Strehlow Research Centre, Alice Springs, 2004; Susan Cochrane and Max Quanchi (eds), *Hunting the Collectors: Pacific Collections in Australian Museums, Art Galleries and Archives*, Cambridge Scholars Publishing, Newcastle upon Tyne, 2014.

Flierl II could not work with Hörlein, Walter could not tolerate Emo in Broome, Gsell's confreres would rather be anywhere else but with him, and Schwarz and Poland created a strategic distance between their separate mission sites at Cape Bedford.

With practically everything in scarce supply, the staff jealously watched each other's privileges, such as working hours and the quality of goods from the mission store. At Bloomfield, it was about who got the better grade of flour and whose wife was more often incapable of contributing. Not everything that a mission had to offer was free of charge, either. At Killalpaninna, the staff paid school fees of £1 per child to send their own children to the school.

Their relative poverty created tensions, but it also created bonds. The women helped out if one of them fell ill and might even take in each other's children, and in retirement missionaries in many cases kept in contact with each other's families. Furnishings were circulated and we can see Anna Siebert wearing the same wedding dress as Pauli Reuther a few years earlier (both photographs were taken in Tanunda, and at that time villagers in Germany often hired out their wedding dress for a fee).

Separation of families

The separation of children from their families was commonplace. A mission placement was always necessarily a separation from kith and kin and, in the interest of obtaining the best possible education, the children of missionaries were often sent far away to boarding colleges. Lutherans who sent their children for schooling into the Lutheran communities in South Australia and Germany paid for their children's education out of their own pocket. Pastor Reuther constantly pleaded for assistance and special indulgence to afford the off-mission schooling of his seven sons at Eudunda and Neuendettelsau.

The primary classrooms on Protestant missions catered for a mixed audience. At Ramahyuck mission under the Moravian Frederick Hagenauer in 1881, five of the 47 pupils in the government school were Hagenauer children between the ages of 6 and 14 (of whom two failed to pass the government inspector's test, while almost all Indigenous children, including Samuel Pepper, passed).²² The Schwarz children were educated at Cape Bedford Lutheran mission school where their mother was the government teacher.

The German-speaking Moravian missionaries normally schooled their children free of charge in the Moravian boarding school at Kleinwelka near Herrnhut. Rev. Hey, writing from Mapoon, mentioned how anxious his wife already was about the impending departure of their two youngest girls to Germany, and the director at Herrnhut attempted to show some sympathy:

> I am touched by what you write about Sr Hey's difficulty in getting over the impending parting with her children. It is one of the hardest trials of missionary life, but not a monopoly of that service. Tell Sr. Hey she must not impair rest and health by brooding. The same afflictions are accomplished in her sisters, who are in the flesh. Sr Townley at Makkovik is sadly missing her girl and boy, left behind in England. I was over at Kleinwelka the other day, and saw the children there, over whom many a heartache has been dissolved in prayer from parents' lips. So pass on to your good wife the very human comfort that others have felt the same, along with the Divine comfort that the Heavenly Father knows what it is to part with a beloved and only begotten son on our behalf, and so to speak for the sake of Missions. May the Angel of the Covenant bless your lassies!²³

Such separation from families led, among the children of missionaries, to a phenomenon dubbed 'third culture kids'. This term refers to the children of missionaries, military personnel and other expatriates who grow up between two cultures, languages and nations, feel displaced in both and are scarred by rootlessness and unresolved grief.²⁴ Missionary children often harbour a deep resentment against their parents who had time to

---

22   Ramahuck School Gippsland, Inspector's Register Book 1871–1874, MSF 10401, State Library of Victoria.
23   Th. Bauer, Head of Unitätsdirektion, Berthelsdorf to Hey, 24 December 1903, Missionsdirektion, Personalakten Mission, Nicolaus Hey, MD825, Archiv der Brüderunität (Herrnhut Archives). Presumably, 'sisters in the flesh' means actual siblings, as distinct from 'sister' as the usual address between Moravian women.
24   David Pollock and Ruth van Reken, *Third Culture Kids: Growing Up among Worlds*, Nicholas Brealey, London, 2001.

care for the children of strangers, but not for their own. Signs of such intergenerational strain appear in reminiscences such as John Strehlow's account of his father Ted Strehlow and grandfather Carl Strehlow.[25]

Missionaries were able to compensate for the pain of separation from their children by placing it in the framework of a higher purpose – obtaining the best possible education for their children and serving the greater glory of God. They expected the same sacrifice of the mission residents. However, the mission residents did not have the same ambit of choice.

Commitment for life: The Pallottines

Neither did Catholic missionaries consider the separation of families as a major issue. Joining a Catholic society or order meant taking leave from one's natural family and a commitment for life, which raised its own challenges. Before they made their 'eternal profession', they entered a fixed-term profession of one or three years. The lifelong profession the Pallottines signed varied slightly over the years, but, as an example, Johann Graf in 1903 professed to the greater glory of God, to the honour of the blessed virgin and all angels and saints, and to the salvation of his own soul and the souls of those around him. He professed to dedicate his life to the imitation of the Lord Jesus Christ according to the rules of the society, in poverty, chastity and obedience dedicated to the communal life and never to accept any other honours than that of being a member of the society.[26]

Considering the impoverished background of many of the Brothers, entering the monastery was indeed an honour. When Br Franz **Nissl** decided to join the Pallottines, he had already lost both parents and had damaged a foot in an accident. He had spent his childhood in poverty, strict discipline and hard work, so a vow of poverty, chastity and obedience was hardly a lifestyle change, but the 'palatial Limburg monastery' certainly was. Nissl left for Limburg without informing his five siblings 'and for the first time in his life felt free'.[27]

---

25 John Strehlow, *The Tale of Frieda Keysser, Volume I: 1875–1910*, Wild Cat Press, London, 2011. Eric Flierl (pers. comm.) told a similar story about himself and his sister.
26 The Professformel signed by Johann Graf at Beagle Bay, 1903, in Graf, Johann (Br), P1 Nr 22, ZAPP.
27 Francis Byrne, *A Hard Road: Brother Frank Nissl 1888–1980: A Life of Service to the Aborigines of the Kimberleys*, Tara House, Nedlands, 1989.

Freedom hardly seems an apt description for the communal monastic life. The initial decision to join the society, and follow their faith, was for many Brethren their last free decision. For the remainder of their lives, the Brothers and Fathers were dependent on the provisions made for them and on the decisions their superiors made about them.

The Pallottine Brothers who worked in the first few years at Beagle Bay under the direction of Fr Georg Walter demonstrate this dependence (Zach, **Wesely**, **Sixt**, **Graf, Herrmann**). Walter was from a wealthy background and had little talent for getting on with the Brothers, but neither did Limburg dedicate their most promising Brothers to the Australian mission. The Brothers engaged in income-earning and productive activities, and therefore had very close contact with the mission residents. Br Rudolf Zach was a peculiar character and showed a preoccupation with death and dying. Every year he dedicated a lengthy homespun poem to his former superior Max Kugelmann to wish him a marvellous hour of death. Zach's morose descriptions of his emotional intimidation of Indigenous girls may well be the reason why he was recalled from mission service. (See Chapter 7 – 'Hitting children and child abuse', or Rudolf Zach for his anecdotes of domineering interactions and ghostly encounters with mission girls.)

Br Raimund Wesely asked for a copy of the Pallottine house rules a few months after his arrival at Beagle Bay to see for himself where it prescribed that one must wear the thick black habit during outdoor work in the tropics. In 1906, Wesely was sent home 'for reasons of health'. He was hoping for a placement at the Rome headquarters near the former Limburg superior Kugelmann, whom all the Brothers in Australia revered, and therefore expressed misgivings about returning to Limburg. To his utter dismay, he was told that he would be placed neither in Rome nor in Limburg, nor anywhere else with the Pallottines. He pleaded that he wanted to live and die as a son of Vincent Pallotti, and would rather lose everything than his beloved profession. Wesely finally succeeded in getting a placement at the Rocca Priora, the Pallottine house in Rome, but when he was offered the eternal profession he declined. In his case, the lure of adventure may have been greater than the call of the Spirit. Later, Wesely worked for the Franciscan Fathers in America and many years afterwards he wrote from California: 'Since I left your Society dear Father I have never omitted the prayers which are said in that Order and up to date I hold them dear and am sure many blessings have come to me'. The Limburg administration was not impressed. Wesely's letter, accompanied by a money order to read some masses, was curtly annotated: 'Done'.²⁸ At Limburg, the shadow of a *persona non grata* tends to hang over those who left the society.

Br August Sixt, also in Fr Walter's team, was expelled from Beagle Bay after an argument during which he had slapped one of the Fathers (probably Walter). Sixt obstinately refused to repatriate to Germany and instead remained close to Beagle Bay. At first, he stayed with the Marcelino family, and then he set up a market garden and remained in contact with the mission and became one of its staunch supporters until his death. At the time of his expulsion, superior Fr Walter feared that Br Sixt may claim the back-payment of wages. The court case of an expelled convent Sister elsewhere in Australia had already shown that Australian courts would not uphold the voluntary relinquishment of wages in work contracts. This was in 1907, the year when the **Harvester judgment** granted males a basic wage and workers' rights ranked uppermost in the national conversation as the basic plank of a White Australian future. Perhaps for this same reason, Walter reluctantly recommended the admission of one of the other Brothers, Johann Graf, to the eternal profession of the society: 'Although the good man is hardly of any use to the mission society, his conduct and character are such that the Society can hardly refuse him the eternal profession after five years of work'.²⁹

Br Alfons Herrmann also left the society during Walter's watch. He came to Beagle Bay mission in 1904 and left in 1907 due to 'poor health'. In 1911, Herrmann was posted to Cameroon where, during World War I, he joined a volunteer corps and took part in a daring operation that ended in his arrest and internment at Cotonou and Le Mans. He returned to Limburg in 1918 with an Iron Cross and malaria. No longer able to participate in the monastic routines, he left the society in 1921, and entered into lengthy negotiations about a pay-out, listing all the items that he had brought to the monastery 20 years earlier: four suits, six blue linen work suits, two woollen blankets, a dozen each of sheets, towels, serviettes, collars, cuffs and other personal wear. He also brought 500 Mark to Limburg and a gold watch, which he said he gave to the superior. Hermann wanted to recoup 1,650 Mark and the society offered 1,000 Mark. As in most divorce proceedings, neither party was happy about the outcome.

---

28 Raimund Wesely file, ZAPP.
29 File note, Beagle Bay, 25, 6. 1902, in Johann Graf file, ZAPP.

To enter into a mission institution, candidates were supposed to join their wealth with that of the society. Fr Jean-Marie Janny, for example, brought 150,000 Francs to the Trappist monastery at Sept Fons at which his brother became Superior.[30] To the question about a financial contribution on the application form, Brother August Sixt answered that at the moment he had nothing, but after the death of his mother the Pallottine mission society in Limburg would get his 'entire fortune' ('mein ganzes Vermögen'), which presumably meant one-sixth of very little because he was one of six surviving siblings in an impoverished family.[31] Eventually, however, Sixt delivered on this promise. He financed a chapel for the sodality of the Children of Mary, the first Pallottine attempt at an Indigenous church in Australia in 1938, and, in 1954, he left his farm and cottage, actually his entire fortune, to the St John of God Sisters in whose care he died at the Beagle Bay mission, 57 years after his unlikely promise.

In 1949, Br Bernhard **Stracke** also faced the spectre of repatriation to Germany against his will. Like Sixt before him, he decided to leave the society and stay close by: 'I got a dispensation from my promises. I left the mission with practically nothing, touching forty'.[32] Stracke married a young woman who had grown up in the Beagle Bay mission dormitory. They raised a family in Broome and maintained close links with the Catholic community.

The case of Br Bernhard **Hoffmann**, also one of the pioneers of Beagle Bay, became a traumatic experience for the Limburg motherhouse in the attempt to make convivial financial provision for a dismissed Brother. Hoffmann was a competent master carpenter, who subsequently served in Cameroon where he was referred to as 'Sango Doktor' at Engelberg mission. But 'his apostolic completeness left much to be desired'. He went out drinking dressed in his habit, was seen smoking in the streets of Freising, sent his apprentices to fetch beer and secretly ordered illustrated books (of possibly dubious content), but was always treated leniently.[33] The crunch came in Limburg in 1926, when police intercepted his *poste restante* correspondence with a young woman, which gave rise to the suspicion of human trafficking ('Mädchenhandel' – no further details are

---

30 Brigida Nailon, *Emo and San Salvador*, Brigidine Sisters, Echuca, 2005, Vol. 1, p. 91.
31 Fragebogen, in Sixt, August (Br – Ex), P1 Nr 28, ZAPP.
32 Chris Jeffrey, an Interview with Bernhard Stracke, (age 73), 6 August 1981, Battye Library Oral History Programme, transcript, State Library of Western Australia.
33 Antonia Leugers, *Eine geistliche Unternehmensgeschichte: Die Limburger Pallottiner-Provinz 1892–1932*, EOS Verlag, St Ottilien, 2004, pp. 100, 144, 176.

available in the Limburg archives). The Pallottines managed to suppress prosecution and offered a generous severance package in return for his immediate voluntary resignation from the society in order to stifle negative publicity. A monthly pension of 100 Mark was probably paid for 26 years until Hoffmann took the society to court and achieved an increase to 120 Mark. Within a few years, Hoffmann requested another increase, based on the increased expense of the aged care home in which he now lived approaching 80, but in December 1952 the Provincial sent a stern and final refusal. The next month Hoffmann was dead.

This episode shows how symbiotic the relationship between the society and its members could become. Having invested all their future options, the members of the society felt that they had only the society to fall back on. Even if a member returned to Germany to be near his family, the Pallottine Society was still expected to pay for ambulance, hospital and funeral costs.

It was often difficult to find something to do for ageing Fathers and Brothers who could no longer be useful on missions. A Father might be placed as the assisting priest on a mission station, or become a resident priest in a hospital, where he himself could be cared for. In many cases, they would be repatriated to Limburg where some less strenuous occupation might be found for them; however, after a few decades in foreign mission, the reintegration into the uneventful collective routines of the motherhouse could be difficult.

A few managed to live out their lives on the mission. Br Johannes Graf, the man who was 'of hardly any use to the Society' in Walter's opinion in 1902, lived at Beagle Bay until January 1951. He invented a machine for the mission girls to make brooms out of sorghum (broomcorn) for sale in Broome. For many years, he was in charge of the 500 head of goats, the goat milking and the coconut and banana plantations. He also rang the 5 am mission gong, which was actually a hubcap suspended from his hut. Fr Ernst Worms describes Graf as:

> A gaunt figure with sharp face behind which lurks roguishness, friendliness and piousness. Black beard tinged with grey. Gardener, goatherd, and philosopher besides … He assiduously collected the cattle manure, especially from the goats, on an antediluvian wood cart with massive timber disks as wheels, pulled by the young boys with great commotion. His garden sat across several springs, very peculiar in this dry continent. He constantly adjusted the irrigation. Next to a permanent spring he had

built a small Lourdes grotto which he daily decorated with fresh flowers. Daily for forty years – the meaning of perseverance. … Beneath the eucalypts, on the edge of a glade drawing down to the bay, lay a large tree trunk. 'That's Brother John's place', the children told me. There he prayed in undisturbed silence.[34]

Clearly some Brothers were able to carve out a little private space for themselves on the mission. Br Heinrich **Krallmann** also died at Beagle Bay in June 1951. He was a carpenter and inventive bush mechanic known for his well-digging and wool presses, always with the rosary by his side. One day Krallmann wanted all hands commandeered for the shearing, but Fr Hügel wanted to keep back one of the Brothers for other tasks, to which Krallmann retorted that in that case maybe Fr Hügel himself could help in the shearing shed. Fr Hügel relates, 'At the end of the day my good Br Heinrich came to me, kneeled down and asked for forgiveness'.[35] This incident speaks volumes about the oath of obedience and internal mission hierarchy.

Lifelong commitment, forbearing and melting oneself into the commune were the expectation. Sickness was the only honourable exit from mission service, and there was no provision for old age if one left a Catholic society. Some of the staff felt that they were letting down their families at home through their long absence. Fr Nicholas Emo, for example, became depressive after receiving news of the miserable condition of what were presumed to be his sister and niece.

Another curious case is that of Br Franz Herholz, who achieved dispensation from the Kimberley for health reasons. Herholz arrived home in the midst of the Depression and unemployment of 1933, only to find that after 10 years away he had no claim to public assistance or to a job assignment. His letters from Danzig describe that he was one of 17 siblings whose father had died and his mother had descended into debility. When they lost the family home and were over their ears in debt, one of the younger sons ran amok with a pistol, and the mother tried to drown herself in the river. With three operations behind him, Herholz was not capable of hard work and thought he could work as a water diviner. He sent a hundred begging letters to acquaintances in Germany and overseas, to which he received only three apologetic responses. Clearly

---

34   Handwritten MS (in German) in Worms, Ernst (Pater), P1 Nr 27, ZAPP.
35   P.F. Hügel, 'Memories of Br. Heinrich Krallmann' in Krallmann file, ZAPP.

unable to provide for himself, let alone help others in the family, Herholz still felt it was by the Lord's guidance that he was sent home to watch over his family. His Limburg superiors wisely decided to let this man go, in the interest of the Pallottine society, since 'congenital mental conditions were known to manifest more easily in a religious community'.[36]

Br Rudolf Wollseifer was sent back from the Kimberley to Limburg for what everyone thought should be a deserved rest, but he became torn with misgivings, expressed in a stream of letters, and achieved reposting to the Kimberley. This was an indulgent decision by the Limburg superiors. The St John of God Sisters who nursed Wollseifer at Beagle Bay were also tending to children, leprosy patients and any other medical conditions. They conducted the school and shouldered many other responsibilities. Wollseifer began to feel that he was being neglected and, on a strict diet for his intestinal troubles, that he was being starved to death, after he himself had created such a fruitful garden and had helped to grow the sheep and cattle herds to such bountiful numbers. In his last weeks, Wollseifer was attended by an old Nyul Nyul woman who prayed the rosary and sang with him.

Wollseifer had become a colourful institution at Beagle Bay. According to a description by Fr Ernst Worms, he inhabited a whitewashed cottage with cement floor and plain furniture, in which he suspended tobacco leaves for drying, mostly for his own consumption, since nobody else dared to smoke his 'cuckle-cuckle'. In his earlier days, he was always the first in church for the 5 am morning prayer, and sloshed barefoot along the path to his garden every day, from where he liked to distribute sugarcane as a treat for the children. On Sundays, he also played a trumpet 'mottled with verdigris'. Wollseifer loved music but hardly excelled at it:

> He liked to play the reed organ to accompany the native Christians in the hymns during holy mass. But because he never studied organ-playing and harmony, the right hand would hold the proper melody whereas the left one would flit up and down the keyboard driven more by instinct and without always hitting on the right accompaniment. The pace was fairly idiosyncratic but because he always sang along himself with a loud voice, the song-loving blacks had become used to his peculiar rhythm. Thus hymn after hymn would drawl along in voluptuous length through the holy mass and right up to the blessing to the doubtful exaltation of the

---

36   File annotation, 6 February 1934, Herholz, Franz (Br – Ex), ZAPP.

choral-loving Br. Huegel [whose father was an opera singer in Leipzig] and testing the patience of the most reverend music connoisseur Bishop Raible. But it went on for years.[37]

Br Frank Nissl was also one of those who refused to retire. He celebrated his 80th birthday at Beagle Bay, and in retirement at Millgrove he still hammered away in the shed of his piggery at age 89.[38] He had spent much of his time in the bush working with mission residents, and Fr Byrne recollected about Nissl and his Indigenous aides:

> Whenever I visited them in the bush, it was an uplifting experience. At night they would gather quite naturally to recite the Rosary and the Litany to Our Lady just as they would if they were back at the mission.[39]

Such Brothers refused to be relegated to the role of mere stock workers and saw themselves directly engaged in teaching and preaching.

The problem of retirement was eased after World War II, when priests who were naturalised and retired in Australia could qualify for a government pension. But the Catholic hierarchy was used to making decisions for and on behalf of subordinates, and its superiors were not required to indulge in consultation. Fr Alfons **Bleischwitz** was suddenly pensioned off as soon as he turned 65. He had 25 years of mission service at Balgo (1937–56) and Lombadina (1969–74), as well as a period as director of the Manly college (1956–69), and as parish priest in Wyndham (1974–84). He began to suffer from depression, describing himself as a lonely man, with nobody to talk to. He found Wyndham 'rather depressing', and reflected on the 'sad experiences of the last 25 years': 'Where are we going – where is our religious discipline. Sometimes I think we have thrown everything away because it came from the past and hence it was outmodelled'. The Pallottines were no longer dominating the Catholic presence in the Kimberley, with a Redemptorist parish priest at Kununurra, a Carmelite in Broome and Jesuit students at Balgo, moreover church attendance was minimal: 'Many [priests] find it hard to say mass every day if there are no people there'. The Limburg Provincial Ludwig Münz, who had himself served in Australia, tried to cheer Bleischwitz up and wrote tongue-in-cheek:

---

37 Handwritten MS (in German) in Worms, P1 Nr 27, ZAPP.
38 Byrne, *Hard Road*, p. 109.
39 Byrne, *Hard Road*, p. 110.

You might have great difficulty in spending all that [pension] money in Wyndham. There's only the pub to spend money in. Perhaps you will, at your age, become a RC (regular customer) at the pub.[40]

Bleischwitz yearned for the mission years and the inspiration obtained from the company of fellow religious, such as Frank Nissl, in whose honour he wrote a history of the Balgo mission during his last year in Wyndham. Who better to appreciate the small and large sacrifices made by such men than their own Brethren, particularly as public opinion was turning against them yet again.

Motivation – driven by faith

Even the positive spin of mission newsletters did not promise a comfortable lifestyle. The publicity and recruitment machine made no secret that missionaries faced tropical diseases, natural disasters like floods, droughts and cyclones, and even hunger and starvation (e.g. Zion Hill, **Stradbroke Island**, Daly River, Cape Bedford, Bloomfield). It was clear that they would be remote from facilities such as hospitals, dental care or help for difficult childbirth. They knew they would not be well paid, not comfortably housed and not well supplied with luxuries. Self-advancement could simply not have been a strong motive for volunteering into missions. What drove so many young people into remote mission service?

Only a few academic historians like Katharine Massam and Christine Lockwood patiently engage with the expressions of faith in the mission records, and insist that faith needs, after all, to be taken seriously if we wish to understand what powered the mission movement. As shown in Chapters 1 and 2, Germany had a strong Awakening movement but no empire except for three short decades. The strong religious vocation inspiring these volunteers is reflected in the titles published by missionaries and their confessional historians, such as *My Life and God's Mission* (Johann Flierl), *Led by the Spirit* (John Lümmen), *For Faith and Freedom* (Everard Leske) and *Venture of Faith* (Philipp Scherer).

---

40   Ludwig Münz to Alphonse Bleischwitz, 14 October 1975, and Bleischwitz to Münz, 24 August 1976, in Bleischwitz, Alfons (Pater), P1 Nr 13, ZAPP.

This language of faith, together with the twentieth-century standard lexicon of cultural superiority, can be a taxing fare for today's secular researchers who are plumbing missionary records for historical evidence. Readers who are tempted to slash away expressions of faith that seem to thrive like a jungle of weeds around the hidden gems of historical data may find they are left with very little. A particularly illustrative (and relatively short) example is a letter from a missionary of the pietist Gossner Mission (*Gesellschaft zur Förderung der evangelischen Missionen unter den Heiden*) to New Zealand Bishop G.A. Selwyn requesting the Church of England instructions for his mission on the Chatham Islands in January 1845. To decipher such a handwritten letter to the point where one is relatively confident of having read it correctly can take a few days, but it is easily summarised in a couple of lines: Rev. Franz Schirmeister (who later came to Australia) apologises for his poor English (modelled in some respects on the King James Bible), insists on the common purpose of the Anglican and the Lutheran Church, and continually reiterates his task – the redemption of souls for the greater glory of God:

> My Lord,
>
> Not longer delay we to address our humblest supplications to Your Lordship, steadfastly convinced that Ye, by the love of Christ which dwelleth in You, full indulgence connive our infashioned and imperfect English expression, only regarding the holy interests of the Kingdom of Christ.
>
> Sent out by the "German Mission's Society evangelical for spreading of Christianity among natives of heathen-lands" was pointed out us of the Lord Jesus this Island to workfield by wonderous guidances.
>
> In deepest humbleness supplicate we Your Lordship trustfully; to protect the Mission's work, also, among us; that we, called by the Church of Christ of Germany to be servants and witnesses of Christ Jesus among heathen, under the near and high protection of the Lord Bishop of the Church of Christ of England, may work, by God's grace, the work of the Lord with so much the more confidence and the banner of the holy Cross might be planted in many hearts, that the abundant grace might through the thanksgiving of many redound to the glory of God.
>
> May it please Your Lordship to deliver unto us the Liturgy and the Prayer-book of the Church of England.

> Forgive us, where we have missed the expression and form of a strange tongue. The Spirit of Christ Himself may be our interpreter in the holiest matter, which concerneth the redemption of the souls, who are bought with a precious price.
>
> Of Your Lordhip's lowest servants, F. Schirmeister, German Missionary, in conjunction with four Mission's brethren.

The Prince of the High Anglican Church in New Zealand did not respond (perhaps he had as much trouble reading the letter as I did), so Schirmeister followed up with another note apologising for establishing a mission station so close to the Wesleyans, which he repeatedly asserts was done 'by wonderous guidances of the Lord Jesus', and reaffirming his task 'to save immortal souls by Christ and for Christ', 'so that by our weak labour, prayers and tears may be gathered for him his blood – gain out of our miserable heathen-brethren to their ever-lasting salvation, and the glory of God the Father'.[41]

It is tempting to dismiss the bulwark of scriptural references, expressions of faith and insistence on a common purpose in these letters as mere diplomatic noise. But, taken seriously – as one eventually must when this self-representation emerges again and again – the missionary task is the eternal salvation of as yet unconverted souls and not the material improvement of living conditions, while the ultimate purpose of achieving grace for humans is to serve the greater glory of God, and not, conversely, bringing Christianity to people in order to achieve something for them. The ultimate purpose of mission is not anthropocentric but spiritual, as Christine Lockwood is at pains to explain.

Much more is packaged into this lamentatious message. Non-Christians (heathens) are 'miserable', which means that they are deserving of pity (*misericordia*), and they are brothers, children of the same God, for whom Jesus shed his own blood, so that they must be gathered in to honour that sacrifice. The missionaries sensed that they were taking on an enormous task, a battle that could only be fought and never ultimately won. Therefore, they celebrated small victories, such as a request for baptism, a question about the gospel or a show of affection.

---

41 Letters by Franz Schirmeister at Chatham Island to Bishop Selwyn, 2 January 1845 and 14 April 1845, Gossner G1, 0813, Archiv der Gossner Mission, Evangelisches Landeskirchliches Archiv, Berlin.

Conclusions

Interesting and challenging as the missionary life tended to be portrayed in autobiographies and mission publications, it was also full of hardships, trials, social isolation and criticism. It was not a secure or financially rewarding career, and required skills of adjustment, obedience and community adaptation. Those who were from better-off backgrounds, and from English-speaking ones, rose more easily through the ranks of colonial society. Even missionaries who took a keen interest in science and ethnography, discussed in Chapter 7, were generally treated as repositories of free information rather than as serious interlocutors.

To justify a life of economic dependence, lack of privacy and social isolation, the missionaries had only their faith to fall back on. They were exposed to diseases to which they had no resistance and their daily lives were regimented by the mission bell. There was no after-hours private life, so that their alcohol consumption and sexual conduct were matters for public comment and committee deliberation. The mission societies screened allegations of moral transgressions from public view to protect the reputation of development aid dependent on grassroots support, but sexual misconduct, or allegations of it, generally spelled the end of a mission, or at least of a mission career. Like eco-warriors throwing themselves before a high-powered whaling ship on the open ocean, missionaries were motivated by a set of ideas that had very wide currency, and they were ready to sacrifice for the cause.

7

The German difference

Hitler's men

A man from the Kimberley missions once told me that 'we were educated by Hitler's men'. One of his teachers had been Fr John **Lümmen** at the Pallottine training centre in Rossmoyne, Perth. Lümmen mused that 'I was somehow seen as authoritarian, but how could it be different when I had been a German officer, trained in a German army'.[1]

Certainly, some missionaries in South Africa and New Guinea applauded the Third Reich politics. Christine Winter found that members of the Neuendettelsau Mission Society in Germany became 'intoxicated' with Nazi ideology.[2] However, Nazi policies rendered it increasingly difficult to carry on mission, and a honeymoon period of collaboration ended in increasing attacks on the mission societies. Restrictions on foreign currency exchange hindered the transfer of funds between countries, and the mission colleges were drained of candidates and teachers who were drafted into the military. The Hitler Government pressured the Protestant

---

1   John Luemmen and Brigida Nailon, *Led by the Spirit: Autobiography of Father John Luemmen SAC*, Imprinti Potest Provincial of the Pallottines in Australia, Rossmoyne, 1999, p. 57.
2   Christine Winter, 'The NSDAP stronghold Finschhafen, New Guinea', in Emily Turner-Graham and Christine Winter (eds), *National Socialism in Oceania: A Critical Evaluation of Its Effect and Aftermath*, Peter Lang, Frankfurt am Main, pp. 31–47; Christine Winter, *Looking After One's Own: The Rise of Nationalism and the Politics of the Neuendettelsauer Mission in Australia, New Guinea and Germany (1921–1933)*, Peter Lang Verlag, Frankfurt am Main, 2012.

mission societies to join the Reichskirche (State Church), which ended its assemblies with 'Sieg Heil' instead of prayer, and only the Reichskirche was allowed to conduct collections of donations.

This political landscape gave rise to internal tensions that became particularly evident in the Hermannsburger Missionsgesellschaft (HMG). Its director at Hermannsburg, Christoph Schomerus, disagreed with co-director Winfried Wickert, who was based in South Africa. Wickert's mission stations flew the swastika, performed Horst Wessel's Nazi party anthem *Die Fahne hoch* ('The Flag on High') and sent donations to the Volkswohlfart (people's welfare). Wickert promoted shares in the South African Mercedes Benz subsidiary to circumvent the foreign currency restrictions and to promote the economic goals of the Third Reich. Schomerus expressed concern about Wickert's policy. He feared that embracing the Third Reich ideology was dangerous for the HMG's members abroad, such as in Australia. Many German Lutherans of Jewish descent appealed to the HMG for help with emigration, but with a divided leadership the HMG was unable to assist.[3] In South Africa, the Lutherans splintered, with the South-West Synod joining the Reichskirche, while the Johannesburg Synod held fast to the Lutheran Freikirche (free church).

Eventually, Schomerus resigned from the Reichskirche senate and Nazi pressure on the HMG increased. The HMG newsletter was subjected to censorship and had to be suspended in 1940. The secret state police (Gestapo) refused permission for the mission festival in 1939 on the grounds that it coincided with the NSDAP (National Socialist German Workers' Party) assembly and had not been applied for 'properly'. The HMG festival was rescheduled and this time the premises that Schomerus requested were refused. On the day when the mission festival was finally held, several HMG students received their military call-up.[4]

The Pallottines suffered far more than such bureaucratic bullying. They evacuated their German headquarters to Switzerland, but in Limburg about 60 Pallottines were arrested for refusing military service and 13 imprisoned at Dachau, where Fr Reinisch was beheaded. By late 1942, 50 Pallottines had died, several in concentration camps.[5]

---

3   Ernst-August Lüdemann (ed.), *Vision: Gemeinde weltweit – 150 Jahre Hermannsburger Mission und Ev. Luth. Missionswerk in Niedersachsen*, Verlag der Missionshandlung, Hermannsburg, 2000.
4   Lüdemann, *Vision: Gemeinde weltweit*.
5   Brigida Nailon, *Nothing is Wasted in the Household of God: Vincent Pallotti's Vision in Australia 1901–2001*, Spectrum, Richmond, 2001, pp. 129–30.

The Ehrenbreitstein monastery was looted and destroyed and several Pallottine houses, including the motherhouse in Limburg, had been confiscated and occupied by the Gestapo. It is true that the Pallottines who arrived in Australia after the war had been in uniform, including Bishop John Jobst. Much as most Indigenous people had little choice but to participate in Christian missions, the young German men had little choice but to follow the military call-up of the Third Reich.

Many former mission residents used words like 'strict' and 'tough' to describe their missionaries. In Lümmen's case, even his assistant priest at Riverton, Fr Eugene San (who later rose to Australian Pallottine Regional), 'found Fr. John to be a tough taskmaster'.[6] Cecilia Little also described Lümmen as strict: 'although Fr. John was strict, he was more a mentor to the boys and girls [at Rossmoyne] and many maintained their friendship with him throughout his life'.[7] The Rossmoyne training centre, strongly assimilationist, removed high achieving students from their communities in order to receive training in Perth and produced several students who later rose to prominence as cultural activists: Harold Little became a Western Australian AFL premiership footballer, Peter Yu became chair of the Kimberley Land Council, Jimmy Chi became a well-known playwright, and Steven Albert, also known as actor and musician Baamba, himself became a strong proponent of Aboriginal education – but on the new paradigm of self-determination (see **Lümmen**).

Lümmen was invited to the premiere of Jimmy Chi's award-winning 1990 musical *Bran Nue Dae*, a cheeky take on the mission era. One of its central characters, Father Benedictus, was 'loosely modelled' on Fr John Lümmen, who later recalled Stephen Albert, a main actor in the play, telling him, 'Pop, if we had not learnt discipline at Rossmoyne by you, we would never have been able to go through the training of this play'.[8] At Lümmen's funeral in Perth in January 2014, a large delegation from Broome, including Albert and Chi, were present to pay their final respects. This show of respect sits oddly with the 'Hitler's men' comment. Presumably, the comment was more about the strictness and discipline

---

6   'Father John Lümmen SAC', Obituary read by Fr Eugene San SAC, Kimberley Community Profile, April 2014, p. 13, broomediocese.org/wp-content/uploads/2016/02/KCP-2014-01.pdf (accessed August 2017).
7   Mark Reidy, '**Brand New Day for Fr. John Luemmen**', *The Record*, 9 February 2014.
8   Luemmen and Nailon, *Led by the Spirit*, p. 60.

often shown by former military personnel, and often ascribed to Germans, rather than an allegation of adoration of the Führer and national socialist ideas.

German mission culture

A German flavour is undoubtedly present on the missions supervised by Germans, and such traces of German culture are perhaps more recognisable to those who share it, from the boiled and coloured Easter eggs at **Tardun** to the harvest festival at Hopevale, to *Stille Nacht* resounding through Christmas Eve at **Hermannsburg**. At Hermannsburg, we find reference to the mouth organ, violin, clarinet and zither, and the German women baked Lebkuchen and Springerle (ginger bread and rock ammonia biscuits) and the Christmas trees were decorated with toys, biscuits, sweets and treats. At Tardun in the 1950s, the Catholic Schoenstatt Sisters organised the children for processions just like the German Catholic children at home, carrying self-made paper lanterns for St Martin's Day and candles for occasions such as blessing the crops or blessing a new shrine. On 1 May, they wheeled any carts and wheelbarrows – loaded with teddy-bears – around to the workshops for the blessing of the vehicles on St Joseph's Day, Patron Saint of workers. For Advent, they translated and fervently intoned the *Herbergsuch* ('Searching for Shelter') portraying a pauper searching for shelter and being turned away at each door. The Kimberley children probably understood no more about these rituals than did children like myself in the Catholic villages of rural Germany, who focused only on the little flame we carried in our lantern or on the flower petals we gathered for Corpus Christi, which the Sisters turned into artful flower carpets that were as short-lived as a sand painting in the desert. The Brothers at Beagle Bay played the popular card game of Skat,[9] and Br Johannes **Graf** subjected himself to water cures in the popular tradition of the German Dr **Kneipp**, which seemed radical and harsh to observers. The Brothers in the Kimberley erected Lourdes grottos so popular in German Catholic villages, and built churches on European patterns, in which women sat on one side and men on the other just like at home. The layout of Lutheran missions resembled a German rural village, with the church and public buildings at the centre, surrounded by cottages bordering the fields. The

---

9   Skat takes its name from the Italian *scarto* because some cards are discarded at the beginning of each round.

Moravian missions may have had less of a German outward appearance, but at **Ebenezer** the colony cottages were getting scrubbed every Saturday (in keeping with the German housewifery routine) and at **Ramahyuck** Hagenauer said grace at mealtimes: 'Komm Herr Jesu sei unser Gast und segne was Du bescheret hast'.[10] Occasionally, the missionaries reverted to speaking German to each other so that mission residents would not understand what they were saying,[11] a small privilege most bilingual migrants now and then claim for themselves.

Just like the productive economies of German rural households geared for self-sufficiency, the Lutheran women at Hermannsburg mission baked their own bread, produced Hefekuchen for Sundays and taught the young girls to mend, sew and knit. Cabbages were pickled as sauerkraut; milk from cows, sheep and goats was turned into butter, cheese and quark. From the butchered animals, the men produced mettwurst, leberwurst, blutwurst, speck and schmalz (metwurst, liverwurst, black pudding, smoked ham and drippings).[12] At Beagle Bay, the Brothers competed with each other over who turned out the best sausages.

Another German trait was the practice of homeopathy, a treatment philosophy developed by Dr Samuel Hahnemann in the 1830s, based on the principle *similia similibus curantur* (like cures like). Hermann Vogelsang at Hermannsburg and Pastor Wolfgang Riedel at **Killalpaninna** were practitioners of this self-help appropriate technology, and Pastor Carl Gottfried Hellmuth, Pastor Georg Heidenreich,[13] Pastor Carl Strehlow and Fr Georg Walter also subscribed to it. Johann Flierl reported that his wife cured an ox with homeopathic medicine, and that Dr Johann Zwar at North Rhine and the Tanunda doctors treated mission staff free of charge with homeopathic remedies.[14] In Germany, chemists (apothecaries) still sell homeopathic medicines along with allopathic ones, and herbal remedies such as those based on the medieval teachings of Hildegard von Bingen also enjoy wide medical credibility.

---

10   Franz Barfus, 'A visit to the mission station Ramahyuck at Lake Wellington, Gippsland (Victoria)', 1882, MS 12645, Box 348612, State Library of Victoria.
11   Felicity Jensz, *Moravian Missionaries in the British Colony of Victoria, Australia, 1848–1908: Influential Strangers*, Brill, Leiden, 2010, p. 82.
12   Judy Gale Rechner, *GJ Rechner and His Descendants: Rechner, Fischer/Fisher, Stolz and Reuther Journeys*, Rechner Researchers, Adelaide, 2008, p. 234.
13   St John's Lutheran Church, *100 Years of Grace: St John's Lutheran Church, Bundaberg, Qld.: 1877–1977*, the Church, Bundaberg, 1977.
14   Susanne Froehlich (ed.), *Als Pioniermissionar in das ferne Neu Guinea – Johann Flierls Lebenserinnerungen*, 2 vols, Harrassowitz Verlag, Wiesbaden, 2015, Vol. 1, pp. 150, 188.

Cultural animosities

Cultural differences, of course, went deeper than these visible surface traits, and were not unanimously welcomed. Chapter 2 referred to the Anglo-German bible and mission networks that began to deteriorate from the 1820s and, by the time German-speaking missionaries arrived in Australia after the 1836 Church Act,[15] cultural animosity was already surfacing. Dr Louis Giustiniani commented on the xenophobic colonial society he found at Swan River colony in 1836. He was refused naturalisation and the allocation of mission land, and was driven out of Western Australia in a 'period of intense British nationalism and patriotism'.[16]

At Wellington Valley, too, considerable tension developed from the start between the German and Anglo-Saxon staff. The latter made dismissive comments about Germans, or foreigners in general, who resisted submission to a bishop, and Watson himself 'had from observation not much reason to admire missionary zeal in any German with whom [he] was acquainted', meaning Johann **Handt** and Jakob **Günther**.[17] In 1842, the New South Wales governor withdrew financial support from the two German-staffed missions in the colony and redirected funds towards the efforts of English speakers.[18] This does not look like a mere coincidence. J.D. Lang was criticised for importing German missionaries, and their qualifications were later called into question (see **Zion Hill**). Such tensions continued to fester. In the 1890s, the Immanuel Synod accepted the view that the media campaign against Pastor Carl **Meyer** surrounding a 'crimping incident' at **Bloomfield** (see below) was based on anti-German sentiment, and Meyer's successor, Pastor Johann **Hörlein**, felt that much of the resistance from settlers arose because 'the English gentlemen just don't like this German mission, and where they can harm us it pleases them to the utmost'.[19] Acrimonious differences emerged

---
15   *An Act to promote the building of Churches and Chapels and to provide for the maintenance of Ministers of Religion in New South Wales 1836* (NSW).
16   Lesley J. Borowitzka, 'The Reverend Dr Louis Giustiniani and Anglican conflict in the Swan River Colony, Western Australia 1836–1838', *Journal of Religious History* 35.3 (2011): 357.
17   Third Annual Report of the Apsley Aboriginal Mission, supported & conducted by the Reverend William Watson, 30 December 1843 441898, CSIL, Archival Estrays (DL CSIL/6), cited in Barry John Bridges, 'The Church of England and the Aborigines of New South Wales, 1788–1855', PhD thesis, University of New South Wales, 1978, p. 654.
18   Watson's mission replaced the one jointly run with Günther, while Zion Hill mission was disbanded and Handt was snubbed in favour of an English priest at Moreton Bay.
19   Hörlein to Rechner, 30 August 1891, Immanuel Synod, Bloomfield Mission Correspondence, 1887–89 (henceforth Bloomfield Correspondence), Lutheran Archives Australia (LAA).

between Chief Protector Neville and Bishop Otto **Raible** in Western Australia, between ethnographer Baldwin Spencer and missionary Carl **Strehlow** in the Northern Territory, and between the Rev. Nicholas **Hey** and Commissioner Archibald Meston in Queensland.[20] The Italian Fr Vaccari fared no better with Bishop Polding in the 1840s, and the Italian Passionists explained the tensions between Polding and Vaccari as cultural differences: Vaccari evidently found it difficult to 'exercise that patience which is necessary in dealing with English people'.[21]

Cultural discomfort was mutual. Pastor Hörlein had reservations about the English wife of the mission teacher, because Bloomfield mission was 'supposed to be German Lutheran' and should not be 'stained with an English patina'. Pastor Hey, too, commented in retirement about the university-trained 'English gentlemen' who had succeeded his Brethren at Weipa. They were 'very educated but not suitable for the work' and their wives 'never went out without gloves for fear of being touched'.[22] This comment was after World War I, when several pastors were traumatised by the hostility they had encountered.

An argument often raised during World War I was that the missionaries were spreading 'German sentiments'. This allegation owed much to the language approach of the German missionaries, who translated their German hymns and rhymes into the local languages, with the result that mission residents learned popular German tunes.[23]

Language policy

Most German missionaries felt it best to acquire a local language, for both practical and philosophical reasons. The practical reasons were that most of the newly arriving Germans struggled with English and neither were the mission residents fluent in grammatical English, having become used to the pidgin used in their interactions with colonisers. The common

---

20 Hey, Annual Report for Mapoon for 1910, MF 186, Australian Institute of Aboriginal and Torres Strait Islanders (AIATSIS).
21 Barberi in London to Testa in Rome, 4 May 1847, in Osmund Thorpe, *First Catholic Mission to the Australian Aborigines*, Pellegrini & Co., Sydney, 1950, p. 203.
22 Hey to Hennig, 7 October 1920, Missionsdirektion, Personalakten, Nicolaus Hey, MD825, Archiv der Brüderunität (Herrnhut Archives).
23 A.W. Hurley, 'German-Indigenous musical flows at Ntaria in the 1960s: Tiger Tjalkalyeri's rendition of "Silent Night," or what is tradition anyway?', *Perfect Beat* 15.1 (2014): 7–21.

language was to be the language in which at least most of the mission residents were competent. Competition with English speakers also played into the turn towards the vernacular. Fr Anton **Strele** recommended using a vernacular mission language in the Northern Territory missions because he thought it was just as easy for the Jesuit Fathers to learn a local language than to learn English and '(much more important) the way is kept closed to the [Anglican] ministers'.[24] Until World War I, most Lutheran missions had a substantial German-speaking staff, so that in many cases separate religious services were held in German, and in Indigenous languages. Schooling, too, was attempted in local languages, and missionaries proudly gathered the evidence of vernacular literacy that their students produced in the form of letters, poems or gifts.

The philosophical reason for the turn towards the vernacular is one that has been much emphasised by the Lutheran Church – that it was a fundamental premise of Lutheranism to make the word of God available to peoples in their own language following the example of Martin Luther, who first translated the Bible into German published in 1534. This Lutheran position was reinforced by the German intellectual tradition of the eighteenth century, to which we will return below.

Despite their fundamental cultural commitment to vernacular languages, the case-by-case review below shows that the implementation of this language policy was uneven among the German-speaking missionaries. Colonial governments did not support these efforts of language maintenance and made it a condition of public funding that schools were conducted in English. Also, in several instances, we see that a lack of English as a *lingua franca* must have made it more difficult for Europeans to start learning a vernacular language.

Lutherans in south-east Queensland and northern New South Wales

At **Wellington Valley**, William Watson and Handt began in 1835 to translate short Bible passages and commenced a Wiradjuri grammar and dictionary.[25] However, the school was conducted in English and Watson

---

24   Strele 1884 in Anton Strele, *Annual Letters from the Jesuit Mission in North Australia 1886–1889*, translated by F. Dennett SJ, Archives of the Society of Jesus, Hawthorn.
25   John Harris, *One Blood: 200 Years of Aboriginal Encounter with Christianity: A Story of Hope*, Albatross, Sutherland, NSW, 1990, p. 60.

claimed that his German Brother Handt, who was still struggling with English, was 'desultory' in language acquisition.²⁶ Presumably learning two foreign languages together (English and Wiradjuri) rendered Handt's task more difficult. Later in Brisbane, Handt reputedly helped the Zion Hill missionaries to learn Turrbal. Among the missionaries at Zion Hill in the late 1830s, only Christopher **Eipper** spoke English and was able to learn Yaggera while the others were struggling to learn English and took turns to conduct their religious services in German.²⁷ The Italian Catholic missionaries on **Stradbroke Island**, who also lacked English save for the Swiss member Joseph Snell, were unsuccessful in acquiring a local language.

South Australian Lutherans

However, things stood differently with their contemporaries in South Australia. C.G. **Teichelmann** and C.W. **Schürmann** from the Dresden Mission Society arrived with a sound background in languages, including English, and quickly learned Kaurna. Within 18 months of arrival in Adelaide, they published a substantial vocabulary with a sketch grammar and sentences. Teichelmann continued this work with a substantial grammatical manuscript. At the Piltawodli school Schürmann taught in Kaurna (1839), and both missionaries translated German hymns into Kaurna. The governor closed this school in 1845 and transferred the children to the government 'Native School' where all instruction was in English (see **Piltawodli**). Subsequently, the Dresden missionaries continued to pioneer language work. Schürmann documented the Parnkalla language at Port Lincoln, and **A.E. Meyer** began work on the Ramindjeri (see **Encounter Bay**). Their linguistic methods employed with Kaurna, Parnkalla and Ramindjeri were adopted by others, including the Lutheran missionaries working on Dieri, and Protector **Matthew Moorhouse** and John Weatherstone working on the Ngayawang language on the River Murray.²⁸ Linguist Rob Amery and his students and colleagues in Adelaide have also put the records of these missionaries to good use. Amery drove the project for language reclamation resulting in

---

26   Bridges, 'The Church of England and the Aborigines of New South Wales', pp. 413–14.
27   Yaggera is also spelled as Jagara, Jagera, Yuggera. Turrbal is spelt as Turrubul, Dyirbal.
28   Rob Amery, 'Piltawodli', German Missionaries in Australia, Griffith University, missionaries. griffith.edu.au.

the re-emergence of fluent speakers and the reintroduction of the Kaurna language into public life in Adelaide.[29] Amery maintains that 'The real success of the German missionaries lay in their linguistic work'.[30]

The Far North

The Italian Catholic Fr Angelo Confalonieri also left a significant legacy for language research. During his short period at Port Essington (1846–48), he began to document the Iwaidja language and translated prayers and parts of the New Testament. He produced a dictionary and a tribal areas map. Many of the terms Confalonieri gathered were actually Macassan words such as Limba Piu for a place the Macassans called Limba Peo ('mud bay' – near Cape Don), or Limba Bina for the Macassan Lemba Binangaja (literally 'river bay', aka Trepang Bay).[31] Linguist Nicholas Evans used this work to examine linguistic adaptations of Macassan words and found the Iwaidja languages to be the linguistic equivalent of a well-stratified archaeological site. Evans was able to identify four distinct historical layers in the adoption of Macassan loanwords and suggests that the earliest adaptations occurred before the split between the Mawng and Iwaidja languages, which means over a millenium ago, and well beyond the timeframe of Macassan–Australian contacts currently accepted.[32] Like so much early language work, the use to which this work has been put far exceeds the hopes originally invested in it.

Moravian missions in Victoria

The Moravian missionaries worked in association with the Presbyterian Church and spent much less effort on local languages. At **Lake Condah**, formed in 1867, a board teacher arrived in 1871 and taught in English. At Ebenezer, the children of settlers and missionaries attended school together with Aboriginal children, and references to Jardwadjali are scarce. According to Werner, the missionaries instructed in 'simple English',

---

29 '**Language revival**: Securing the future of endangered languages', University of Adelaide.
30 See Rob Amery, *Warrabarna Kaurna! Reclaiming an Australian Language,* Swets & Zeitlinger, Lisse, Netherlands, 2000.
31 Regina Ganter, Julia Martinez and Gary Lee, *Mixed Relations: Asian–Aboriginal Contact in North Australia*, UWA Publishing, Crawley, 2006; Stefano Girola, 'Fr. Confalonieri's Legacy in the Australian Church', *L'Osservatore Romano*, Weekly Edition in English, 28 October 2009.
32 Nicholas Evans, 'Macassan loans and linguistic stratification in western Arnhem Land', in Patrick McConvell and Nicholas Evans (eds), *Archaeology and Linguistics: Aboriginal Australia in Global Perspective*, Oxford University Press, Melbourne, 1997, pp. 237–60.

and Friedrich Hagenauer, Adolf Hartmann and J.F.W. Spieseke collated word lists, but did not embark on translations.[33] However, Spieseke was able to translate a 'hymn' composed by Nathanael Pepper (presumably in a Wergaia language, see Chapter 5). At Ramahyuck, the school was conducted on the government curriculum in English and excelled on all registers. At **Mapoon**, Rev. Nicholas Hey published a Nggerikudi grammar in 1903, but the children are reported as learning English hymns in 1893, and the German wife of Pastor Edwin Brown became the government-funded schoolteacher in 1909, which must mean that she also taught in English.

Central Australian Lutherans

At Killalpaninna, all the Lutheran missionaries were expected to learn Dieri (Dyari). Within three years of arrival in 1866, the first HMG-trained missionaries published a tiny reader with catechism for use by the staff, and with the help of this booklet even the lay assistants Heinrich Vogelsang and Ernst Jakob at Kopperamanna and Etadunna outstations held daily prayers and Sunday service in Dieri. Pastor Johann Flierl described Dieri and Aumeni as closely related dialects along Cooper's Creek, while the languages that the Dieri called Wonkangpara and Wonkanguru (*Wongkan* meaning 'language' and *uru* meaning 'other') were spoken from Salt Creek and Kalakupa Creek to Lake Eyre and into Queensland. Flierl had a universal primer printed in 1880 with a simplified form of Luther's small catechism and some Bible stories, including 'a few songs that had grown out of our sandhills'. It also included a few popular rhymes, such as the children's evening prayer 'Müde bin ich geh zur Ruh, mache meine Äuglein zu', which became 'Matja ngani mokali, moka turala anai'.[34] These efforts produced a generation of literate Dieri speakers. By the time Johannes **Pingilina** left Killalpaninna in 1886, he was perfectly literate in written Dieri.

---

33   August Bernhard Werner, *Early Mission Work at Antwerp Victoria*, Banner Print, Dimboola, 1959, p. 1.
34   Froehlich, *Pioniermissionar*, Vol. I, p. 225; Everard Leske, *For Faith and Freedom: The Story of Lutherans and Lutheranism in Australia 1838–1996*, Open Book publishers, Adelaide, 1996, p. 98. The well-known children's evening prayer 'Müde bin ich geh zur Ruh' is part of the spiritual opus of Luise Hensel (1798–1876), a well-connected friend of Clemens Brentano.

A complete translation of the New Testament went into print in 1898 (produced by Georg **Reuther** and Carl **Strehlow**), which was the first complete translation of the New Testament into any Australian language. On Sundays, Reuther preached first in Dieri and then in German. The school at Cooper's Creek (later Killalpaninna) included the children of the missionaries and at least some of the instruction was in German until H.J. Hillier became schoolteacher (1892–1905) and, according to Christine Stevens, all classes were conducted in English from then on.[35] Linguist Luise Hercus, who engaged in great detail with the Dieri language material produced by the Lutherans, noticed that new words quickly disappear from a language once culture contact is over. For example, the Dieri word for sourdough bread, which was translated as meaning 'eyes locked up', is no longer understood among Dieri speakers.[36]

It was much the same at Hermannsburg, where Pastor A.H. Kempe in 1875 had settled on Aranda (Arrernte) as the most dominant language around the mission. Christine Stevens claims that when Harry Hillier arrived as teacher at Hermannsburg (circa 1906–10), there was a German classroom and an Aranda classroom, and Aboriginal people learned both German and English.[37] Certainly, a separate Sunday sermon was delivered in German for the mission staff.[38] However, school instruction for Indigenous children was in Aranda. Kempe had printed an Aranda reader within five years of his arrival, and a decade later (1891) the HMG printed a substantial book with Bible texts, songs, prayers and catechism. Carl Strehlow, who was at Hermannsburg from 1894 to 1922, continued the work of Kempe. Strehlow translated parts of the Bible and produced a complete translation of the New Testament. Strehlow strained to correct the oft-repeated allegation that Aranda children were taught in German and insisted that they were only ever taught in Aranda and English.

---

35   Christine Stevens, *White Man's Dreaming: Killalpaninna Mission, 1866–1915*, Oxford University Press, Melbourne, 1994, p. 143.
36   Luise Hercus, 'Reuther's Diari: Looking at the Detail', paper presented at The German Anthropological Tradition in Australia, Nicolas Peterson and Anna Kenny, ANU, 18–19 June 2015.
37   Stevens, *White Man's Dreaming*, p. 143.
38   On 18 November 1901 (Wettengel to Kaibel), Immanuel Synod, FRM Box 5, Correspondence Wettengel (transcriptions and translations).

North Queensland Lutherans

The Lutheran missionaries in Queensland had much less impact on language conservation. The Danish/German committee in charge of **Mari Yamba** mission near Prosperine insisted on teaching in English (and reporting in German as well as in Danish) while the Lutherans further north struggled against government policy. The missionaries at Hopevale (**Cape Bedford**) and Bloomfield River tried briefly to introduce German and a vernacular as the language of instruction. Pastor C.A. Meyer arrived with the Dieri Johannes Pingilina to help with learning Guugu-Yimidhirr at Hopevale, and subsequently Pingilina taught in Guugu-Yimidhirr with Pastor J.G. Pfalzer. But then Meyer took Pingilina to Bloomfield (1887–92) where he translated some Bible stories into Kuku Yalanji. The Bloomfield school was conducted by lay helper Ernst Jesnowski in English from about 1887 to 1890, in German from about 1891 to 1895, and in English by Pastor Christian Mack from 1895 to 1900.

After Meyer and Pfalzer left Hopevale, Pastors Georg Schwarz and Wilhelm Poland were also teaching in Guugu-Yimidhirr with the help of some older mission girls until the police magistrate threatened in 1890 to withdraw the subsidy unless English was taught. The Hopevale subsidy was indeed withdrawn in 1893 over another policy issue, and this made room to teach in whatever language the teachers saw fit, including German, Guugu-Yimidhirr and English. In 1898, the director of the Neuendettelsau Mission Society received a beautifully composed letter in Guugu-Yimidhirr from one of the mission girls (see Cape Bedford). In 1900, an English-speaking government schoolteacher arrived and the language question was settled.

Catholics in the north

On the **Daly River**, the Austrian Jesuits taught in Malak-Malak for nearly a decade (circa 1886 to May 1895) until the amalgamation of language groups and the shrinking populations of native speakers rendered this unviable. Meanwhile, Fr Nicholas **Emo** compiled a Spanish dictionary and small grammar of the Yawuru of Broome, and the French Trappist Fr Alphonse Tachon, who learned Nyul-Nyul in Derby in 1890, began to preach in Nyul-Nyul at **Beagle Bay**. The German Pallottine Fr Joseph **Bischofs** (who was at Broome and Beagle Bay from 1905 to 1920) observed that some of the words the Trappists had gathered were not familiar to the Beagle Bay residents and must be from the language of **Disaster Bay**.[39]

Under the Pallottine watch, the Beagle Bay mission residents sang 'Fürst des Waldes' in Nyul-Nyul and 'Wacht am Rhein' in English, and the Australian Institute of Aboriginal and Torres Strait Islanders (AIATSIS) also holds recordings of German songs with accordion accompaniment from 1910.[40] Here, too, the language of instruction had shifted to English by the 1920s, under pressure from the government and the force of population changes as children were removed from various language regions to Beagle Bay.

Nevertheless, in the 1930s, Bishop Raible engaged two linguists to support the missionary work in the Kimberley. Fr Ernst **Worms** SAC arrived in November 1930 and began working on the Yawuru language in Broome under the guidance of his mentor Hermann **Nekes** in Limburg. Worms spoke German, English, French and Latin, and was very awake to the cultural influences and dramatic changes being wrought on the Kimberley communities by the lugger industries that brought so many Asians to the northern ports and provided easy mobility for its Indigenous workers. Broome, in particular, had become a second home to many workers from Timor, Roti and other nearby islands.[41] By May 1933, Worms urgently requested a Malay grammar. Dr Hermann Nekes SAC, known for his work in Cameroon on tonology and foreign influences in the Bantu languages, arrived in 1935 and brought with him sophisticated phonographic equipment provided by Dr Marius Schneider from the sound archives of Berlin's ethnographic museum. The Völkerkundemuseum already held prewar recordings from Beagle Bay, and Worms and Nekes sent at least nine more wax cylinders with transcriptions and partial translations of songs to Schneider.[42]

---

39   Joseph Bischofs SAC, The Pious Society of Missions, Milwaukee (Wisconsin), to Pater Nekes, 28 November 1927 in Nekes, Hermann (Pater), P1 Nr 16, Zentralarchiv der Pallottinerprovinz (ZAPP).
40   North-West Australian phonograms recorded by Beagle Bay missionaries, 1910. Ellis was informed that the sound recordings held at the Museum für Völkerkunde in Berlin may have been produced by Hermann Klaatsch. Catherine J. Ellis, Report to AIATSIS on research in Germany during study leave 1990, unpublished MS, PMS 4981, AIATSIS.
41   Sarah Yu, 'Broome Creole Aboriginal and Asian partnerships along the Kimberley Coast', in Regina Ganter (ed.), *Asians in Australian History, Queensland Review* 6.2 (1999): 49–73.
42   Ellis, Report to AIATSIS on research in Germany during study leave 1990, AIATSIS.

Their language work quickly overtook the purpose intended by Raible. Nekes produced a Nyul-Nyul translation of the Pater Noster and Ave Maria,[43] but his energies were vested in a grammar and dictionary of Nyul-Nyul and related languages, and Worms eventually became more interested in ethnography. By April 1939, it already became evident that their large emerging dictionary manuscript of 2,590 handwritten pages, with an etymology of close to 7,000 words, would be difficult to place with a publisher in Australia. Their magnus opus on *Australian Languages* was completed in January 1946, and it took until 1953 for it to appear in microform, and until 2006 to be re-edited and published as a book (with CD-ROM). Nekes conducted his work in German, using German phonetics, and then translated it into English, and his work was not very well-received by Australian scholars. A review of his 1938 article mentioned only that it was a 'long piece' and that his editor, anthropologist A.P. Elkin, corrected Nekes' spelling of Nyol-Nyol to Nyul-Nyul. Worms, too, gradually shifted from the Anthropos alphabet, which was unpopular with English speakers, in order to approximate the forms used by English-speaking anthropologists. Bill McGregor, who carefully edited the 2006 republication, found Worms' spelling to be inconsistent and points out that Worms himself did not master any of the Kimberley languages.[44]

The linguistic efforts of the Catholics in the Kimberley have been substantial. The monastic lifestyle of Catholic orders has always been able to support intellectual and cultural pursuits, and under Bishop Raible the Pallottines had enough Brothers to afford such a division of labour. In the 1950s, Pallottines at **La Grange** mission still tried to engage with local languages. Fr Kevin McKelson translated the Lord's Prayer into five local languages and 'Silent Night' into Njanumada. He also published a booklet of prayers in the local languages, a collection of Bible stories and an outline of the kinship terms in the community languages.[45] By this time, the faith-based Summer Institute of Linguistics was becoming interested in Pacific languages and has since done an enormous amount of work on Aboriginal languages.

---

43 Hermann Nekes, Kimberleys language material: Daro, Nol Nol etc., 1931–47, MS 35, AIATSIS.
44 William B. McGregor, '**Frs. Hermann Nekes and Ernest Worms's Dictionary of Australian Languages**, part III of Australian Languages (1953)', in Ilana Mushin (ed.), Proceedings of the 2004 Conference of the Australian Linguistics Society; William B. McGregor, 'Frs. Hermann Nekes and Ernest Worms's "Australian languages"', *Anthropos* 102.1 (2007): 99–114.
45 Margaret Zucker, *From Patrons to Partners, A History of the Catholic Church in the Kimberley 1884–1984*, University of Notre Dame Press, Broome, 1994, p. 177.

All of this makes a checkerboard of German approaches to language, arising from denominational differences, but also from the social environment of the missions. Still, in general, German-speaking missionaries were more likely to acquire local languages and promote literacy in vernacular languages rather than English. Lutherans claim a particular reputation for acquiring local languages in order to translate the Bible and other religious texts into Indigenous language, but in fact only two complete translations of the New Testament were undertaken by the Lutheran missionaries in Australia, into Dieri and Aranda. Meanwhile, non-Lutheran missionaries also engaged to significant degrees with Indigenous languages, including partial Bible translations. The German Moravians, who collaborated with the Presbyterian Church, were much less preoccupied with vernacular languages, while the German Catholics were less concerned about Bible translations. In what sense, then, can we speak of a 'German difference'?

German training

Several authors have observed that the German-speaking and Anglophone traditions emerged from vastly different philosophical and cultural assumptions. While British thought was deeply influenced by John Locke and John Stuart Mill, the German-speaking intelligentsia bore the imprint of Kantian idealism, Hegelian metaphysics and cultural romanticism. These broader intellectual traditions favoured an emphasis on philology and linguistics among German speakers, while among English speakers the emphasis was on political economy and utilitarian explanations of culture. The cultural romanticism of Wolfgang von Goethe and Johann Gottlieb Herder emphasised the validity of folk traditions as important cultural phenomena worthy of study and conservation, and inspired important collections of folk songs and folk traditions. Herder and Wilhelm von Humboldt formulated the centrality of language in the cultural traditions that are defining features of nations, positing language as the 'soul of the people'. From this arose a strong and lasting philological orientation in German education, and serious academic interest in folk cultures and their regional variations.

These different philosophical traditions were embedded in different political circumstances. Whereas the German Empire referred primarily to forging a nation out of disparate states, the idea of the British Empire referred primarily to colonialism. These settings produced different imaginaries of the indigenous that are decipherable in the practice of anthropology and particularly in the approach to ideas of evolution. The Anglophone engagement with indigenes was mediated primarily through settler societies, and Paul Turnbull observes that both polygenist and Darwinist approaches to evolution resonated well with that experience in predicting the demise of Indigenous populations.[46] G.W. Stocking points out that in Germany debates about racial difference acquired their particular salience from debates over the nature of Jews – Europe's internal Other. The 'Jewish question' was how to account for physical, cultural and social differences between Jews and Gentiles. Such questions could not be approached with evolutionary thought, neither did the polygenist explanation of cultural difference gain much traction in Germany.[47]

The production of anthropological knowledge was never a disinterested enterprise but tied to intellectual fashions, religious conversion and administrative governance. Evolutionary thought gripped the Anglo-Saxon intelligentsia after the 1859 publication of Charles Darwin's *Origin of Species*, whereas it did not become as dominant in German-speaking circles. The functionalist explanation of culture in British thought led to a static view of societies, so that most British anthropologists embraced the idea of gradual cultural evolution, whereas German speakers, including missionaries Worms and Strehlow, tended to favour the more dynamic and interactionist *Kulturkreise* (cultural circles) view of cultures promoted by Fr Wilhelm Schmidt as editor of the *Anthropos* journal.

German science contributed a wealth of research, in particular on Indigenous Australian body morphology, life-ways and culture, and to anthropology in general. But rivalry and debate over evolution tended to eclipse the influences of leading figures in Germany like Rudolf Virchow, Adolf Bastian, Ernst Häckel and Hermann Klaatsch. Alfred Haddon's *History of Anthropology* in 1910 gave short shrift to Virchow and studiously ignored the 'four-field anthropology' implemented by Franz Boas in 1899 at Columbia University. German speakers continued to distinguish between 'anthropology' arising from medicine and 'ethnology' arising from 'Völkerkunde' (the study of local folklore). In English usage, on the other hand, 'anthropology' became an umbrella

---

46   Paul Turnbull, 'British anthropological thought in colonial practice: The appropriation of Indigenous Australian bodies, 1860–1880', in Bronwen Douglas and Chris Ballard (eds), *Foreign Bodies: Oceania and the Science of Race 1750–1940*, ANU E Press, Canberra, 2008, pp. 205–28.
47   George Stocking, *Functionalism Historicized: Essays on British Social Anthropology*, University of Wisconsin Press, Madison, 1984, p. 5.

term accommodating both physical and cultural anthropology. Barbara Murray finds that such differences are also discernible in the different instructions to scientific travellers given in German and English in the nineteenth century.[48] Susanne Zantop adds that Germans gained particular unpopularity because with a very truncated German colonial period Germans could afford to 'sit on the sidelines' and felt 'free to critique other colonial powers'.[49]

Walter Veit also discerns deep-running cultural differences. He observes that due to significant differences in the hermeneutic conditions of the two language environments, 'German writings are read differently in Australia than in German-speaking countries'.[50] Veit's edited collections have done much to render the German missionaries interesting in the Australian field, and Anna Kenny followed up with her detailed examination of Carl Strehlow, showing how much Strehlow's work and approach owes to German scientific preoccupations.[51] The same might be said about Ernst Worms, Georg Reuther and Otto **Siebert**.[52]

And yet, when we look at overall patterns rather than striking instances, the 'German difference' seems to dissipate under the gaze of historical empiricism. In practice, the demands of mission work made it difficult to pursue scholarly interests. First, missions were notoriously underfunded and had to generate income, therefore much of a pastor's attention was directed at productive activities and farm and station management. Chapter 6 showed that the missionary life was a busy one even without conducting research.

---

48 Barbara Murray, 'Georg Balthasar von Neumayer's directives for scientific research', in Walter Veit (ed.), *The Struggle for Souls and Science: Constructing the Fifth Continent: German Missionaries and Scientists in Australia*, Occasional Paper No. 3, Strehlow Research Centre, Alice Springs, 2004, pp. 130–42.
49 Susanne Zantop, *Colonial Fantasies: Conquest, Family and Nation in Precolonial Germany, 1770–187*, Duke University Press, Durham, NC, 1997.
50 Walter Veit (ed.), *The Struggle for Souls and Science: Constructing the Fifth Continent: German Missionaries and Scientists in Australia*, Occasional Paper No. 3, Strehlow Research Centre, Alice Springs, 2004, p. 92; and Veit collection on Strehlow.
51 Anna Kenny, *The Aranda's Pepa: An Introduction to Carl Strehlow's Masterpiece Die Aranda- und Loritja-Stämme in Zentral-Australien (1907–1920)*, ANU Press, Canberra, 2013.
52 See, for example, Regina Ganter, 'Historicising culture: Father Ernst Worms and the German anthropological traditions', in Nicolas Peterson and Anna Kenny (eds), *German Ethnography in Australia*, ANU Press, Canberra, 2017, pp. 357–79; Regina Ganter, 'Too hot to handle: A German missionary's struggle with ethnography in Australia', *Zeitschrift für Australienstudien* 31 (2017): 57–71.

Second, the committees that oversaw and financially supported the Lutheran missions included lay members of the rural German immigrant communities. Such committees chastised missionaries like Reuther and Siebert, who were interested in ethnographic work beyond the immediate purpose of conversion, for recording 'useless fables'.[53] Indeed, these migrant struggle-towns could not be expected to fund original research of national importance.

Third, missionary training was not conducive to scholastic work, because it was designed as a shortcut to ordination. Chapter 2 showed how the curricula of the German missionary training colleges inflated from very basic to more philological instruction under the pressure to teach Bible languages as a preparation for ordination. As a result, the ordained missionary priests were generally well trained and multilingual, which equipped them for language and translation work. But this only gave them the tools to acquire yet more languages that they needed in their mission field. They might speak Latin but not English, and they had no training in Indigenous languages.

They also had no training in understanding Indigenous cultures. The emerging science of anthropology generally treated missionaries as suppliers of data rather than partners in scientific debate, so missionaries had only the yardsticks of Christian morality to fall back on when forming opinions about Indigenous cultural traits. Bishop **Gsell** commented that he would have found anthropological advice very helpful, had it been available when he arrived in the north.

In fact, on the topic of training, the missionaries also did not bring the practical skills necessary to generate income through tropical or arid zone agriculture and in the seminaries they neither learned to ride a horse nor shoot a gun. Most skills were acquired on the job.

---

53   'Wenn Du für die dicken Stöße Lügenden & Fabeln, welche Du zurecht geschrieben hast, die keinem Menschen etwas nützen – wer wird das Geld zum Drucken daran wenden? – uns monatlich kurze Nachrichten zukommen ließest, erfülltest Du Deine Pflicht, befriedigtest uns und tätest etwas Nützliches.' [If only you would send us some brief monthly reports instead of the fat reams of lies and fables which you write up and which are of no use to anybody – who will spend the money for printing that? – then you would be fulfilling your duty, satisfy us and do something useful.] Kaibel to Reuther, 18 February 1904, Immanuel Synod, Bethesda Mission Box 19, LAA.

Strong-armed intervention

Mission leaders like the Lutheran Pastor Strehlow, the Catholic Fr Gsell or the Moravian Rev. Hey identified problematic trends in Indigenous well-being and diagnosed their causes on the basis of their own training. They mostly felt helpless to address the violence exerted by the settler society and its state apparatus because they themselves were at the mercy and indulgence of the state, and their home organisations would not tolerate political agitation. They focused on the violence that arose from traditional practices and beliefs: revenge killing and ritual violence, infanticide and abortion, child marriage and domestic violence. This the missionaries felt empowered to address both by the state and by the church, and their strong-armed interventions into traditional societies have earned them the main weight of the criticism levelled against them.

Gsell came under criticism for his intervention in child marriages. He purchased the conjugal rights of the girls he took into the mission to release them and their future children from traditional marriage promises. This was a major intervention into a social structure already under pressure from colonial contact. German missiologist Corinna Erckenbrecht calls Gsell's marriage policy 'one of the most bizarre testimonies of overseas mission history'.[54] Recent international interventions in child marriages have not been subjected to such criticism. The detrimental impact of child marriage on health, well-being and education is now well documented, and the United Nations considers child marriage as a violation of human rights. A broad alliance of organisations now pledges to eradicate child marriage. Plan International claims that every two seconds a girl is forced into child marriage, and has implemented the 'Because I am a Girl' movement 'to enable millions of girls to avoid early and forced marriage, stay in school and benefit from a quality education'.[55] A whole raft of development aid agencies, including Red Cross, World Vision, CARE, Good Shepherd and Global Giving currently conduct fundraising campaigns against global child marriage under the slogan: 'It is wrong. It is illegal. But it happens'. Under the impact of neoliberal ideas on

---

54   Diane Bell, *Daughters of the Dreaming*, George Allen & Unwin, Sydney, 1983; Jane C. Goodale, *Tiwi Wives: A Study of the Women of Melville Island, North Australia*, University of Washington Press, Seattle, 1971; Corinna Erckenbrecht, 'Der Bischof mit seinen 150 Bräuten', *Jahrbuch des Museums für Völkerkunde Leipzig* 41 (2003): 303–22.
55   Plan International – Because I'm a Girl – '**Child Marriage**'.

gender equality, human rights and the rights of the child, public attitudes towards strong-armed intervention in what are diagnosed as dysfunctional societies have come full circle.

Gsell, too, wanted to enable girls to 'avoid early and forced marriage, stay in school and benefit from a quality education'. But the missionaries were attempting to implement such human rights before they were formulated in international charters that provided the international finance to protect them. At any rate, the missionaries are not so much criticised for what they tried to do, but for how they went about it. The one attitude for which they have still not been forgiven is their paternalism.

In the twenty-first century, all the mistakes of the nineteenth-century missionaries were repeated with the Northern Territory Intervention designed by the conservative government of John Howard in 2007. It meant to address child abuse in Indigenous communities by sending in the military and quarantining welfare cheques to cover 'first things first' (rent, food and bills), regardless of the parenting style of different families. This strong-arm, top-down approach was entirely devoid of local consultation and targeted people not by need or by deed, but by race, so that the *Racial Discrimination Act 1975* (Cth) had to be actually suspended to implement the scheme. It caused a storm of national and international criticism. In this case, it cannot be claimed that the anthropological know-how was not available, or that the Zeitgeist tolerated paternalism.

Discipline and punishment

So strongly entrenched was the parent/child image in the humanist imagination that mission societies took it for granted that their missionaries had a 'paternal right of punishment' over the adult and minor population on missions.[56] Physical punishment was ingrained in the idea of 'upbringing' – the German word *Erziehung* literally means pulling up, not as Indigenous people generally say 'rearing up', which denotes nurturing. One must wonder about the character formation provided by the training methods of Louis Harms at the HMG, for example, who treated his candidates as his children and required them to thank him for the punishments he meted out to them. Not only physical punishment,

---

56 W.H. Ryder (Under Secretary) to P. Robertson, Presbyterian Church Brisbane, R15.V.II.a.3, Herrnhut Archives.

but also public humiliation comes into play – the bending of the body and the spirit, the breaking of resistance and sense of self: techniques perfected in military training, concentration camps and other total institutions.

The meanings of punishment

Body discipline, a central plank of Western European pedagogy in the nineteenth century, was also used in the workplace, particularly on apprentices, who were typically younger than their masters and stood in an inferior relationship to them. The cattle stations also meted out punishment, as Hermannsburg residents told Pastor Strehlow. Strehlow observed that 'before our time they were mauled and educated with the whip or cane' meaning that Indigenous people were already exposed to physical punishment by settlers before they came to the mission.[57] At home it was a phenomenon of patriarchy, but in the colonial context corporal punishment became an extension of colonial violence. On missions, where the state apparatus that could enforce the colonial order was usually far out of reach, physical punishment was the most fundamental expression of hierarchy and authority. Therefore, counter-hegemonic violence could not be tolerated, such as a pupil hitting a teacher (Mrs Ward at Mapoon), or a Brother hitting a Father (Fr Walter at Beagle Bay) or a lay assistant hitting a pastor (Pastor Mack at Bloomfield). Whether on a mission or in a nation state, violence exerted by authority was deemed legitimate, whereas counter-hegemonic violence was rebellious, illegitimate, offensive and punishable. Social distance on missions was scaffolded with a hierarchy of mission superior, assistant priest, lay helpers, wives or Sisters, and gradations between Indigenous people – Christians, colony residents, camp dwellers and occasional visitors. These social circles also occupied definable spaces on the mission. Hierarchical relationships were propagated with restricted access zones such as altars, vestries or the mission house. Jane Lydon has examined the socio-spatial arrangement of Ebenezer mission.[58]

---

57 'Zum andern sind sie vor unserer Zeit mit der Peitsche oder Stock traktiert u. erzogen worden, wie sie uns selber gesagt haben.' Carl Strehlow in the letter from Carl and Frieda Strehlow to Pastor Rechner and his wife, 26 February 1898, Immanuel Synod, FRM Box 3, Correspondence 1895–99, LAA.
58 Jane Lydon, *Fantastic Dreaming: The Archaeology of an Aboriginal Mission*, Rowman AltaMira Press, Lanham, MD, 2009.

Physical discipline and punishment was also central to Indigenous law enforcement. Missionaries strongly objected to violence based on Indigenous custom and often heroically inserted themselves in tribal fights or family retribution. In the European moral compass, violence should not be exerted by men against women, or against defenceless bodies, except by authority. The suppression of ritual violence was a denial of Indigenous authority. It asserted both a new morality and a new authority.

Missionaries understood themselves as the liberators and protectors of Aboriginal women. Lisa Curtis-Wendlandt agrees that male violence towards women was endemic in the traditional societies of the Hermannsburg region, for example, but argues that the mission regime actually reinforced the subordination of women by confining them to a closed community and therefore exposing them even more to the physical violence of their husbands.[59] With the mission records as my major source, I am unable to comment on this interesting observation except to point out that missionaries did not force women to stay on missions unless they had been brought in by police, and that patriarchal chains of command are not a credible mechanism for the liberation of women.

Also in the European moral compass, the corporal punishment of adults was degrading, while the corporal chastisement of children was character forming. Indigenous societies, in complete reversal, were comfortable with the physical punishment of adults, including women, but not of helpless little children who could not yet be expected to know all the laws and rules. They considered corporal punishment of children as abusive.

Different ideas about the legitimacy of various types of corporal punishment (hitting, spearing, axing or killing versus caning, beating, shaving, chaining or tarring) posed irreconcilable cultural differences between missionaries and Indigenous people. Like most missionaries, Frieda Strehlow was convinced that 'the local blacks cannot be educated entirely without beatings', and often called on her husband to intervene 'if necessary with beatings'.[60] Similar comments can be gleaned from most mission histories, but, in general, physical punishment was an unspoken, taken for granted aspect of mission life.

---

59   Lisa Curtis-Wendlandt, 'Corporal punishment and moral reform at Hermannsburg mission', *History Australia* 7.1 (2010): 7.1–7.17.
60   Letter from Frieda Strehlow to Frau Inspektor [Magda Deinzer], undated [after July 1899], Carl Strehlow Correspondence 1898–99, Strehlow Research Centre, cited in Curtis-Wendlandt, 'Corporal punishment and moral reform at Hermannsburg mission', note 11.

Hitting children and child abuse

The mission diaries and correspondence only mention corporal punishment if it resulted in some rebellious response (such as the frequent absconding on the Daly River), led to a public inquiry (such as at Mapoon) or could be narrated as an amusing incident. For example, at Hermannsburg Carl Strehlow found that the schoolboys who had missed some days of school already anticipated punishment and came dressed in multiple layers of clothing to soften to blows of the cane:

> Since this idleness became more and more prevalent, I first used the cane. This method achieved the desired success for some time. They tried to weaken the impact of it by wearing multiple items of clothing over one another. One day, I arrive at the school; it is a hot summer's day; sweat erupts from every pore. There, some of the boys sit on their benches, dressed as if it was icy cold ... of course, these are the wrongdoers who had missed school for a few days and had already prepared for the anticipated punishment.[61]

Child-rearing issues were particularly contentious. Chapter 5 cited threats of violence against missionaries over the question of children at Stradbroke Island and Hermannsburg, and to protest responses on the Daly River missions. Missionaries often found Indigenous parents too indulgent, like Pastor F.W. Albrecht during his first year at Hermannsburg:

> In front of the dining hall the usual uproar. There the women sit with their little ones who cry most awfully. I think all these little fellows are terribly spoilt, since a mother never disciplines them, especially the boys. And these do what they like with their mothers.[62]

Pastor Hörlein had the same impression during his first years at Bloomfield:

> It is very sad when one has to see the disobedience of the children toward their parents too without the former being punished for it. The black people overlook everything where the children are concerned even if they strike their own parents. Child rearing is something quite unknown to them.[63]

---

61 Carl Strehlow, 'Unsere australische Mission. Bericht von Hermannsburg', *Kirchen und Missions Zeitung* 33.13, Tanunda (19 July 1897): 100.
62 Albrecht mission diary, 25 April 1926: 'Vor dem Esshaus der übliche Trubel. Da sitzen die Frauen mit ihren kleinen Kindern, die ganz entsetzlich schreien. Ich glaube alle diese kleinen Kerle sind verzogen, vor allem den Jungens tut ja eine Mutter nichts. Und diese machen mit der Mutter, was ihnen beliebt.'
63 Report by Missionary Hoerlein on the Bloomfield Station in Queensland, 1893, Hörlein Family History, unpublished MS, courtesy of Ian Hoerlein, North Epping.

In one instance, Hörlein 'boxed the ears' of a visiting young boy known as 'Blanket', who became so enraged that he threw stones at him and then charged him with spears. If a child started to yell under Hörlein's punishment, 'then all blacks gathered in the yard and made a scene'. An old woman might 'join in the howling' 'or the rainmaker threatens that he will make no more rain, should the children be spanked again, or he would make so much rain that we should all be drowned'.[64]

The Catholic Brother Rudolf **Zach** boasted about the emotional sway he held over the Beagle Bay mission girls. He felt that the Sisters were not thorough enough in their flagellations of the girls, and 'neither can the priest proceed quite like a square-built Brother'. Zach claimed that at the direction of the Lord himself he ignored the injunction of his 'sissy' mission superior:

> It must be noted that in some regards I am even softer than the Sisters.
>
> It's not within my rights to flay these virgins but I have pondered it beforehand before the Lord and he directs. The Father who is so against it is sissy, the thing works. I can and do wait for a while. The girls know this and therefore improve if I only say 'watch it, if I catch you just once on the cheap, then …' But I only use this medicine for hardy types.[65]

Soon after writing this frank reflection, and of the ghost of a recently departed mission girl that appeared to him, Zach was recalled to Limburg. There is no doubt that mission residents were sometimes exposed to very disturbed and unbalanced characters.

A much publicised incident at Mapoon unfolded after one of the mission girls assaulted the schoolteacher (presumably Mrs Ward) in class in 1907. According to missionary Hey, lay assistant Martin Baltzer administered between 18 and 20 lashes with a stingray tail. A ring of tar was drawn

---

64 Report by Missionary Hoerlein on the Bloomfield Station in Queensland, unpublished MS.
65 'Es ist noch zu bemerken, dass ich in mancher Beziehung noch weicher bin als die Schwestern, z. B. wenn die Schwestern ein Mädchen durchbläuen gelingt es ihnen selten bis auf den Grund zu kommen. Die Mädchen widersetzen sich, werfen sich auf die Erde, schlagen mit allen 4 um sich und erfüllen die Luft mit einem Geheul dass alles zusammenläuft – Auch der Priester kann nicht vorgehen wie ein so 4-schrötiger Br. weil er eben Priester ist. – Jungfrauen durchzubläuen habe ich kein Recht aber lange zuvor schon überlege ich deshalb die ganze Sache vor dem Herrn und er lenkt dann; der P. der so dagegen ist, ist verweicht; die Sache klappt. Warten kann und tue ich lange. Die Mädchen wissen das, und bessern sich daher, wenn ich blos sage: Gib Acht! Wenn ich dich ein mal billig erwische dann'.

Diese Medizin gebrauche ich aber nur für Rossnaturen. Zach at Beagle Bay to Kugelmann, 15 August 1912, in Zach, Rudolf (Br), P1 Nr 24, ZAPP.

around her neck, which Hey described as a symbol of shame such as worn by widows to express grief. Baltzer related his version of this story to his sister in Strasbourg, from where it was eventually cabled around world news networks and caused a parliamentary inquiry. According to the press story, the girl was tied to a post for five days and whipped with a leash until she fainted. She was taken down and was howling for two days in pain, unable to lie down or stand up, and with her eyes covered in tar. The inquiry obtained witness statements from the mission girls and concluded that the press reports had been exaggerated. However, the punishment had exceeded the normal expectations of school discipline and was 'not beyond objection'.[66] This incident is reminiscent of malpractices in Northern Territory youth detention centres widely debated in 2016.[67] As Hey had stated a few years earlier, 'we are now a penitentiary'.[68] This incident impugned the reputation of the entire Moravian mission effort, and in July 1907 the Herrnhut director felt compelled to circularise the friends of the Moravian mission with a position statement. He pointed out that Mapoon was not under the direction of Herrnhut but of the Presbyterian Church in Australia, and that Pastor Hey 'rarely' used his 'paternal right of punishment' on girls above age 12. He also discredited the news reports with the suggestion that Baltzer may be suffering from *Tropenkoller*. *Tropenkoller*, or tropical spleen, was a fashionable German term around the turn of the century to describe a mental condition associated with excessive punishments in colonial settings. Baltzer was suspended from the mission for nine months. Evidently Baltzer, who had administered the punishment, had been acting on orders from Hey and became the scapegoat of the incident. He afterwards sent a personal apology to Herrnhut, stating that Pastor Hey, Mrs Hey and Mrs Ward had now forgiven him for sending that letter to Strasbourg, and expressed the 'hope that this letter will attain its purpose, namely that I shall be forgiven, and that Mr Hey shall stand free again'.[69] The apology was for publicising the affair, and not for the excessive punishment of the Aboriginal girl.

---

66   W.H. Ryder (Under Secretary) to P. Robertson, Presbyterian Church Brisbane, R15.V.II.a.3, Herrnhut Archives.
67   Caro Meldrum-Hanna, Mary Fallon and Elise Worthington, '**Australia's shame**', *Four Corners*, ABC TV, 25 July 2016.
68   Walter Roth, Annual Report of the Chief Protector of Aborigines, *Queensland Votes and Proceedings*, 1903, Vol. 2, p. 470.
69   Baltzer to Berthelsdorf (Moravian Mission Board), 30 August 1908, R15.V.II.a.3, Herrnhut Archives.

7. THE GERMAN DIFFERENCE

At Hopevale (Cape Bedford), corporal punishment by Pastor Kevin Kotzur led to two public inquiries in 1964 and 1967. In this case, the result was that the role of the missionary was separated from that of mission manager and an Aboriginal Council was formed.

Sexual misdemeanor and assault

Sexual misconduct played a major role in the termination of mission stations, though this is not evident in the mission narratives. At the first German-speaking mission, on the New South Wales frontier at Wellington Valley, sexual transgressions were underplayed with hardly a mention of the 11-year-old Aboriginal girl who contracted venereal disease during her time on the mission. Two servants (presumably convicts) were handed over to police for sexual offences, but in 1842 the lay assistant William Porter was also dismissed for 'improper relations' with at least one Wiradjuri woman.[70] Public funding was withdrawn in mid-1843.

Bloomfield mission foundered on the allegation of sexual offences much more directly. The lay assistant bachelor H.G. Steicke was known to be 'too friendly with the Aborigines'. He came under investigation as early as 1891, after he was allegedly seen crawling into an Aboriginal woman's hut at night. But the Aboriginal eyewitnesses refused to implicate him. Steicke spoke Kuku Yalanji and reputedly got on very well with Aboriginal people. In 1900, Pastor Hörlein had to travel south and appointed Steicke as acting manager rather than the man next in line of command, assistant missionary Pastor Mack, with whom Hörlein was not on speaking terms. Steicke battened down in the mission house with the girls and prevented them from attending the school conducted by Mack. When Pastor Mack confronted him, Steicke slapped Mack. Mack claimed that Steicke was sexually abusing mission girls and that 'When the police inquired whether he had any connection with the girls [Steicke] unhesitatingly said, yes'.[71] This admission in a dramatic confrontation may mean many different things. Steicke was living with a black woman at nearby Ayton, and may have seen himself as the paternalistic protector of his female affinal kin. The mission committee concluded that Steicke conducted himself dishonourably. Not only are the mission sources protective of private

---

70   Broughton to Günther, 13 June and 25 June 1842, cited in Bridges, 'The Church of England and the Aborigines of New South Wales', p. 714.
71   Ordained missionary Mack to Committee, 15 April 1900, Bloomfield Correspondence, LAA.

stories, but Aboriginal oral history also. Roger Hart mentioned, without going into detail, that one of the mission staff at Bloomfield fathered a child with an Aboriginal woman in 1900.[72]

Pastor Mack himself was in a difficult position and his mental health, too, is in doubt, which weakens his eyewitness credibility. He was in dispute with mission superior Hörlein, accused Steicke of misconduct, and alleged that his superiors in South Australia were embezzling mission funds. He was soon afterwards whisked away to America. Mack's complaints about Steicke brought Chief Protector Walter Roth to Bloomfield mission. This was the third official visit during which the ordained mission superior was absent. Roth found that a stockman (Steicke) was in charge and ordered the closure of the mission or, rather, as the Immanuel Synod mission committee minuted, 'gave us a broad hint to withdraw from Bloomfield'.[73]

On the Daly River, the Jesuit superior imposed a clausura when three mission girls were pregnant and one of them gave birth to a white baby in 1894. This meant that the Brothers and Fathers were locked in after dark and during lunch breaks, and the Brothers' interactions with the mission females had to be in company with a priest. The girls' dormitory was disbanded and the girls were placed with Indigenous resident families. An attempt was made to gain witness statements from Aboriginal women, but these women resented the interrogation and most of the mission people moved away. One of the Brothers was dismissed in dishonour and eventually other Brothers under suspicion were also removed on various pretexts. Finally, the superior was also replaced and the Daly River Jesuits felt that this was the end of their mission. After a number of official visitations, permission to introduce Sisters was not granted, and the mission wound down four years later, in 1899. In this case, there were also strategic reasons at play, as suggested in Chapter 3, but sexual transgressions no doubt played a part in the closure of the mission.

At Beagle Bay, it was clearly sexual misdemeanour that ended the Trappist mission. In 1899, the Trappist mood became explosive under allegations of sexual misconduct from Fr Emo. Emo's first line of response was to remove the staff about whom he had suspicions of homosexual attachment and improper dealings with mission females. However, Emo

---

72 John B. Haviland with Roger Hart, *Old Man Fog and the Last Aborigines of Barrow Point*, Crawford House Publishing, Bathurst, 1998, pp. 81, 100.
73 Immanuel Synod, Mission Commitee Minutes, 8 May 1900, LAA.

did not notify his superiors until well after he had dealt with the situation himself, by which time he himself was on the defensive because he had exceeded his powers (see Chapter 3).

At **Aurukun**, the Presbyterian/Moravian mission was not closed as a result of sexual offences against 10-year-old girls, but Aboriginal people themselves killed the offender Peter Bee in 1908. A virtual war between the mission residents and tribal people ensued from the scandal. The tribal avengers threatened to burn down the whole mission and intimidated the wife of the offender. They were captured and an Aboriginal mission assistant shot two of these men in custody, for which he served a nine-month banishment from Mapoon to Yarrabah. In this story, the circle of victims is large, and the reach of justice is indistinct. Presumably the mission itself was not called into question in the public arena because the offender was a lay assistant of Pacific Islander descent and therefore the missionaries could be seen as sufficiently culturally different not to become implicated. However, the old Aboriginal men lost all respect for the missionaries and most former residents avoided the mission in the wake of the Peter Bee affair.

Illegitimate children, cohabiting, improper relationships

Being 'too friendly with the Aborigines' like Steicke was a risky attitude for a missionary. Fr Emo had two young protégés, and in Broome there was a suspicion that one of them was Emo's own child.[74] But, according to Mary Durack, he accepted responsibility for the child of a Trappist novice, and there is some credibility in Durack's version. The Trappists accepted at least two locals as novices, Constable Cornelius John Daly (Brother Xavier) and James Montague (Br Jacques). When Emo was temporarily in charge of Beagle Bay mission, he found that one of the Brothers (not named) was suffering from venereal disease but was reluctant to have him treated in Broome for fear of gossip. Instead, Emo designated this man for Palestine, upon which:

> he flew into such a tantrum that he flung himself into my room pale as a corpse, shouting so loudly and so upset that I was quite surprised … he was not going to El Athroun, he wanted to stay in Broome with the policeman (his compatriot) and that he was going to let the Brothers

---

74   Harris, *One Blood*, p. 445.

know everything that had happened at the mission etc. etc. and the public would judge afterwards ... I knelt before him a long time to calm him down and clasped his feet.[75]

Perhaps this was the moment when Emo took on responsibility for a child. Durack suggests that Emo's falling out with the Benedictines at Drysdale River some years later was over the question of the mixed-descent boys he had brought to the mission, and whom he wanted to repatriate.

The Catholic insistence on celibacy necessitated many obfuscations, lies and misrepresentations. Protestant mission societies, on the contrary, had a strong policy of posting married pastors because it was never considered acceptable for an unmarried missionary male to have charge of Aboriginal children. Pastor Hörlein, who like most missionaries considered himself above reproach, perhaps underestimated the force of this opinion when he unselfconsciously narrated in the mission newsletter that he and Pastor Bogner, both bachelors, had 'little daughters' who lived with them in the mission house, spoke a little German, helped in the kitchen and 'cheer us up'. Pastor Meyer and his family had taken these children into the mission home, but this story acquired uncomfortable undertones once the Meyers and their children had left. Suspicions also cloud the Lutheran missions in South Australia and the Northern Territory. At Hermannsburg, the lay assistant P. Zander was dismissed for 'unchaste behaviour' in 1897,[76] and at Killalpaninna the rumour emerged in 1905 that lay helper Kokegei had fathered a child with mission resident Paula. Pastor Reuther advised her to name an Aboriginal father.[77]

At around the same time, 45-year-old Reuther himself was accused of having a child with Frieda, a mixed descendant suffering from consumption, who lived in the Reuther household.[78] With evident affection, Reuther called her 'our Frieda', '*mei Mädle*' (me lassie) and 'Mother's adopted daughter'. Frieda had spent some time at Lights Pass as a domestic for the Reuther

---

75   Emo to Sept Fons, 6 January 1901, in Brigida Nailon, *Emo and San Salvador*, Brigidine Sisters, Echuca, 2005, Vol. 1.
76   Immanuel Synod, Mission Commitee Minutes, 1 December 1897, LAA.
77   It is not clear which Kokegei is meant. A Heinrich Kokegei was engaged in 1897 and sent to Killalpaninna instead of the Finke. In 1900, he had four small children and another Kokegei child was born in 1904. An F.J. Kokegei was dismissed in September 1901.
78   It is possible that Frieda spent only a short while in the Reuther household. In a letter to Paul Reuther, who left home in February 1903, Reuther explained that Frieda was the adopted daughter of 'Mother'. Frieda was still in the mission house in September 1903, then spent a period at Lights Pass, and had her confinement back at the mission in 1905. By January 1907, she had already died.

sons and then returned to Killalpaninna with Reuther. Her childbirth at Killalpaninna was conducted in secrecy. Frieda explained her pregnancy as a night-time rape and maintained that she had no idea who the offender was. Nor did she absolve Reuther, and Reuther's colleagues felt that he tried to cover up instead of initiating investigations.[79] After Frieda's death, the Reuthers adopted her baby Laura. Reuther was called to a hearing before the mission committee, at which most of his confreres accepted his innocence, but Reuther further implicated himself by suddenly leaving his mission service in the midst of these allegations.

Reuther had for years hinted at concerns about his mental health. He explained his sudden withdrawal from the mission with reference to his 'nervous condition', attested to by his physician who had told him that he must either withdraw from the mission work or face a lunatic asylum. He had successfully bid for a block of land for which the government required actual occupation, and said that he only meant to move his family and then return to the mission until another missionary could take his place, but the committee prevented him from returning. Realising that he had made a mistake, he kept explaining himself for years.

As with most of these stories of sexual transgressions, we have allegations, counter-allegations, refutals, vested interests, protected reputations and a lingering notion that Indigenous girls were not safe from unwanted solicitations either in traditional society or on missions, even if they were locked up at night.

Improper conduct

Other forms of improper conduct involved firing warning shots to defend the garden crops, as reported from Beagle Bay and from Zion Hill, where the military demanded an explanation.

At Bloomfield, Pastor Meyer incurred bad press when he hired out some workers to a fisheries recruiter and accepted £15 as the wages down-payment. Meyer said he was unaware that this violated the government policy. John Douglas as government resident at Thursday Island was particularly keen to put a halt to unsupervised recruiting and had supported the establishment of Cape York missions precisely to protect

---

79 Reuther to Neuendettelsau, 14 January 1907, 1 June 1904, 17 June 1905, in 1.6. 35 Reuther, Georg, 1861–1912, Pers. Korresp. Vorl. Nr. 4.93/5, Archiv de Neuendettelsau.

Aboriginal workers from the fisheries. This 'crimping incident' led the government to withdraw funding from the mission until Meyer was replaced in 1892. The mission committee investigated the affair and inspected Meyer's records, but 'we find it impossible to make head or tail of them'. Still, they concluded that the action brought against Meyer stemmed from enmity against the mission.[80]

Another allegation, of the embezzlement of mission funds, was raised against the mission director Pastor Julius Rechner, twice. In 1890, Flierl II (a namesake cousin of Johann Flierl) alleged that Rechner had embezzled £800. Flierl II was threatened with libel action, church penance (Kirchenbuße) and expulsion from the synod. Flierl II was given an explanation, apologised to Rechner and left for the United States.[81] In January 1900, Mack at Bloomfield made a similar accusation, which was minuted as 'slanderous'. A synod member also supporting the allegation checked Rechner's financial accounts in May 1900. Shortly after Rechner's death in August 1900, Missionary Mack retracted his comments, apologised and left for San Francisco. Two years later, it was minuted that the 'heirs of Pastor Rechner still owe the mission £99'.[82] The Lutheran mission community was as closely knit through kin and marriage as the Aboriginal communities on the missions.

Conclusions

How violent was life on the missions? Were German missions more prone to discipline and punishment than other missions? Current standards of organisational behaviour define serious misconduct differently from the standards used on missions, where there was no private sphere, no 'time off work'.[83] In addition to fraud, theft, assault, endangerment and intoxication at work, serious misdemeanours on missions included the production of illegitimate children, cohabiting and any unsupported allegation of criminal behaviour. Using this catalogue, this study turned

---

80 Immanuel Synod, Mission Commitee Minutes, 10 September 1890, 16 December 1890, LAA.
81 Immanuel Synod, Mission Commitee Minutes, 1 July 1891, 30 September 1891, 21 October 1891, LAA.
82 Immanuel Synod, Mission Commitee Minutes, 12 January 1900, 8 May 1900, 14 September 1900, 8 January 1902, LAA.
83 The *Fair Work Act 2009* (Cth) defines as 'serious misconduct' incidents of theft, fraud, assault, intoxication at work, causing a risk to a person, behaviour inconsistent with the employment contract and refusal to carry out a reasonable instruction consistent with the employment contract.

up 28 misconduct incidents on the German-speaking missions. These include any credible allegation of sexual misconduct involving staff, physical abuse such as excessive punishment, illegal behaviour (cohabiting, crimping, embezzlement, espionage and illegitimate offspring) and overt threats of violence. The latter includes instances where missionaries themselves came under direct threats of violence – perhaps because of some prior violence, transgression or threat on their own part.

Trying to quantify such data is always hazardous, but a statistical approach provides a rough guide. The 28 incidents took place on 13 of the 35 mission locations covered in this study, which means nearly one-third of the German-speaking missions were beset by some serious trouble at least once. (It would be interesting to compare this to the record of other types of institutions, such as universities.) The 35 missions of various duration add up to 446 mission-years, so that around 6 per cent of German mission-years were tainted with controversy while 94 per cent of German mission-years passed without reportable incident. The 35 missions employed about 180 German-speaking staff. Over 169 calendar years (between 1831 and 2000), about 16 German-speakers (9 per cent) were threatened by Indigenous violence, and about 11 (6 per cent) were accused of misdemeanour, so that 94 per cent of the German-speaking staff were never under allegation of misconduct. This compares favourably with current organisational surveys of misconduct that also rely on self-reporting of incidents, and roughly accords with the findings of the 2017 report of the Royal Commission into Institutional Responses to Child Sexual Abuse, which found that 7 per cent of Catholic priests working in Australia between 1950 and 2009 have been accused of sexual abuses.[84]

Undoubtedly, there is something like an overarching German culture, traces of which were imparted onto the missions by German speakers, but the ethnic origin of the missionaries could not overdetermine language policy in the long run. The German cultural background of missionaries was fissured with differences: between the class backgrounds

---

84 Mark McGraw, 'The decline of workplace misconduct', HRE Daily, 19 February 2014, blog.hreonline.com/2014/02/19/the-decline-of-workplace-misconduct/ (accessed July 2016, site discontinued); KPMG Fraud and Misconduct Survey 2010 Australia and New Zealand, www.wiseworkplace.com.au/_literature.../KPMG_Fraud_and_Misconduct_Survey_2010 (accessed 12 January 2018, site discontinued); Clare Blumer, Rebecca Armitage and Simon Elvery, 'Child sex abuse Royal Commission: data reveals extent of Catholic allegations', ABC News, 8 February 2017, www.abc.net.au/news/2017-02-06/child-sex-abuse-royal-commission:-data-reveals-catholic-abuse/8243890 (accessed 13 December 2017).

of missionaries, between the practices of various denominations, and also under the impact of the sociopolitical environment of missions. The Lutheran and German predilection for engagement with languages was difficult to maintain in the face of government opposition and where there was close collaboration with English-speaking churches. Moreover, during the twentieth century, which was Australia's century of missions, the fundamental differences in intellectual traditions and approaches between the English- and the German-speaking intelligentsias evaporated along with the different founding orientations of the missionary training colleges. In the twentieth century, the Australian states and territories implemented increasingly intrusive Aboriginal management policies and tied funding for missions to their policy goals. The German Catholics Nekes and Worms became the last German-speaking missionaries to conduct significant language work. Fr Worms became one of the founding members of the Australian Institute of Aboriginal Studies, established as the prime repository for ethnographic, linguistic and historical records on Australian Indigenous people.

8
Conclusions

Driven by faith

In the nineteenth century, a proliferation of missionary training colleges aiming to produce specialised professionals drew most of their candidates from impoverished backgrounds on the European continent. Some of them may have been attracted by a monastic lifstyle of prayer, study, work and celibacy, or by the expectation that a short period of training would be followed by everlasting summers in exotic locations. The multiphased acceptance procedures for mission colleges and the discretionary selection principles for mission placements were quite efficient in weeding out young lads who were merely looking for a free fare to adventure. What the college directors were looking for, and mostly succeeded in obtaining, was total commitment, for life. This is reflected in the curriculum vitae that the candidates were required to submit for acceptance into the seminaries and before their departure into mission.

The mission movement itself, and the majority of its front-line of volunteers, was essentially driven by faith, by the deep-seated conviction in a common humanity united in God, capable of salvation of the soul and eternal life after death. Evangelical 'labourers in the vineyard of God' were required to enlist and convert non-believers. The equivalent secular humanist assumption is that there are basic human rights that justify, and even demand, interventions in families, organisations or nations, whether by persuasion, compulsion or force. These unshakeable and unquestionable assumptions, which underpinned the purpose in life of missionaries, armoured them against external criticism. That they remained vulnerable to criticism from their own ranks shows in the moving letters of Pastors **Reuther** and **Hörlein**.

External criticism came from many quarters. Missionaries were often under suspicion of improper conduct, ranging from excessive physical punishment, improper dealings with minors, cohabiting, illegitimate children, molestation, crimping, embezzlement, to espionage. In most cases, determining the truth of the allegations is impossible on the basis of extant records, since rumour and innuendo surround the events and often the misdeeds themselves were not enunciated. One must be careful not to judge by the institutional policies that are now in place for dealing with suspected transgressions or by what now counts as improper conduct. Illegitimate children, extramarital affairs, cohabiting, miscegenation and homosexual relations have all disappeared from the modern register of ethical misdemeanours within less than a century. At the same time, new misdemeanours have appeared in the moral compass, including patronising Indigenous adults, corporal punishment, bullying and deprivation of liberty. It is this new moral compass that casts a long shadow on the mission histories.

In these shifting territories, there were also vast mismatches between Indigenous and Christian ethical standards. The missionaries accused Indigenous people of polygamy, abortion, infanticide and violence against women. Indigenous people accused missionaries of arranging wrong marriages, violations of avoidance rules, incarcerating children and violence against children. In other words, the contest was over the maintenance and erosion of cultural traditions and standards, typical of the colonising process. Yet missionaries thought of themselves as guardians against the worst excesses of colonisation, rather than as colonisers themselves, and were often amazed when Indigenous people treated them as just one of the 'bosses'. They understood themselves not as dominating the lives of others but as sacrificing (*sacer facium* – making holy) their own, as acting for a cause that was spiritual rather than material, that aimed for conversion rather than colonisation. Chapter 6 details that the missionary profession generally did not offer a brilliant career, or an attractive wage, or a secure retirement. The prime motivation of volunteers must have been faith, and not self-advancement.

Gratitude and other cultural conventions

Against the backdrop of vast differences in ethics, expectations and self-definition, the missionaries highly prized any show of affection or gratitude from Indigenous people. Bishop **Gsell** was comforted by the lifelong support from Martina, the woman who had inspired his signature policy, and who during World War II at Channel Island expressed the 'fervent wish' to see him once more.[1] Fr **Lümmen** enjoyed even more support from Edith Little at Rossmoyne. Fr Wilhelm **Droste** was showered with letters from his 'aunties', 'children' and 'friends' at Beagle Bay and Broome, addressed to their Ibal (father) who had returned to Germany. After 20 years in the Kimberley, these affectionate letters must have been a great comfort to him two months before his death in December 1929. Another moving description is the great wailing that accompanied the arrest of the Pallottine Brethren at **Beagle Bay** in 1940. At that moment of removal under police guard, nobody knew what might happen to the missionaries who were arrested – a situation all too familiar to Indigenous people. Fr Francis Byrne describes how the Elders gathered on the grass in front of the mission house and wept:

> As the missionaries, with their few personal belongings, were being loaded onto the truck and police vehicles, a mournful lament began in the Aboriginal camp. It was an eerie wail which seemed to permeate every building, every tree, every plant, every soul.[2]

There was also a great show of sorrow when Pastor F.W. Spieseke died at age 56 at **Ebenezer** in 1876, and some Aboriginal men walked all the way to Dimboola to buy his coffin.[3] When Pastor Carl **Strehlow** was carried off the mission, struck down with illness after nearly 30 years at Hermannsburg, the entire congregation accompanied him with a farewell song for a stretch of the way. For missionaries, such expressions of grief meant that they were accepted as an important part of the community, that there was gratitude for their efforts, and that there was some basic human affection.

---

1   Frank Flynn, *Distant Horizons: Mission Impressions as Published in the Annals of Our Lady of the Sacred Heart,* Sacred Heart Monastery, Kensington, 1947, pp. 67, 74.
2   Francis Byrne, *A Hard Road: Brother Frank Nissl, 1888–1980: A Life of Service to the Aborigines of the Kimberleys*, Tara House, Nedlands, WA, 1989, p. 83.
3   Ebenezer Diary, 24 June 1876, microfilm, MF 171–73, Australian Institute of Aboriginal and Torres Strait Islanders (AIATSIS).

But this is not necessarily what they meant for Indigenous people. When Brother Eberhard fell sick in 1882 at **Rapid Creek**, after only less than a year in the north, Fr Strele was very moved by the loud lamentations raised by Aboriginal people, who showed distress and continually inquired about his state. It is quite possible that this show of concern was primarily a way of averting blame and revenge killing in case Br Eberhard died.

To visit the dying was a widespread custom that deflected blame in Indigenous societies where death had to be accounted for. When Nathanael Pepper was told in 1877 that he only had days left to live, he sent for every inhabitant of **Ramahyuck** to come to his bedside.[4] It was much the same with Br **Krallmann** in 1951 at Beagle Bay:

> His heart wanted to give up, he sat in front of his hut with the rosary – a simple room and hard bed. Friendly chat with each passing Blackfellow. The end was slowly approaching. Without invitation all the Blacks now came in long queues to say farewell. With his weak voice he had a good word for each of them. Everyone was crying. When it was over he told the Bishop [Raible] and Brothers who were present, 'what a comfort to encounter such gratitude.'[5]

Perhaps these farewell rituals were also part of an increasingly syncretic middle ground where a shared platform of meaning was intuited from two very different sets of cultural connotation – absolution from blame and guilt in one culture, and devolution of responsibilities and material inheritance in the other. Perhaps there was a measure of gratitude – the missionaries certainly expected it. Gratitude would compensate for the hardships, difficulties and abstinences typical of a missionary life. But gratitude is not a currency that is traded between equals, and therefore the missionaries never saw enough of it to compensate for their sacrifices. This does not mean that Indigenous people failed to acknowledge the work of the missionaries. Their world was rapidly and uncontrollably changing, and they were in need of support and assistance under the onslaught of massive historical changes.

---

4   Hagenauer, 17 March 1877, Annual Reports of the Central Board for Aborigines, B332/0 1861–1924, Victorian Archives Centre.
5   Handwritten manuscript in Worms, Ernst Alfred (Pater), P1 Nr 27, Zentralarchiv der Pallottinerprovinz (ZAPP), translated by Regina Ganter.

8. CONCLUSIONS

Perspectives on mission history

Pat Grimshaw reports an Aboriginal woman as saying: 'Only for the missionaries there wouldn't be so many Aborigines walking around today. They're the ones that saved the day for us'.[6] Missionary histories make similar claims. But, after all their efforts, it cannot be taken for granted that missions actually played a major role in the continued survival of Aboriginal people in Australia when few missions were able to provide an abode that lasted for more than a generation, and only between 5 and 7 per cent of Indigenous people had access to missions until after World War II.

In view of all the dysfunctions, it seems difficult to fashion a reconciliatory mission history that takes into honest account the intentions, processes and outcomes at play. The question of intentions has been the prerogative of histories written from within the churches that are bent on giving due credit for effort. A focus on the process tends to be the domain of Indigenous memories of mission life that are inclined to emphasise pain. The outcomes, finally, are more in the viewfinder of academic treatments that leverage critical analysis in the framework of empire and colonialism. This book has attempted to span these perspectives, not working deductively from a theory or model, but inductively sorting through a massive amount of detailed record. That it confined its scope to missions staffed by German-speaking and other Continental missionaries should not diminish that effort.

Indigenous accounts of missions are largely in the form of oral history, and without access to German materials. A community history of Mapoon focuses on the displacement from the old mission under the pressure of mining development and the disappointing lack of support from the church at that crucial moment. A collection of oral histories from Beagle Bay was produced under the editorship of Sister Brigida Nailon and Fr Francis Hügel. Their book, *Beagle Bay – This is Your Place*, contains hardly a trace of criticism of the mission period, but neither is the praise for the missionaries very liberal in the testimony of former mission residents. Others do make some acknowledgement of a certain indebtedness, and in church publications we find many Indigenous

---

6 Patricia Grimshaw, *Creating a Nation 1788–1990*, McPhee-Gribble, Melbourne, 1994, p. 135.

voices that are positive about the mission past. Glenyse Ward placed her autobiography, *Wandering Girl*, under the banner of her character-forming mission childhood at Wandering Brook, with fond memories of the German Sisters and wistful references to the cloistered mission years. As an academic stepping well beyond oral and family history, Noel Pearson also squarely confronted the Lutheran background of his home community at Hopevale, and has since commented on the benefits his community derived from its mission.[7]

Anger and frustration speak from between the lines of many former missionaries or their descendants, who have found the mission efforts under the microscope of armchair critique from secular academics.[8] Ordained religious like Dr John Harris and Paul Albrecht also know how to wield an incisive knife of critique, but they share with the missionaries about whom they write a fundamental commitment to Christian faith and the bedrock of conviction that missions were intended for the benefit of Aboriginal people. Secular approaches, canvassed in the Preface, emphasise, on the contrary, that missions served the interests of colonising states.

That the empire-building of the different confessions was driven by faith is much less credible than the argument advanced here about individual motivations. Even Lutheran historians understand that the dogmatic disputes that delayed the formation of a Lutheran Church in Australia until 1966 owed more to personality clashes than to unbridgeable confessional differences.[9] The tensions described in Chapter 1 within the Catholic Church and between Protestant and Catholic mission

---

7   Brigida Nailon and Francis Huegel (eds), *This is Your Place: Beagle Bay Mission 1890–1990*, Beagle Bay Community, Broome, 1990; Glenyse Ward, *Wandering Girl*, Magabala Books, Broome, 1988; Noel Pearson, 'Ngamu-ngaadyarr, Muuri-bunggaga and Midha Mini in Guugu Yimidhirr History: Dingoes, Sheep and Mr Muni in Guugu Yimidhirr History: Hope Vale Lutheran Mission 1900–1950', Honours thesis, University of Sydney, 1986; Geoffrey Stephen Wharton, 'The Day They Burned Mapoon: A Study of the Closure of a Queensland Presbyterian Mission', Honours thesis, University of Queensland, 1996.

8   This is particularly evident in John Strehlow, *The Tale of Frieda Keysser: Frieda Keysser & Carl Strehlow: An Historical Biography. Volume 1, 1875–1910*, Wild Cat Press, London, 2011.

9   Th. Hebart, *The United Evangelical Lutheran Church in Australia (U.E.L.C.A.): Its History, Activities and Characteristics, 1838–1938*, (Trans. Johann J. Stolz), Lutheran Book Depot, Adelaide, 1938; F. Otto Theile, *One Hundred Years of the Lutheran Church in Queensland*, UELCA Qld. District, Brisbane, Lutheran Publishing House, Adelaide, 1938 (facsimile reprint 1985); Everard Leske, *For Faith and Freedom: The Story of Lutherans and Lutheranism in Australia 1838–1996*, Open Book publishers, Adelaide, 1996; Everard Leske (ed.), *Hermannsburg: A Vision and Mission*, Lutheran Publishing House, Adelaide, 1977.

endeavours have the character of a competitive carving of spheres of influence, also typical of the colonising process. All these mission empires eventually collapsed because they had no secure land tenure to buffer them against secular policy changes. Nobody could foresee that in the end the enormous productive activity on missions and the personal investments and leadership of missionaries would lead Aboriginal communities only into large-scale welfare dependence. Traditional lifestyles, leadership structures and access entitlements were successfully eroded to make room for a new age, but security of tenure for Indigenous communities in the new system was not achieved, a national calamity with which Australia is still wrestling.

God was here before the missionaries!

The early Australian mission efforts seemed doomed from the beginning, and most of them were judged failures. The end of the mission era became a bitter contest between the aspirations of Indigenous people, the ambit claims of states, the emerging powers of the federal government and the mission societies. Despite all this, the emergence of ordained Indigenous pastors and priests and Indigenous churches with a strong following have achieved the aims of the mission movement. John Harris estimated that by the 1930s a greater proportion of black than white Australians were actively Christian, and a study by Noel Loos of the emergence of an Aboriginal Church affirms that Christianity is now an important part of contemporary Aboriginal culture.[10]

The emerging Indigenous churches in Australia devised their own syncretic adaptations, some of which were trialled as 'inculturation' in the final Catholic mission phase explored in Chapter 5. The Christian church became transformed with the addition of saints, icons, processions, bishops and other rituals, and the social hierarchies in Europe. Aboriginal people, too, located the gospel within their own frames of reference, including the allocation of a place in country to gospel stories. In the Kimberley missions, reports circulated about a figure of Christ in an

---

10   John Harris, *One Blood: 200 Years of Aboriginal Encounter with Christianity: A Story of Hope*, Albatross Books, Sutherland, NSW, 1990, p. 659; Noel Loos, *White Christ Black Cross: The Emergence of a Black Church*, Aboriginal Studies Press, Canberra, p. 175.

intertidal creek,[11] at Hermannsburg (Ntaria) there are the Footprints of Jesus near the Finke River, and believers proclaim that 'God was here before the missionaries'.[12]

These days, Aboriginal Christians do not perceive a conflict between participation in traditional ceremonies and church rituals, both of which 'validate a spirit-filled universe'.[13] In the 1980s, anthropologist David Thompson found that at the former Anglican mission of Lockhart River 'sincere Aboriginal Christians … find a harmonious identity through being active participants to both Bora and Church'. They emphasised parallels and similarities, and to explain elements of bora to outsiders they used English terms like godparent, baptism or confession.[14] Translations have always involved a certain latitude in interpreting the gospel. For example, Fr Gribble discovered that his Pacific Island assistant Willie Ambryn promised the Yarrabah people a heaven with 'no sickness, no pain, no sorrow, and no white people'.[15]

White bishops have been cautious about emerging forms of Aboriginal Christian spirituality. In 1972, Anglican Bishop of Carpentaria Donald Shearman felt that 'only a few have a real commitment to Jesus Christ'.[16] Darwin's Catholic Bishop F.X. Gsell boasted more than 700 names on his baptismal register in the 1940s, but when asked how many of the them were true believers, he reputedly said: 'none. Their religion goes deeper than ours'.[17]

---

11 A undated file note in Worms, Ernst Alfred (Pater), P1 Nr 27, ZAPP suggests that soon after his arrival in the north in December 1930, Fr Ernst Worms followed up the report of the figure of Christ. A scribbled note on re-used paper reads: '15 November, Br. Kasparek, self and Clem went by lorry to Ten Mile Mill to look at the curious stones. Found petrified trees, especially one as if sawed through twice. Didn't see the so-called Figure of Christ (was already covered with water). Saw rabbit tracks for the first time. The name of the place is: –'. (Worms didn't specify the name of the place.) In the original German: 'Nov. 15th. Br. Kasp., ich, Clem. waren per lorry nach 10 Mile Mill, um nach den sonderbaren Steinen zu sehen. Fanden petrified Bäume besonders einer, wie zeimal durchgesägt. Die sogenannte Christus Figur sahen wir nicht. (Schon mit Wasser bedeckt). Sahen zum ersten Mal Rabbit-track. Der Platz heißt: –'.
12 *The Dream and the Dreaming*, 2003, ABC TV.
13 Loos, *White Christ Black Cross*, p. 163.
14 David Thompson, *Bora is Like Church: Aboriginal Initiation and the Christian Church at Lockhart River, Queensland*, Australian Board of Missions, Sydney, 1985, Foreword.
15 Loos, *White Christ Black Cross*, p. 146.
16 Loos, *White Christ Black Cross*, p. 154.
17 Douglas Lockwood, *The Front Door: Darwin, 1869–1969*, Rigby, Adelaide, 1968, p. 116.

Noel Loos provides a detailed study of the emergence of an Indigenous church inside Anglicanism, which shows a parallel development to those covered in this study.[18] In the 1970s, Edward River and Lockhart River missions were 'on the verge of introducing a language program'. Bishop Donald Shearman pronounced how important it was 'to deliver the gospel in the language of the people' after linguist Bruce Sommer had found in 1969 that at Kowanyama (Mitchell River) only about 58 per cent of English was understood. For example, the indistinct difference between the English 'a' and 'e' resulted in a blurring between 'blessing' and 'blaspheming'. In various ways, the gospel was either misunderstood or reinterpreted in the framework of Indigenous understandings.[19] Gospel stories became identified with a place, and therefore with a clan that owned the story and became responsible for maintaining it and for performing its associated church rituals. At Kowanyama, God was identified as the mythic culture hero Poonchr who lived in the sky and occasionally visited the earth in human form. This is reminiscent of the invocation of 'Mahmamorack' in Nathanael Pepper's hymn discussed in Chapter 5.

Loos mentions several syncretic adaptations, including the use of damper as holy host, the inclusion of the totemic sea eagle in the coat of arms of the James Noble Fellowship at Yarrabah, and, conversely, the incorporation of a traditional smoking ceremony in important church functions such as the General Synod and National Conference. Some traditional ceremonies fell away, such as increase ceremonies that became superfluous once local stores opened their doors, others were adjusted, such as mortuary rites that began to include Torres Strait music and dance for 'house opening' ceremonies after a death, and some church ceremonies became reinscribed, such as baptism to replace initiation and adult baptism bestowed on new arrivals to render them part of the community.[20] In the same way, it has been observed that Aboriginal people have transformed Lutheranism as much as Lutheranism transformed Indigenous people.[21]

---

18   Loos, *White Christ Black Cross*.
19   Australian Board of Missions, Board Minutes, 24–26 October 1972, Chairman's Report; J. Taylor, 'Goods and gods: A follow-up study of "Steel Axes for Stone Age Australians"', in Swain and Rose, p. 447 cited in Loos, *White Christ Black Cross*, pp. 159, 154.
20   Taylor, 'Goods and Gods', in Swain and Rose, p. 447 cited in Loos, *White Christ Black Cross*, pp. 154, 168–72.
21   Jim Cox et al., Religion and non-Religion among Australian Aboriginal Peoples, Roundtable Discussion, Religion and Society Research Centre, University of Western Sydney, August 2014; see also Jim Cox and Adam Possamai (eds), *Religion and non-Religion among Australian Aboriginal Peoples*, Routledge, Abingdon, 2016.

Contrary to histories written from within the churches,[22] Loos emphasises that 'the innovators have always been Aboriginal people' and that such adaptations were achieved through struggle against centralised church structures.[23] The Aboriginal churches grew out of local initiatives, and were not a High Church decision.[24] Anglican Bishop Wood observed 'a gradual emergence of Aboriginal congregations throughout Australia', but Loos observes that this was not in the denominations to which they once belonged. In the fringe camps of galvanised iron shacks without running water, the Aborigines Inland Mission, the United Aborigines Mission and the Assembly of God attracted large followings.[25]

At the Anglican mission of Yarrabah, an important catalyst and role model was James Noble, who became the first Aboriginal deacon in the Anglican Church in 1925. He, along with several others, helped Rev. Ernest Gribble establish the Anglican missions at Yarrabah in 1898, the Roper River mission in 1908, the Forrest River mission and the Mitchell River mission. It took until 1970 for another Aboriginal person to be ordained in the Anglican Church.[26] Noble had a conversion experience at a place now called 'Vision Creek'. By the 1980s, in the wake of the Christian renewal of the 'born-again Christian' movement of the late 1970s, visions became widespread at Yarrabah, with images of Jesus appearing in clouds, trees, children's paintings or curtain folds, and Yarrabah's Rev. Wayne Connolly observed that 'our people are starting to see our Lord Jesus Christ in everything'.[27]

Grappling with problems of alcohol, drugs, gambling, domestic violence and sexual promiscuity, more and more Yarrabah people proclaimed how their lives were changed by a conversion experience.[28] In 1985,

---

22 For example, Margaret Zucker, *From Patrons to Partners: A History of the Catholic Church in the Kimberley 1884–1984*, University of Notre Dame Press, Broome, 1994; Brigida Nailon, *Nothing Is Wasted in the Household of God: Vincent Pallotti's Vision in Australia 1901–2001*, Spectrum Publications, Richmond, 2001.
23 Loos, *White Christ Black Cross*, p. 159.
24 Loos, *White Christ Black Cross*, p. 171.
25 Bishop Wood, *Church Scene*, 1992 cited in Loos, *White Christ Black Cross*, pp. 172, 170.
26 Loos, *White Christ Black Cross*, p. 146ff. In 1970 Patrick Brisbane was ordained and worked at Lockhart River and Cowal Creek in relative obscurity. In November 1973, Gumbuli Wurramurra (Michael Gumbuli) was ordained at the former Church Mission Society (CMS) Roper River mission at Ngukurr. Loos, *White Christ Black Cross*, p. 152.
27 Wayne Connolly, *National Boomerang*, August 1986, cited in Loos, *White Christ Black Cross*, p. 164.
28 Loos mentions several of these conversions as reported in the church newsletters, *National Boomerang* and *Yaburru*.

Aboriginal Bishop Arthur Malcolm ordained nine Yarrabah residents as deacons, priests and Eucharistic assistants.[29] Ordained men with their wives were sent out from Yarrabah to Palm Island, Wyndham, Forrest River, Oenpelli, Cherbourg and Woorbinda. By 1986, the mid-week meetings of the James Noble Fellowship at Yarrabah drew up to 250, and Sunday communion up to 170 participants. The Yarrabah church began to see itself as a 'mother church for Aboriginal people around Australia'.[30] Important networking occurred through workshops, conferences, ecumenical functions, fellowship meetings and clubs and societies such as the Mother's Union and Girls Friendly Society, and through the Nungalinya theological training college established in Darwin in 1973 and Wontulp-Bi-Buya in Cairns.[31]

The presence of indigenous ministers from the Pacific and Torres Strait Islands was also an important catalyst for the emergence of Indigenous churches. Unable to recruit sufficiently from its white congregations, the Uniting Church brought the 'Melanesian Brothers' from Vanuatu and the Solomon Islands in 1976, and the Anglican Church placed Torres Strait Islanders on its mainland communities.[32] But these worked under the direction of white bishops and white community administrators.

Loos observes that the Anglican Church rendered itself practically irrelevant by failing to offer leadership on issues that most affected Indigenous lives in the north. The Australian Council of Churches had resolved in 1965 to support land rights and compensation for lost land, but during the difficult land rights negotiations with the Queensland Government in the 1980s the church leaders remained aloof. The question of alcohol split the Yarrabah Anglican Church almost in half for many years, with a breakaway congregation (Juyuga Ministries formed in 1989) advocating

---

29 Bishop Arthur Malcolm from Yarrabah attended Church Army College near Newcastle in 1952, then completed four years of theological training and graduated as a Church Army officer. He married Colleen, another church army officer, and in 1974 Bishop Lewis appointed these two to replace Rev. Cyril Brown, to develop an Indigenous ministry. Loos, *White Christ Black Cross*, pp. 168, 163.
30 Wayne Connolly, *National Boomerang*, August 1986, cited in Loos, *White Christ Black Cross*, p. 164.
31 Nungalinya college offered a one-year certificate of theology leading on to a Diploma of Theology, as well as courses in Community Development, Language Studies, Cultural Orientation and Theology, and drew many students from Queensland until Wontulp-Bi-Buya (the words for 'light' in Wik Mungkan and two Torres Strait languages) opened as a training college in Cairns supported by Uniting, Lutheran, Catholic and Anglican churches. Two of its graduates, James Leftwich and Saibo Mabo, are now bishops. Loos, *White Christ Black Cross*, pp. 151–53.
32 Loos mentions William Namok, Poey Passi, Sailor Gabey, Tom Savage, and Kebisu and Kosia Ware as assistants from Torres Strait at Lockhart River.

complete abstinence. By 2007, the congregation had reconciled with almost all Yarrabah Christians abstaining from alcohol, and not accepting the authority of the Anglican Church on this question. Alcohol and church had become alternatives to each other.[33] The Indigenous church that emerged, with Aboriginal leadership of congregations, engages with questions of sacred sites protection, stolen generation, mandatory sentencing and reconciliation.

Formal emancipation within the churches developed under the impetus of indigenous churches observed in New Zealand and Papua New Guinea. Māori Christians had already taken control of their churches, and national Aboriginal bodies began to emerge inside the churches, showing themselves unwilling to accept white domination in their denominations. In Australia, an Aboriginal Evangelical Fellowship was formed in 1971, and national Aboriginal bodies also developed in the Uniting Church in 1980 (Uniting Aboriginal and Islander Christian Congress) and in the Catholic Church in September 1991 (the National Aboriginal and Islander Catholic Council). Lagging behind other denominations and behind developments overseas, the Anglican Church tried to contain Aboriginal self-determination within the church by establishing Aboriginal bishoprics 'within the structure and ethos of the church'.[34] Finally, Yarrabah's Aboriginal Bishop Arthur Malcolm and the Aboriginal Administrator of Tranby college, Kevin Cook, established a National Aboriginal Anglican Council 'to celebrate Aboriginal culture, language and lifestyle within the Anglican church', which the General Synod formally adopted in February 1992.

Aboriginal churches now operate outside mainstream institutional church and mission structures, embrace place-based spirituality and kinship-based ministry.[35] These adaptations draw strength from the Old Testament, which belongs to the Torah and the Qur'an as much as to the Christian Bible, and which contains stories from deep in the dreaming of Western civilisation, like the story of the great flood and ark of Noah, which can be traced back as far as the legend of Gilgamesh, King of the Mesopotamian city of Uruk in about 2,500BCE.[36] David Thompson

---

33   Loos, *White Christ Black Cross*, pp. 168, 151.
34   Loos, *White Christ Black Cross*, p. 173.
35   Steve Bevis in Jim Cox et al., Religion and non-Religion among Australian Aboriginal Peoples, Roundtable Discussion.
36   Joshua Cole and Carol Symes, *Western Civilisations. Vol. 1: Their History and their Culture*, Wiley/Norton, New York, 2013.

during fieldwork at Lockhart River in the 1970s found a high level of compatibility between Aboriginal and Christian world-views and rituals, but on the whole the traditional world view was 'more akin to that of the early Israelites'.[37] At Yarrabah, Rev. Wayne Connolly likened the healing pool at King's Beach to the cleansing pool at Jerusalem and pronounced that Aboriginal religion contained good spirits and evil spirits – Godhead and Angels – in short, Aboriginal people 'had the gospel all the time'.[38]

This message is now so well embraced that it also finds expression in popular culture. Gurrumul Yunupingu's 2015 *Gospel Album* in Yolngu and English is so redolent of ancient meanings, with the gradual introduction of Yolngu terms for sun, blood, death and rebirth, that it 'defies translation'.[39] Seaman Dan, too, has several albums celebrating mission history and the gospel.

Among the foremost Indigenous theologians is Rev. Dr Djiniyini Gondarra from Galiwin'ku, a community that also experienced a strong Christian revival movement. The Elcho Island 'adjustment movement' led to the disclosure of much secret/sacred knowledge surrounding precolonial contact with Muslim Macassan visitors. Gondarra studied theology in Papua New Guinea to become a Uniting Church minister, taught at Nungalinya college in Darwin (partnered by the Catholic, Anglican and Uniting Churches) and rose to become a moderator of the Uniting Church. His reflections on Aboriginal theology – *Let my people go* – include a chapter entitled 'Father you gave us the Dreaming', which likens the relationship between Aboriginal religion and Christianity to that between the Old Testament and the New Testament, with Christianity as the fulfilment of Aboriginal religion. However, he critically engages with what he sees as the shortcomings of white Christian theology, such as its emphasis on individualism and lack of spiritualism.[40]

Initiatives like the 'adjustment movement' at Elcho Island under the leadership of Methodist Rev. Donald Shepherdson in the 1940s, the 'inculturation' pioneered by Catholic Fr Werner Kriener in the Kimberley

---

37 David Thompson, *Bora is Like Church*, Foreword; Loos, *White Christ Black Cross*, p. 154.
38 Wayne Connolly addressing the Queensland Synod in 2003 and 2004, in Loos, *White Christ Black Cross*, p. 166ff.
39 Nicholas Rothwell, 'Gurrumul's gospel songs reflect the legacy of Christian missions', *The Australian*, 2 July 2015, Arts.
40 Gondarra, Djiniyini, *Series of Reflections of Aboriginal Theology: Four Reflections Based on Church Renewal, Christian Theology of the Land, Contextualization and Unity*, Bethel Presbytery, Northern Synod of the Uniting Church in Australia, Darwin, 1986.

in the 1970s, or the tentative incorporation of Aboriginal ritual on the Anglican missions described by Loos, 'were trying to graft on to the white Christianity an Aboriginal presence and input that had been deliberately excluded previously'.[41] Despite these efforts, White churches have not served Indigenous needs very well, with patronising attitudes perhaps too deeply embedded. An example is the history of the Catholic Church in the Kimberley commissioned by Bishop John Jobst. It is entitled *From Patrons to Partners* to flag a fundamental shift in relationships, but its photo captions belie this shift: white persons, including visitors, are invariably fully identified by name, while Aboriginal persons are typically identified as 'a member of the community'. Nevertheless, Indigenous people now overwhelmingly identify as Christian, though with a downward trend. In the 2006 census, 73 per cent of Indigenous respondents identified as Christians, 24 per cent as having no religion and only 1 per cent as adhering to an Aboriginal traditional religion.[42] By 2011, there was a 41 per cent increase in Indigenous atheism (outstripping the growth of atheism in the general population), though actual numbers reporting 'no religion' remained small at 1,230 Indigenous respondents. An almost equal number (1,142) of Indigenous respondents identified as Muslim.[43]

It must be concluded that the mission movement achieved its basic aims, of spreading Christianity and seeding Indigenous churches. According to Loos, the Anglican national Aboriginal body (now National Aboriginal and Torres Strait Islander Anglican Council [NATSIAC]) has its centre of gravity in the north (where the mission effort had been most intensive) and the only state not represented is Tasmania (which never had missions). With its brief to 'go into the world and make disciples of all nations', and Yarrabah's Rev. Lloyd Fourmile announcing that 'we must teach whites reconciliation to inspire them to commit to Christ',[44] the flow of evangelist teaching from white to black people is now reversed. The adoption in 1992 of the Christian principle of Reconciliation as a national policy agenda under the leadership of a former Catholic priest, Patrick Dodson, now known as the 'Father of Reconciliation', crowns the achievement of the mission movement.

---

41 Loos, *White Christ Black Cross*, p. 157.
42 Australian Bureau of Statistics, 4713.0 – Population Characteristics, Aboriginal and Torres Strait Islander Australians, 2006.
43 Jim Cox et al., Religion and non-Religion among Australian Aboriginal Peoples, Roundtable Discussion.
44 Loos, *White Christ Black Cross*, p. 166.

Indigenous–white relations have hardened in the wake of postcolonial rethinking, but a reappraisal of missions as players in the force field of interest between settlers, governments and Indigenous people is well underway. Individual missionaries are remembered with gratitude in their communities, and not necessarily placed in the framework of critical analysis. Loos sees the missionaries as 'very ordinary people doing the best they could to spread the faith that had made their own lives significant'. Unlike the heroic apostles who brought Christianity to Europe, the Australian missionaries 'have become the fringe dwellers of the Aboriginal past', according to Loos, who observes that of former mission residents, 'most express a magnanimity towards these ruthlessly loving cultural imperialists and an appreciation of the mission communities they brought into being as refuges'.[45] At the centenary of the Yarrabah mission in 1992, there was 'not a black armband in sight'.[46] Indigenous communities draw strength from their faith, and when they turn around their lives as a result of visions, white people's disbelief 'doesn't worry us'. Their faith allows them to 'Stand up as equals, all made in the image of God',[47] and no believer could argue against the emancipatory claim that 'God was here before the missionaries!'

---

45   Loos, *White Christ Black Cross*, p. 157.
46   Loos, *White Christ Black Cross*, p. 170.
47   Connolly, *National Boomerang*, 1986, cited in Loos, *White Christ Black Cross*, p. 165; and NATSIAC document, 2000, cited in Loos, *White Christ Black Cross*, p. 174.

Bibliography

Archives

Archiv der Berliner Missionsgesellschaft, Berlin

Correspondence, Berliner Missionsgesellschaft, Signatur 572, Evangelisches Landeskirchliches Archiv, Berlin

Archiv der Brüderunität, Herrnhut (Herrnhut Archives)

Missionsdirektion, Personalakten, Nicolaus Hey, MD825

Various – Baltzer–Hey, 1905–1909, R15.V.II.a.3

Archiv der Gossner Mission, Berlin

Gossner G1, Signatur 0813, Evangelisches Landeskirchliches Archiv, Berlin

Archiv der Neuendettelsauer Missionsgesellschaft, Mission Eine Welt, Neuendettelsau

Reuther, Georg, 1861–1912, Persönliche Korrespondenz, Vorl. Nr. 4.93/5, 1.6. 35, Neuendettelsau (now Landeskirchliches Archiv, Nürnberg)

Archives of the Pallottine Community, Rossmoyne

La Grange Mission Chronicle 1/1/55–2/6/63, #14284

Archives of the Society of Jesus, Hawthorn

Dalton, Paddy J., 'History of the Jesuits in South Australia 1848–1948', unpublished MS, 1948

Daly River Mission Diary (DRM)

Strele, Anthony, 'History of the Mission to the Aborigines in the part of Australia which is called Northern Territory', translated from Latin by F.J. Dennett SJ, ca 1895

Strele, Anton, Annual Letters from the Jesuit Mission in North Australia 1886–1889, translated by F. Dennett SJ

Australian Institute of Aboriginal and Torres Strait Islanders (AIATSIS), Canberra

Christie, Ernest MacGregor, 'Angelo Confalonieri: first missionary to Port Essington, North Australia', 1942, typescript ca 1950, PMS 3686

Ellis, Catherine J., Report to AIATSIS on research in Germany during study leave, 1990, unpublished MS, PMS 4981

Kristen, Adolf, 'Aboriginal Language', 1899, MS 1239

Nekes, Hermann, Kimberleys language material: Daro, Nol Nol etc., 1931–47, MS 35

The Moravian Mission in Australia Papers, 1832–1916, microfilm, MF 163–88

Annual Reports for Mapoon to the Moravian Mission Board, microfilm, MF 186–87

Annual Reports for Weipa to the Moravian Mission Board, microfilm, MF 186–87

Ebenezer Diary, microfilm, MF 171–73

North Australia, North Queensland, microfilm, MF 186–87

Battye Library, State Library of Western Australia, Perth

Jeffrey, Chris, An Interview with Bernhard Stracke, (age 73), 6 August 1981, Battye Library Oral History Programme, transcript

Berndt Museum, University of Western Australia, Perth

Made by Mambur, Elcho Island 1961, Nr 931 Berndt Collection

Chevalier Resource Centre, Kensington, NSW (MSC Archives)

Caruana, Anthony, 'Reflections on hundred years of MSC mission work in the Northern Territory 1904–2004', unpublished MS, 2004

Lutheran Archives Australia (LAA), Adelaide

Biographical Collection – Meyer, C. A.

Biographical Collection – Moses Uraiakuraia – 'Our Australian Mission'

Biographical Collection – Schoknecht, Rev CHM

Immanuel Synod – Bethesda Mission, Box 19

Immanuel Synod – Bloomfield Mission Correspondence, 1887–89

Immanuel Synod – Finke River Mission, Box 3 – Correspondence 1895–99

Immanuel Synod – Finke River Mission, Box 5 – Correspondence Wettengel (transcriptions and translations)

Immanuel Synod – Mission Committee, Correspondence book of Pastor GJ Rechner 1886–1892

Immanuel Synod – Mission Committee, Minutes 1875–1883

Immanuel Synod – Mission Committee, Minutes 1884–1894

Immanuel Synod – Mission Committee, Minute Book, 1895–1901 (translated)

Immanuel Synod – Mission Committee, Meetings: Kaibels' notes, 1901–1914

Immanuel Synod – Mission Committee, Minutes 1902–27 (translated)

Lohe, M., 'Pastor Haussmann and Mission Work from 1866', translation of unpublished articles in *Australiche Kristenbote*, unpublished MS, 1964

United German and Scandinavian Lutheran Synod of Queensland (UGSLSQ) – Mission Committee, Minute Book 1887–1903

Weiss, Peter, Short General and Statistical History of the Australian Lutheran Church, Lutheran Archives Australia, 2001–2007 (Weiss index)

Mitchell Library, Sydney

John Dunmore Lang Papers Lang, 1837–67, A2240 Vol. 20, item 82

R. Windeyer (Chair), Parliamentary Committee on the Condition of the Aborigines, 1845, Q. 572.9 P.A. 1

National Archives of Australia (NAA), Canberra

Alien Registration of Alfonso Aboliro, 24 October 1916, MT269/1, barcode 6561190

Alien Registration of Mary Aboliro, 26 October 1916, MT269/1, barcode 6561191

Bathurst Island Mission Reports 1910–1915 A431, 1951/1294, barcode 66600

Beagle Bay Mission, Broome, Western Australia, A885, B77 PT1

Father Bischoff – German Mission Station at Beagle Bay A367, 1917/50, barcode 61882

Port Keats, Catholic Mission, Northern Territory (1934–55), A452, 1955/98, barcode 75384

Schwarz, Report on Prisoner of War, MP1104/2, Q490, barcode 9902270

State Library of Victoria, Melbourne

Barfus, Franz, 'A visit to the Mission station Ramahyuck at Lake Wellington, Gippsland (Victoria)', 1882, MS 12645, Box 348612

'Mission Work among the Aborigines at Ramahyuck, Victoria, Report for 1894', McCarron Bird & Co. Printers, Melbourne, 1895

Ramahyuck School, Gippsland, Inspector's Register Book, 1871–1884, MS 10401

Spieseke, J.F.W., Mission Station, Wimmera – Extracts from *Periodical Accounts relating to the Missions of the Church of the United Brethren*, compiled by C.W. Schooling, ca 1975, MS 9896

Victorian Association in Aid of Moravian Missions to the Aborigines of Australia, *Further Facts relating to the Moravian Missions in Australia. Sixth Paper*, Fergusson & Moore, Melbourne, 1867, pp. 7–17, handle.slv.vic.gov.au/10381/173013

State Records Office, Western Australia, Perth

MacFarlane, Helen and John Foley, 'Kimberley Mission Review – Analysis and Evaluation of Church and Government involvement in the Catholic Missions of the Kimberley', n.d., ca 1981

Victorian Archives Centre, Melbourne

Annual Reports of the Central Board for Aborigines, B332/0, 1861–1924

Zentralarchiv der Pallottinerprovinz (ZAPP), Limburg

Australien 1900–1907 B7 d.l. (3)

Bleischwitz, Alfons (Pater), P1 Nr 13

Bleischwitz, Alphonse, 'Geschichte der australischen Mission', MS, B7d,r (18)d

Diary of Wilhelm Droste (Pater), P1 Nr 17 (Droste diary)

Droste, Wilhelm (Pater), P1 Nr 17

Graf, Johann (Br), P1 Nr 22

Herholz, Franz (Br – Ex)

Hügel, P.F., 'Memories of Br. Heinrich Krallmann' in Hügel, Franz (Pater), P1 Nr 19

Nekes, Hermann (Pater), P1 Nr 16

Report by Missionary Hoerlein on the Bloomfield Station in Queensland, 1893, Hoerlein Family History, unpublished MS, courtesy of Ian Hoerlein, North Epping

Sixt, August (Br – Ex), P1 Nr 28

V. Kopf PSM Provinzial und Visitat, 2. 3. 1909 in Sixt, August (Br – Ex), P1 Nr 28

Wesely, Raimund (Br – Ex)

Worms, Ernst Alfred (Pater), P1 Nr 27

Zach, Rudolf (Br), P1 Nr 24

Publications

Ahrens, Theodor, 'Concepts of power in a Melanesian and Biblical perspective', *Missiology: An International Review* 5.2 (1977): 141–73.

Ahrens, Theodor, 'On grace and reciprocity: A fresh approach to contextualization with reference to Christianity in Melanesia', *International Review of Mission* 89.355 (2000): 515–28. doi.org/10.1111/j.1758-6631.2000.tb00241.x.

Albrecht, Paul, *From Mission to Church, 1877–2002: Finke River Mission*, Finke River Mission, Hermannsburg, 2002.

Amery, Rob, *Warrabarna Kaurna! Reclaiming an Australian Language*, Swets & Zeitlinger, Lisse, Netherlands, 2000.

Amery, Rob, 'Beyond their expectations: Teichelmann and Schürmann's efforts to preserve the Kaurna language continue to bear fruit', in Walter Veit (ed.), *The Struggle for Souls and Science: Constructing the Fifth Continent: German Missionaries and Scientists in Australia*, Occasional Paper No. 3, Strehlow Research Centre, Alice Springs, 2004, pp. 9–28.

Anderson, Christopher, 'A case study in failure: Kuku-Yalanji and the Lutherans at Bloomfield River, 1887–1902', in Tony Swain and Deborah Bird Rose (eds), *Aboriginal Australians and Christian Missions: Ethnographic and Historical Studies*, Australian Association for the Study of Religions, Bedford Park, SA, 1988.

Anderson, Christopher (ed.), *Politics of the Secret*, Oceania Monograph 45, University of Sydney, Sydney, 1995.

Anderson, Jon Christopher, 'The Political and Economic Basis of Kuku-Yalanji Social History', PhD thesis, University of Queensland, 1985.

Archibald, T.S., *Yorke's Peninsula Aboriginal Mission: A Brief Record of its History and Operations*, Hussey and Gillingham, Adelaide, 1915.

Australian Bureau of Statistics, 4713.0 – Population Characteristics, Aboriginal and Torres Strait Islander Australians, 2006.

Ballantyne, Tony, 'Colonial knowledge', in Sarah Stockwell (ed.), *The British Empire: Themes and Perspectives*, Blackwell Publishers, Oxford, 2008, pp. 177–98.

Ballantyne, Tony, 'Humanitarian narratives: knowledge and the politics of mission and empire', *Social Sciences and Missions* 24.2–3 (2011): 233–64.

Ballantyne, Tony, 'Paper, pen, and print: The transformation of the Kai Tahu knowledge order', *Comparative Studies in Society and History* 53.02 (2011): 232–60. doi.org/10.1017/S0010417511 000041.

Barry, Amanda, Joanna Cruickshank and Andrew Brown-May (eds), *Evangelists of Empire? Missionaries in Colonial History*, Melbourne University Conference series Vol. 18, eScholarship Research Centre in collaboration with the School of Historical Studies and with the assistance of Melbourne University Bookshop, Melbourne, 2008.

Bell, Diane, *Daughters of the Dreaming*, George Allen & Unwin, Sydney, 1983.

Bischofs, Joseph SAC, The Pious Society of Missions, Milwaukee (Wisconsin), to Pater Nekes, 28 November 1927 in Nekes, Hermann (Pater), P1 Nr 16, Zentralarchiv der Pallottinerprovinz (ZAPP).

Borowitzka, Lesley J., 'The Reverend Dr Louis Giustiniani and Anglican conflict in the Swan River Colony, Western Australia 1836–1838', *Journal of Religious History* 35.3 (2011): 352–73. doi.org/10.1111/j.1467-9809.2011.01075.x.

Bourke, D.F., *The History of the Catholic Church in Western Australia*, Archdiocese of Perth, Perth, 1979.

Brady, John, *A Descriptive Vocabulary of the Native Language of W. Australia*, Rome, 1845, reprinted in *Royal Geographical Society of Australasia Journal* 6.1 (1896): 8–18.

Brady, P.J., 'Forty faithful years – Derby farewells Father Lorenz in style', *KCP Magazine*, September/October 2004, broomediocese.org/wp-content/uploads/2016/02/KCP-2004-07.pdf.

Brauer, Alfred, *Under the Southern Cross: History of the Evangelical Lutheran Church of Australia*, Lutheran Publishing House, Adelaide, 1985.

Bridges, Barry John, 'The Church of England and the Aborigines of New South Wales, 1788–1855', PhD thesis, University of New South Wales, 1978.

Brock, Peggy (ed.), *Indigenous Peoples, Christianity and Religious Change*, Brill, Leiden, 2005.

Brock, Peggy, 'Negotiating colonialism: The life and times of Arthur Wellington Clah', in Amanda Barry, Joanna Cruickshank and Andrew Brown-May (eds), *Evangelists of Empire? Missionaries in Colonial History*, Melbourne University Conference series Vol. 18, 2008, p. 23.

Brock, Peggy, 'Jealous missionaries on the Pacific northwest coast of Canada', *Journal of Religious History* 39.4 (2015): 545–56. doi.org/10.1111/1467-9809.12266.

Buchanan, Robyn, *Logan: Rich in History, Young in Spirit. A Comprehensive History*, Logan City Council, Logan, 1999.

Byrne, Francis, *A Hard Road: Brother Frank Nissl 1888–1980: A Life of Service to the Aborigines of the Kimberleys*, Tara House, Nedlands, 1989.

Carey, Hilary M., 'Companions in the wilderness? Missionary wives in colonial Australia, 1788–1900', *Journal of Religious History* 19.2 (1995): 227–48. doi.org/10.1111/j.1467-9809.1995.tb00257.x.

Carey, Hilary and D.A. Roberts, WellPro Directory, The Wellington Valley Project, 2002.

Choo, Christine, *Mission Girls: Aboriginal Women on Catholic Missions in the Kimberley, Western Australia, 1900–1950*, University of Western Australia Press, Perth, 2001.

Christmann, Helmut, Peter John Hempenstall and Dirk Anthony Ballendorf, *Die Karolinen-Inseln in deutscher Zeit: eine kolonialgeschichtliche Fallstudie*, Bremer Asien-Pazifik Studien Vol. 1, Lit Verlag, Münster, 1991.

Cochrane, Susan and Max Quanchi (eds), *Hunting the Collectors: Pacific Collections in Australian Museums, Art Galleries and Archives*, Cambridge Scholars Publishing, Newcastle upon Tyne, 2014.

Cole, Joshua and Carol Symes, *Western Civilisations. Vol. 1: Their History and their Culture*, Wiley/Norton, New York, 2013.

Cole, Keith, *From Mission to Church: The CMS Mission to the Aborigines of Arnhem Land 1908–1985*, Keith Cole Publications, Bendigo, 1985.

Cox, Jim and Adam Possamai (eds), *Religion and non-Religion among Australian Aboriginal Peoples*, Routledge, Abingdon, 2016.

Cunningham, Anne, *The Rome Connection: Australia, Ireland and the Empire, 1865–1885*, Crossing Press, Darlinghurst, 2002.

Curtis-Wendlandt, Lisa, 'Corporal punishment and moral reform at Hermannsburg mission', *History Australia* 7.1 (2010): 7.1–7.17.

Dixon, R.M.W., *The Languages of Australia*, Cambridge University Press, Cambridge, 1980.

Döring, Detlef, *Katalog der Handschriften der Universitätsbibliothek Leipzig*, Otto Harrassowitz Verlag, Wiesbaden, 2005.

Duelke, Britta, *'Same but Different': Vom Umgang mit Vergangenheit: Tradition und Geschichte im Alltag einer nordaustralischen Aborigines-Kommune*, Studien zur Kulturkunde 108, Rüdiger Köppe Verlag, Köln, 1998.

Durack, Mary, *The Rock and the Sand*, Corgi, London, 1971.

Eddy, J. 'Therry, John Joseph (1790–1864)', *Australian Dictionary of Biography*, National Centre of Biography, The Australian National University, adb.anu.edu.au/biography/therry-john-joseph-2722/text3835, published first in hardcopy 1967 (accessed 23 September 2015).

Edwards, W.H. (Bill), *Moravian Aboriginal Missions in Australia 1850–1919*, Uniting Church Historical Society (SA), Adelaide, 1999.

Eipper, C., 'Observations made on a journey to the natives at Toorbal, August 2nd 1841 by the Rev. Christopher Eipper, of the Moreton Bay German Mission – Journal of the Reverend Christopher Eipper, Missionary to the Aborigines at Moreton Bay 1841' published in the *Colonial Observer*, www.jenwilletts.com/Rev.Eipper.htm (accessed 1 December 2008).

Erckenbrecht, Corinna, 'Der Bischof mit seinen 150 Bräuten', *Jahrbuch des Museums für Völkerkunde Leipzig* 41 (2003): 303–22.

Etherington, Norman (ed.), *Missions and Empire*, Oxford University Press, New York, 2005.

Evans, Nicholas, 'Macassan loans and linguistic stratification in western Arnhem Land', in Patrick McConvell and Nicholas Evans (eds), *Archaeology and Linguistics: Aboriginal Australia in Global Perspective*, Oxford University Press, Melbourne, 1997, pp. 237–60.

Evans, Raymond, 'The mogwi take mi-an-jin: Race relations and the Moreton Bay penal settlement 1824–42', in Raymond Evans, *Fighting Words: Writing about Race*, University of Queensland Press, St Lucia, 1992.

Evans, Raymond, *A History of Queensland*, Cambridge University Press, Port Melbourne, 2007.

Farnbacher, Traugott and Christian Weber (eds), *Ein Zentrum für Weltmission – Neuendettelsau – Einführung, Zeittafeln, Dokumente, Namen, 1842–2002*, Missionswerk der Evangelisch-Lutherischen Kirche in Bayern, Neuendettelsau, 2004.

Fesl, Eve, *Conned! Eve Mumewa D. Fesl Speaks Out on Language and the Conspiracy of Silence: A Koorie Perspective*, University of Queensland Press, St Lucia, 1993.

Fitz-Gibbon, Bryan and Marianne Gizycki, 'A History of Last-Resort Lending and Other Support for Troubled Financial Institutions in Australia', System Stability Department, Reserve Bank of Australia, Research Discussion Paper 2001–07, October 2001.

Flierl, Johann, *My Life and God's Mission*, translated by Erich Flierl, Lutheran Church of Australia, Board for Church Cooperation in World Mission, Adelaide, 1999.

Flynn, Frank, *Distant Horizons: Mission Impressions as Published in the Annals of Our Lady of the Sacred Heart*, Sacred Heart Monastery, Kensington, 1947.

Flynn, F., '40 ans chez les Aborigènes Australiens – l'évêque aux 150 épouses', *Annales de Notre-Dame du Sacré-Coeur*, December 1960: 266–69.

Foucault, Michel, *Discipline and Punish: The Birth of the Prison*, Vintage, New York, 1977.

Froehlich, Susanne (ed.), *Als Pioniermissionar in das ferne Neu Guinea: Johann Flierls Lebenserinnerungen*, 2 vols, Harrassowitz Verlag, Wiesbaden, 2015.

Gale, Mary-Anne, *Dhanum Djorra'wuy Dhäwu: A History of Writing in Aboriginal Languages*, Aboriginal Research Institute, University of South Australia, Underdale, 1997.

Ganter, Regina, *The Pearl-Shellers of Torres Strait: Resource Use, Development and Decline, 1860s–1960s*, Melbourne University Press, Clayton, Vic., 1994.

Ganter, Regina, 'Letters from Mapoon: Colonising aboriginal gender', *Australian Historical Studies* 29.113 (1999): 267–85. doi.org/10.1080/10314619908596102.

Ganter, Regina, 'Turning the map upside down', *History Compass* 4.1 (2006): 26–35. doi.org/10.1111/j.1478-0542.2006.00301.x.

Ganter, Regina, 'Historicising culture: Father Ernst Worms and the German anthropological traditions', in Nicolas Peterson and Anna Kenny (eds), *German Ethnography in Australia*, ANU Press, Canberra, 2017, pp. 357–79. doi.org/10.22459/GEA.09.2017.

Ganter, Regina, 'Too hot to handle: A German missionary's struggle with ethnography in Australia', *Zeitschrift für Australienstudien* 31 (2017): 57–71.

Ganter, Regina with Julia Martinez and Gary Lee, *Mixed Relations: Asian–Aboriginal Contact in North Australia*, University of Western Australian Publishing, Crawley, 2006.

Gardner, Helen, 'Assuming judicial control: George Brown's narrative defence of the "New Britain raid"', in Diane Kirkby and Catharine Coleborne (eds), *Law, History, Colonialism: The Reach of Empire*, Manchester University Press, Manchester, 2001.

Gibson, Dean, 'War of Hope', NITV, 25 April 2015.

Girola, Stefano, 'Fr. Confalonieri's legacy in the Australian church', *L'Osservatore Romano*, Weekly Edition in English, 28 October 2009.

Gondarra, Djiniyini, *Series of Reflections of Aboriginal Theology: Four Reflections Based on Church Renewal, Christian Theology of the Land, Contextualization and Unity*, Bethel Presbytery, Northern Synod of the Uniting Church in Australia, Darwin, 1986.

Goodale, Jane C., *Tiwi Wives: A Study of the Women of Melville Island, North Australia*, University of Washington Press, Seattle, 1971.

Govor, Elena, *My Dark Brother: The Story of the Illins, a Russian–Aboriginal Family*, University of New South Wales Press, Sydney, 2000.

Gray, Victor, *Catholicism in Queensland: Fifty Years of Progress*, Roberts and Russell, Brisbane, 1910.

Green, Neville, 'Aborigines and white settlers in the nineteenth century', in C.T. Stannage (ed.), *A New History of Western Australia*, University of Western Australia Press, Nedlands, 1981, pp. 86–87.

Griffin, James, 'Verjus, Henri Stanislas (1860–1892)', *Australian Dictionary of Biography*, National Centre of Biography, The Australian National University, adb.anu.edu.au/biography/verjus-henri-stanislas-4777, published first in hardcopy 1976 (accessed 3 May 2017).

Grimshaw, Patricia, *Creating a Nation 1788–1990*, McPhee-Gribble, Melbourne, 1994.

Grimshaw, Pat and Andrew May (eds), *Missionaries, Indigenous Peoples and Cultural Exchange*, Sussex Academic Press, Eastbourne, 2010.

Grimshaw, Patricia and Elizabeth Nelson, 'Empire, "the civilising mission" and Indigenous Christian women in colonial Victoria', *Australian Feminist Studies* 16.36 (2001): 295–309. doi.org/10.1080/08164640120097534.

Grope, Lesley, 'Cedars in the Wilderness', *Lutheran Church of Australia Yearbook*, 1987, pp. 25–57.

Gsell, F.X., '*The Bishop with 150 Wives': Fifty Years as a Missionary*, Angus and Robertson, Sydney, 1956.

Gunson, Niel, *Messengers of Grace: Evangelical Missionaries in the South Seas 1797–1860*, Oxford University Press, Melbourne, 1978.

Habermas, Rebekka, 'Mission im 19. Jahrhundert – Globale Netze des Religiösen', *Historische Zeitschrift* 287 (2008): 629–79. doi.org/10.1524/hzhz.2008.0056.

Haccius, Georg, *Theodor Harms, sein Leben und sein Wirken. Ein Gedenkbüchlein zu seinem 100. Geburtstag am 19.3.1919*, Verlag der Hermannsburger Missionshandlung, Hermannsburg, 1919.

Haddon, A.C. with A. Hingston Quiggin, *History of Anthropology*, Watts & Co., London, 1910.

Hall, Robert A., *Black Diggers: Aborigines and Torres Strait Islanders in the Second World War*, Allen & Unwin, Sydney, 1989.

Harms, Hartwig, *Träume und Tränen – Hermannsburger Missionare und die Wirkungen ihrer Arbeit in Australien und Neuseeland*, Hermannsburg, Verlag Ludwig Harms Haus, 2003.

Harris, John, *One Blood: 200 Years of Aboriginal Encounter with Christianity: A Story of Hope*, Albatross Books, Sutherland, NSW, 1990.

Haviland, John with Roger Hart, *Old Man Fog and the Last Aborigines of Barrow Point*, Crawford House Publishing, Bathurst, 1998.

Haviland, John and Leslie Haviland, '"How much food will there be in heaven?" Lutherans and Aborigines around Cooktown to 1900', *Aboriginal History* 4.2 (1980): 118–49.

Hebart, Th., *The United Evangelical Lutheran Church in Australia (U.E.L.C.A.) Its History, Activities and Characteristics, 1838–1938*, (Trans. Johann J. Stolz), Lutheran Book Depot, Adelaide, 1938.

Henson, Barbara, *A Straight-out Man: F.W. Albrecht and Central Australian Aborigines*, Melbourne University Press, Carlton, Vic., 1992.

Hercus, Luise, 'Reuther's Diari: Looking at the Detail', paper presented at The German Anthropological Tradition in Australia, Nicolas Peterson and Anna Kenny, The Australian National University, 18–19 June 2015.

Hercus, Luise and Kim McCaul, 'Otto Siebert: The missionary-ethnographer', in Walter Veit (ed.), *The Struggle for Souls and Science: Constructing the Fifth Continent: German Missionaries and Scientists in Australia*, Occasional Paper No. 3, Strehlow Research Centre, Alice Springs, 2004, pp. 36–50.

Hey, Rev. J.N., *A Brief History of the Presbyterian Church's Mission Enterprise among the Australian Aborigines*, New Press, Sydney, 1931.

Hoare, Michael, *The Tactless Philosopher: Johann Reinhold Forster (1729–98)*, Hawthorne Press, Melbourne, 1976.

Holzknecht, Philip, 'A priesthood of priests? The German Lutherans in Queensland', in Manfred Jurgensen and Alan Corkhill (eds), *The German Presence in Queensland*, University of Queensland Press, Brisbane, 1988, pp. 155–73.

Hudson, Wayne, 'Religious citizenship', *Australian Journal of Politics & History* 49.3 (2003): 425–29.

Hudson, Wayne and Steven Slaughter (eds), *Globalisation and Citizenship: The Transnational Challenge*, Routledge, London, 2007.

Hurley, Andrew W., 'German-Indigenous musical flows at Ntaria in the 1960s: Tiger Tjalkalyeri's rendition of "Silent Night," or what is tradition anyway?', *Perfect Beat* 15.1 (2014): 7–21. doi.org/10.1558/prbt.v15i1.16668.

Ireland, William, *Historical Sketch of the Zulu Mission, in South Africa, as also of the Gaboon Mission in Western Africa*, American Board of Commissioners for Foreign Mission, Boston, 1865.

Jensz, Felicity, *Moravian Missionaries in the British Colony of Victoria, Australia, 1848–1908: Influential Strangers*, Brill, Leiden, 2010.

Jensz, Felicity, 'Everywhere at home, everywhere a stranger: The communities of the Moravian missionary Mary (Polly) Hartmann', in Regina Ganter and Pat Grimshaw (eds), *Reading the Lives of White Mission Women, Journal of Australian Studies* 39.1 (2015): 20–31. doi.org/10.1080/14443058.2014.989882.

Jones, Philip G., '"A Box of Native Things": Ethnographic Collectors and the South Australian Museum, 1830s–1930s', PhD thesis, Department of History, University of Adelaide, 1997.

Jones, Philip, 'Naming the dead heart: Hillier's map and Reuther's gazetteer of 2,468 placenames in north-eastern South Australia', in Luise Hercus, Flavia Hodges and Jane Simpson (eds), *The Land is a Map: Placenames of Indigenous Origin in Australia*, Pandanus Books, Canberra, 2002, pp. 187–200.

Jones, Philip G., Peter Sutton and Kaye Clark, *Art and Land: Aboriginal Sculptures of the Lake Eyre Region*, South Australian Museum, Adelaide, 1986.

Kenny, Anna, *The Aranda's Pepa: An Introduction to Carl Strehlow's Masterpiece Die Aranda-und Loritja-Stämme in Zentral-Australien (1907–1920)*, ANU Press, Canberra, 2013.

Kenny, Robert, *The Lamb Enters the Dreaming: Nathanael Pepper and the Ruptured World*, Scribe Publications, Melbourne, 2007.

Kidd, Rosalind, *The Way We Civilise: Aboriginal Affairs, the Untold Story*, University of Queensland Press, St Lucia, 1997.

Kirkby, Diane and Catharine Coleborne (eds), *Law, History, Colonialism: The Reach of Empire*, Manchester University Press, Manchester, 2001.

Kneebone, Heidi, 'The Language of the Chosen View: The First Phase of Graphization of Dieri by Hermannsburg Missionaries, Lake Killalpaninna 1867–80', PhD thesis, University of Adelaide, 2006.

Koller, Wilhelm, *Die Missionsanstalt in Neuendettelsau, ihre Geschichte und das Leben in ihr*, Verlag des Missionshauses, Neuendettelsau, 1924.

Larsen, Timothy, *A People of One Book: The Bible and the Victorians*, Oxford University Press, Oxford, 2011. doi.org/10.1093/acprof:oso/9780199570096.001.0001.

Lee, H.I., 'British policy towards the religion, ancient laws and customs in Malta 1824–1851', *Melita Historica: Journal of the Malta Historical Society* 3.4 (1963): 1–14.

Legislative Assembly, *Report from the Select Committee on the Native Police Force and the Condition of the Aborigines Generally*, Fairfax and Belbridge, Brisbane, 1861.

Leonhardi, Moritz von, 'Über einige religiöse und totemistische Vorstellungen der Aranda und Loritja in Zentralaustralien', *Globus* 91 (1907): 285–90.

Leske, Everard (ed.), *Hermannsburg: A Vision and Mission*, Lutheran Publishing House, Adelaide, 1977.

Leske, Everard, *For Faith and Freedom: The story of Lutherans and Lutheranism in Australia 1838–1996*, Open Book publishers, Adelaide, 1996.

Leugers, Antonia, *Eine geistliche Unternehmensgeschichte: Die Limburger Pallottiner-Provinz 1892–1932*, EOS Verlag, St Ottilien, 2004.

Lockwood, Christine, 'The Two Kingdoms: Lutheran Missionaries and the British Civilizing Mission in Early South Australia', PhD thesis, University of Adelaide, 2014.

Lockwood, Douglas, *The Front Door: Darwin, 1869–1969*, Rigby, Adelaide, 1968.

Lohe, M., 'A mission is established at Hermannsburg', in Everard Leske, *Hermannsburg: A Vision and a Mission,* Lutheran Publishing House, Adelaide, 1977.

Loos, Noel, *White Christ Black Cross: The Emergence of a Black Church*, Aboriginal Studies Press, Canberra, 2007.

Lüdemann, Ernst-August (ed.), *Vision: Gemeinde weltweit – 150 Jahre Hermannsburger Mission und Ev. Luth. Missionswerk in Niedersachsen*, Verlag der Missionshandlung, Hermannsburg, 2000.

Luemmen, John and Brigida Nailon, *Led by the Spirit: Autobiography of Father John Luemmen SAC*, Imprinti Potest Provincial of the Pallottines in Australia, Rossmoyne, WA, 1999.

Lydon, Jane, *Fantastic Dreaming: The Archaeology of an Aboriginal Mission*, Rowman AltaMira Press, Lanham, MD, 2009.

McGregor, William B., 'Frs. Hermann Nekes and Ernest Worms's Dictionary of Australian Languages, part III of "Australian Languages" (1953)', in Ilana Mushin (ed.), Proceedings of the 2004 Conference of the Australian Linguistics Society, hdl.handle.net/2123/108.

McGregor, William B., 'Frs. Hermann Nekes and Ernest Worms's "Australian Languages"', *Anthropos* 102.1 (2007): 99–114.

McIntosh, Ian S., 'Missing the revolution! Negotiating disclosure on the pre-Macassans (Bayini) in north-east Arnhem Land', in Martin Thomas and Margo Neale (eds), *Exploring the Legacy of the 1948 Arnhem Land Expedition*, ANU E Press, Canberra, 2011, pp. 337–54.

Mackillop, D., 'Anthropological notes on the Aboriginal tribes of the Daly River', *Transactions of the Royal Society of South Australia* 17 (1892–93): 254–64.

Massam, Katharine, 'Missionary women and work: Benedictine women at New Norcia claiming a religious vocation', in Regina Ganter and Pat Grimshaw (eds), *Reading the Lives of White Mission Women, Journal of Australian Studies* 39.1 (2015): 44–53.

May, Andrew, *Welsh Missionaries and British Imperialism: The Empire of Clouds in North-east India*, Manchester University Press, Manchester, 2012.

Menzel, Heinrich, 'Zum Goldenen Jubiläum unserer Kimberley-Mission in Australien', *Pallottis Werk* 1951/1, p. 16.

Monteath, Peter (ed.), *Germans: Travellers, Settlers and Their Descendants in South Australia*, Wakefield Press, Kent Town, 2011.

Moran, Patrick Francis, *History of the Catholic Church in Australasia: From Authentic Sources*, Frank, Coffee & Co., Sydney, n.d.

Moreton-Robinson, Aileen, *Talkin' Up to the White Woman: Aboriginal Women and Feminism*, University of Queensland Press, St Lucia, 2000.

Mühlhäusler, Peter, 'Exploring the missionary position', *Journal of Pidgin and Creole Languages* 14.2 (1999): 339–46. doi.org/10.1075/jpcl.14.2.05muh.

Mühlhäusler, Peter, *Linguistic Ecology: Language Change and Linguistic Imperialism in the Pacific Region*, Routledge, London, 2002.

Murray, Barbara, 'Georg Balthasar von Neumayer's directives for scientific research', in Walter Veit (ed.), *The Struggle for Souls and Science: Constructing the Fifth Continent: German Missionaries and Scientists in Australia*, Occasional Paper No. 3, Strehlow Research Centre, Alice Springs, 2004, pp. 130–42.

Nailon, Brigida, *Nothing is Wasted in the Household of God: Vincent Pallotti's Vision in Australia 1901–2001*, Spectrum, Richmond, 2001.

Nailon, Brigida, *Emo and San Salvador*, 2 vols, Brigidine Sisters, Echuca, 2005.

Nailon, Brigida and Francis Huegel (eds), *This is Your Place: Beagle Bay Mission 1890–1990*, Beagle Bay Community, Broome, 1990.

Nairn, Bede, 'Polding, John Bede (1794–1877)', *Australian Dictionary of Biography*, National Centre of Biography, The Australian National University, adb.anu.edu.au/biography/polding-john-bede-2557/text3485 (accessed 6 November 2012).

Neumayer, G.B. (ed.), *Anleitung zu wissenschaftlichen Beobachtungen auf Reisen*, Berlin, 1875.

Nicholls, Angus, 'Anglo-German mythologics: The Australian Aborigines and modern theories of myth in the work of Baldwin Spencer and Carl Strehlow', *History of the Human Sciences* 20.1 (2007): 83–114. doi.org/10.1177/0952695106075077.

Nolan, Jeanette, 'Pastor J. G. Haussmann: A Queensland Pioneer, 1838–1901', Honours thesis, University of Queensland, 1964.

O'Kelly, G.J., 'The Jesuit Mission Stations in the Northern Territory 1882–1899', Honours thesis, Monash University, 1967.

Olabimtan, Kehinda, 'Basel Mission', *The Encyclopedia of Christian Civilization*, 25 November 2011. doi.org/10.1002/9780470670606. wbecc0130.

Omasmeier, P., 'Australien', *Pallottis Werk* 1955/4.

Parkinson, Richard, *Thirty Years in the South Seas: Land and People, Customs and Traditions in the Bismarck Archipelago and on the German Solomon Islands*, Sydney University Press, Sydney, 2010.

Pearson, Noel, 'Ngamu-ngaadyarr, Muuri-bunggaga and Midha Mini in Guugu Yimidhirr history: Dingoes, Sheep and Mr Muni in Guugu Yimidhirr History: Hope Vale Lutheran Mission 1900–1950', Honours thesis, University of Sydney, 1986.

Perez, E., 'Griver, Martin (1814–1886)', *Australian Dictionary of Biography*, National Centre of Biography, The Australian National University, adb.anu.edu.au/biography/griver-martin-3674/text5739, published first in hardcopy 1972 (accessed online 2 October 2015).

Pike, Douglas, *Paradise of Dissent: South Australia 1829–1857*, Melbourne University Press, Melbourne, 1957.

Pilhofer, Georg, *Die Geschichte der Neuendettelsauer Mission in Neuguinea*, Freimund Verlag, Neuendettelsau, 1961.

Pohlner, Howard J., *Gangurru*, Lutheran Church of Australia, Adelaide, 1986.

Poland, Wilhelm, *Loose Leaves: Reminiscences of a Pioneer North Queensland Missionary*, Lutheran Publishing House, Adelaide, 1988.

Pollock, David and Ruth van Reken, *Third Culture Kids: Growing Up among Worlds*, Nicholas Brealey, London, 2001.

Proeve, Ernst Heinrich, *Three Missionary Pioneers – A Tribute to J. E. Jacob, H. H. Vogelsang, H. Vogelsang*, Tanunda, 1946.

Rechner, Judy Gale, *GJ Rechner and His Descendants: Rechner, Fischer/ Fisher, Stolz and Reuther Journeys*, Rechner Researchers, Adelaide, 2008.

Redmond, Tony, 'Tracks, Texts and Shadows: Some Intercultural Effects of the 1938 Frobenius Expedition to the North-West Kimberley', paper presented at The German Anthropological Tradition in Australia, Nicolas Peterson and Anna Kenny, The Australian National University, 18–19 June 2015.

Reece, Bob, *Daisy Bates: Grand Dame of the Desert*. Vol. 3, National Library Australia, Canberra, 2007.

Reidy, Mark, 'Brand new day for Fr. John Luemmen', *The Record*, 9 February 2014, www.therecord.com.au/news/brand-new-day-for-fr-john-luemmen (accessed March 2014).

Richards, Jonathan, '"What a howl there would be if some of our folk were so treated by an enemy": The Evacuation of Aboriginal People from Cape Bedford Mission, 1942', *Aboriginal History* 36 (2013): 67–98.

Ritchie, Pat, *North of the Never Never*, Angus & Robertson, Sydney, 1934.

Robin, A. De Q., 'Hale, Mathew Blagden (1811–1895)', *Australian Dictionary of Biography*, National Centre of Biography, The Australian National University, adb.anu.edu.au/biography/hale-mathew-blagden-3689/text5771, published first in hardcopy 1972 (accessed 3 October 2015).

Rose, Deborah Bird, 'Signs of life on a barbarous frontier: Intercultural encounters in north Australia', *Humanities Research* 2 (1998): 17–36.

Rose, Gordon, 'The Heart of a Man: A biography of missionary G.H. Schwarz', *Yearbook of the Lutheran Church of Australia*, 1978, pp. 26–68.

Roth, Walter, Annual Report of the Chief Protector of Aborigines, *Queensland Votes and Proceedings*, 1903, Vol. 2, p. 470.

Roth, Walter, *Royal Commission on the Condition of the Natives – Report*, Watson Government Printer, Perth, 1905.

Rowley, Charles D., *Aboriginal Policy and Practice: The Destruction of Aboriginal Society.* Vol. 1, Australian National University Press, Canberra, 1970.

Salter, Elizabeth, *Daisy Bates*, Angus and Robertson, Sydney, 1971.

Salvado, Rosendo, *Memorie Storiche dell' Australia, Particolarmente della Missione Benedettina di Nuova Norcia*, S. Congreg. de Propaganda Fide, Rome, 1851; translated E.J. Stormon, *The Salvado Memoirs: Historical Memoirs of Australia and Particularly of the Benedictine Mission of New Norcia and of the Habits and Customs of the Australian Natives*, University of Western Australia Press, Nedlands, 1977.

Saunders, Kay (Kay Evans), 'Missionary Effort Towards the Cape York Aborigines, 1886–1910, a Study of Culture Contact', Honours thesis, University of Queensland, 1969.

Saunders, Kay, 'Inequalities of sacrifice: Aboriginal and Torres Strait Islander labour in northern Australia during the Second World War', *Labour History* 69 (1995): 131–48. doi.org/10.2307/27516395.

Scherer, Philipp A. (trans. and ed.), *The Hermannsburg Chronicle, 1877–1933*, Tanunda, SA, 1995.

Schlatterer, W., *Geschichte der Basler Mission 1815–1915*, 3 vols, Basler Missionsbuchhandlung, 1916.

Schmiechen, Joc, 'The Hermannsburg Missionary Society in Australia 1866–1894, a Study in Aboriginal and European Interaction During First Contacts', Honours thesis, University of Adelaide, 1971.

Schubert, David A. and John Potter, *Kavel's People: From Prussia to South Australia*, sound recording, Royal Society for the Blind of South Australia, Gilles Plains, 1990.

Schütte, Heinz, 'Lokale Reaktionen auf evangelische Missionsbemühungen im kolonialen Neuguinea 1887–1914', in Wilfried Wagner (ed.), *Rassendiskriminierung, Kolonialpolitik und ethnisch-nationale Identität*, Bremer Asien-Pazifik Studien Vol. 2, Münster/Hamburg, Lit, 1992, pp. 497–509.

Smallwood, Gracelyn, 'The Role of the Churches from an Indigenous Woman's Perspective', conference paper for World AIDS Day, November 1990, James Cook University, Townsville, 1990.

Spindler, Marc, 'Les missions allemandes: leur liquidation et résilience, 1914–2014', Colloque du CREDIC, Neuendettelsau, 2015.

St John's Lutheran Church, *100 years of Grace: St John's Lutheran Church, Bundaberg Qld. 1877–1977*, The Church, Bundaberg, 1977.

Steele, J.G., *Aboriginal Pathways in Southeast Queensland and the Richmond River*, University of Queensland Press, St Lucia, 1983.

Stevens, Christine, *White Man's Dreaming: Killalpaninna Mission, 1866–1915*, Oxford University Press, Melbourne, 1994.

Stilz, Gerhard (ed.), *Colonies – Missions – Cultures in the English-speaking World*, Stauffenberg Verlag, Tübingen, 2001.

Stockigt, Clara, 'Early descriptions of Pama-Nyungan ergativity', *Historiographia Linguistica* 42.2–3 (2015): 335–77.

Stockigt, Clara, 'Pama-Nyungan Morphosyntax: Lineages of Early Description', PhD thesis, University of Adelaide, 2016.

Stocking, George, *Functionalism Historicized: Essays on British Social Anthropology*, University of Wisconsin Press, Madison, 1984.

Stocking, G.W. (ed.), *Volksgeist as Method and Ethic: Essays on Boasian Ethnography and the German Anthropological Tradition*, University of Wisconsin Press, Wisconsin, 1996.

Stolle, Volker, 'Wozu war ein konfessionelles Hilfswerk nötig?', Lernprozesse für unsere Mission Nr 74, Evangelisches Missionswerk Deutschland (n.d.), www.emw-d.de/publikationen/publikationen.emw/de.shop.emw.126/index.html.

Stolle, Volker, *Wer seine Hand an den Pflug legt: Die missionarische Wirksamkeit der selbständigen evangelisch-lutherischen Kirchen in Deutschland im 19. Jahrhundert*, Bleckmarer Missionsschriften, 1992.

Strehlow, Carl, 'Unsere australische Mission. Bericht von Hermannsburg', *Kirchen- und Missionszeitung* 33.13, Tanunda (19 July 1897): 100.

Strehlow, John, *The Tale of Frieda Keysser: Frieda Keysser & Carl Strehlow: An Historical Biography. Volume 1, 1875–1910*, Wild Cat Press, London, 2011.

Strong, David, *The Australian Dictionary of Jesuit Biography 1848–1998*, Archives of the Society of Jesus, Halstead Press, Rushcutters Bay, NSW, 1999.

Stunt, Timothy, *From Awakening to Secession: Radical Evangelicals in Switzerland and Britain, 1815–35*, Bloomsbury Publishing, London, 2000.

Sutton, Peter, and Bruce Rigsby, 'People with "politicks": management of land and personnel on Australia's Cape York Peninsula.' *Resource managers: North American and Australian hunter-gatherers* (1982): 155–71.

Swain, Tony and Deborah Bird Rose (eds), *Aboriginal Australians and Christian Missions: Ethnographic and Historical Studies*, Australian Association for the Study of Religions, Bedford Park, SA, 1988.

Tampke, Jürgen (ed.), *The Germans in Australia,* Cambridge University Press, Sydney, 2007.

Taylor, John, 'Goods and gods: A follow-up study of "Steel Axes for Stone Age Australians"', in Tony Swain and Deborah Bird Rose (eds), *Aboriginal Australians and Christian Missions: Ethnographic and Historical Studies*, Study of Religions, Vol. 6, Australian Association for the Study of Religions, Bedford Park, SA, 1988.

Taylor, Luke, Graeme K. Ward, Graham Henderson, Richard Davis and Lynley A. Wallis, *The Power of Knowledge, the Resonance of Tradition*, Aboriginal Studies Press, Canberra, 1997.

Theil, Ilse, *Reise in das Land des Todesschattens: Lebensläufe von Frauen der Missionare der Norddeutschen Mission in Togo/Westafrika (von 1849 bis 1899)*, LIT Verlag, Münster, 2008.

Theile, F. Otto, *One Hundred Years of the Lutheran Church in Queensland*, UELCA Qld. District, Brisbane, Lutheran Publishing House, Adelaide, 1938 (facsimile reprint 1985).

Thompson, David, *Bora is Like Church: Aboriginal Initiation and the Christian Church at Lockhart River, Queensland*, Australian Board of Missions, Sydney, 1985.

Thorpe, Osmund, *First Catholic Mission to the Australian Aborigines*, Pellegrini & Co., Sydney, 1950.

Turnbull, Paul, 'British anthropological thought in colonial practice: The appropriation of Indigenous Australian bodies, 1860–1880', in Bronwen Douglas and Chris Ballard (eds), *Foreign Bodies: Oceania and the Science of Race 1750–1940*, ANU E Press, Canberra, 2008, pp. 205–28.

Van Gent, Jacqueline, 'Blickwechsel: Arrernte encounters with Lutheran missionaries in Central Australia', in Hans Medick and Peer Schmidt (ed.), *Luther zwischen den Kulturen*, Vandenhoeck & Ruprecht, Göttingen, 2004, pp. 396–420.

Van Gent, Jacqueline, 'Changing concepts of embodiment and illness among the Arrernte at Hermannsburg Mission', in Peggy Brock (ed.), *Indigenous Peoples, Christianity and Religious Change*, Brill, Leiden, 2005, pp. 227–48.

Veit, Walter, 'In search of Carl Strehlow: Lutheran missionary and Australian anthropologist', in David Walker and Jürgen Tampke (eds), *From Berlin to the Burdekin: The German Contribution to the Development of Australian Science, Exploration and the Arts*, University of New South Wales Press, Sydney, 1991, pp. 108–34.

Veit, Walter, 'Labourers in the vineyard or the uneducated missionary: Aspects of the non-theological education of missionaries', in Michael Cawthorn (ed.), *Tradition in the Midst of Change: Communities, Cultures and the Strehlow Legacy in Central Australia: Proceedings of the Strehlow Conference 2002*, Strehlow Research Centre, Alice Springs, 2004, pp. 136–50.

Veit, Walter, 'Social anthropology versus cultural anthropology: Baldwin Walter Spencer and Carl Friedrich Theodor Strehlow in Central Australia', in Walter Veit (ed.), *The Struggle for Souls and Science: Constructing the Fifth Continent: German Missionaries and Scientists in Australia*, Occasional Paper No. 3, Strehlow Research Centre, Alice Springs, 2004, pp. 92–110.

Veit, Walter (ed.), *The Struggle for Souls and Science: Constructing the Fifth Continent: German Missionaries and Scientists in Australia*, Occasional Paper No. 3, Strehlow Research Centre, Alice Springs, 2004.

Wagner, Wilfried (ed.), *Kolonien und Missionen: Referate des 3. internationalen kolonialgeschichtlichen Symposiums 1993 in Bremen*. Vol. 12, Lit, Münster, 1994.

Walter, Georg PSM, *Australien: Land, Leute, Mission*, Limburg, 1928 and Walter, Georg, *Australia: Land, People, Mission*, Bishop of Broome, Broome, 1982.

Ward, Glenyse, *Wandering Girl*, Magabala Books, Broome, 1988.

Wendt, Reinhard, *Sammeln, Vernetzen, Auswerten: Missionare und ihr Beitrag zum Wandel europäischer Weltsicht*, Gunter Narr Verlag, Tübingen, 2001.

Wendlandt-Homann, Luise, *Zugvögel kennen ihre Zeit: Als Missonarsfrau in vier Erdteilen*, Verlag der Ev. Luth Mission Erlangen, Hermannsburg, 1987.

Werner, August Bernhard, *Early Mission Work at Antwerp Victoria*, Banner Print, Dimboola, 1959.

Western Australia, Royal Commission, *Report of the Royal Commission on the Condition of the Natives*, Government Printer, Perth, 1905.

Wharton, Geoffrey Stephen, 'The Day They Burned Mapoon: A Study of the Closure of a Queensland Presbyterian Mission', Honours thesis, University of Queensland, 1996.

White, Richard, *The Middle Ground: Indians, Empires, and Republics in the Great Lakes Region, 1650–1815*, Cambridge University Press, Cambridge, 1991. doi.org/10.1017/CBO9780511584671.

Wiebusch, C.A., *Koonibba Jubilee Booklet 1901–1926*, Lutheran Publishing Company, Adelaide, 1926.

William, Dom, 'Salvado, Rosendo (1814–1900)', *Australian Dictionary of Biography*, National Centre of Biography, The Australian National University, adb.anu.edu.au/biography/salvado-rosendo-2627/text 3635, published first in hardcopy 1967 (accessed online 2 October 2015).

Wiltgen, Ralph M., *The Founding of the Roman Catholic Church in Oceania, 1825 to 1850*, Princeton Theological Monograph Series, No. 143, Wipf and Stock Publishers, Eugene, OR, 2010.

Winter, Christine, 'The NSDAP stronghold Finschhafen, New Guinea', in Emily Turner-Graham and Christine Winter (eds), *National Socialism in Oceania: A Critical Evaluation of its Effect and Aftermath*, Peter Lang, Frankfurt am Main, 2010, pp. 31–47.

Winter, Christine, *Looking After One's Own: The Rise of Nationalism and the Politics of the Neuendettelsauer Mission in Australia, New Guinea and Germany (1921–1933)*, Peter Lang Verlag, Frankfurt am Main, 2012.

Wurm, Stephen A., Peter Mühlhäusler and Darrell T. Tryon (eds), *Atlas of Languages of Intercultural Communication in the Pacific, Asia, and the Americas*. Vol. 3, Mouton de Gruyter, Berlin, 1996.

Yu, Sarah, 'Broome Creole Aboriginal and Asian partnerships along the Kimberley coast', in Regina Ganter (ed.), *Asians in Australian History*, Queensland Review 6.2 (1999): 49–73.

Zantop, Susanne, *Colonial Fantasies: Conquest, Family and Nation in Precolonial Germany, 1770–1870*, Duke University Press, Durham, NC, 1997. doi.org/10.1215/9780822382119.

Zengotta, Thomas de, 'The functional reduction of kinship in the social thought of John Locke', in George W. Stocking Jr, *Functionalism historicized: Essays on British social anthropology*, University of Wisconsin Press, Madison, 1984, pp. 10–30.

Zucker, Margaret, *From Patrons to Partners: A History of the Catholic Church in the Kimberley 1884–1984*, University of Notre Dame Press, Broome, 1994.

Zweck, Lois, 'Kavel and the missionaries', *Lutheran Theological Journal* 47.2 (2013): 91–101.

www.ingramcontent.com/pod-product-compliance
Lightning Source LLC
Chambersburg PA
CBHW061251230426
43664CB00025B/2926